"An immensely readable romp through the history of Adidas, and thus also the story of international sports politics and the commercial colonization of events."

—*The Independent* (London)

"Where was *Sneaker Wars* when I was doing research for my own book? This book is great for understanding the ins and outs of the industry, particularly for the two brands we used to call 'the Germans' back in the day."

—Bobbito Garcia, author of
Where'd You Get Those?:
New York City's Sneaker Culture, 1960–1987

"Barbara Smit deserves high praise [for *Sneaker Wars*]."

—*The Sunday Telegraph* (London)

"Who knew footwear could be so fascinating? By turns journalism, business history, gripping narrative, and family psychodrama, *Sneaker Wars* is an exceptional work."

—L. Jon Wertheim, senior writer for *Sports Illustrated*
and author of *Running the Table:*
The Legend of Kid Delicious,
the Last Great American Pool Hustler

About the Author

BARBARA SMIT has written for *The Financial Times*, *The International Herald Tribune*, *The Economist*, and *Time*, among other publications. She received her master's degree in international journalism from City University in London. She lives in France.

The Enemy Brothers Who Founded

Adidas and **Puma**

and the Family Feud That Forever

Changed the Business of Sports,

AN  ECCO BOOK

HARPER PERENNIAL

NEW YORK • LONDON • TORONTO • SYDNEY • NEW DELHI • AUCKLAND

sneaker

wars

Barbara Smit

To Lisa, Karen, Fanny, and Marius

HARPER ● PERENNIAL

A hardcover edition of this book was published in 2008 by Ecco, an imprint of Harper-Collins Publishers.

SNEAKER WARS. Copyright © 2008 by Barbara Smit. All rights reserved. Printed in the United States of America. No part of this book may be used or reproduced in any manner whatsoever without written permission except in the case of brief quotations embodied in critical articles and reviews. For information address HarperCollins Publishers, 10 East 53rd Street, New York, NY 10022.

HarperCollins books may be purchased for educational, business, or sales promotional use. For information please write: Special Markets Department, HarperCollins Publishers, 10 East 53rd Street, New York, NY 10022.

FIRST HARPER PERENNIAL EDITION PUBLISHED 2009.

Designed by Sunil Manchikanti

Library of Congress Cataloging-in-Publication Data is available upon request.

ISBN 978-0-06-124658-6

09 10 11 12 13   ID/RRD 10 9 8 7 6 5 4 3 2 1

contents

part three: Multibillion-Dollar Rescue

illustrations

prologue

An army of lawyers, businessmen, and entertainment managers swarmed around the thirty-one-year-old soccer player as he prepared to announce an eye-popping deal: on January 11, 2007, David Beckham opened up multimillion-dollar prospects by revealing that he would move to the United States and play with the Los Angeles Galaxy.

The handshake between the British player and his American employers held the promise of unprecedented excitement for soccer in the United States. While some commentators were quick to deride Beckham as "mostly hype and hair," others marveled at the combination. "Let's be honest: the marketing opportunities here are enormous," one of them put it.

Others had tried it before him. American soccer enthusiasts had resorted to pathetic gimmicks to draw interest in a string of failed soccer leagues. Many believed that soccer had finally come to America in the mid-seventies, when Pelé, the Brazilian soccer genius, played his inaugural game at the New York Cosmos. Europe's finest players, from Franz Beckenbauer to George Best to

Johan Cruijff, had also been lured to the United States, yet American soccer still struggled to take off.

But the increasingly mixed interests of sports, business, and entertainment gave another dimension to David Beckham's move. Tellingly, the deal had been negotiated on Beckham's behalf by Simon Fuller, the producer behind the Spice Girls and *American Idol*. The combination was so intoxicating that Anschutz Entertainment Group (AEG), the owners of the Los Angeles Galaxy, were prepared to reward Beckham with up to $250 million for the next five years.

Along with Hollywood-white smiles and the smell of crisp dollar bills, there was another feature that accompanied Beckham throughout that week: the three stripes of Adidas, the German sports brand. They seemed almost ubiquitous, from the boots on Beckham's feet to the shirts of his teammates at Real Madrid to the outfits of the Los Angeles Galaxy.

Adidas managers could not have dreamed up a more judicious scenario. Since its inception, the brand had witnessed, if not led, all the changes that had turned sports into a glitzy business. Some believed that Beckham could "radically transform the landscape of world sports" yet again—if he induced Americans to embrace soccer at last.

Adidas knew exactly what he could signify for the brand, because the three stripes had been built on such relationships. At a time when money and sports were still two separate worlds, the most admired athletes and soccer players, enjoyed dropping by in the small Bavarian town of Herzogenaurach for a chat with "Adi" Dassler, the ingenious German cobbler behind Adidas.

On the other side of the small river that runs through Herzogenaurach, the guests were just as impressive. Just after the war, Rudolf Dassler had walked over after a blazing row with his brother Adi and set up Puma, a competing brand. Their feud shaped the modern sports business, giving rise to corruption and ever-increasing financial stakes. For several decades, the bickering Dassler brothers ruled over the sports business from their medieval village, their shoes featured in nearly all the most emblematic pictures of sports history.

But the most impressive stronghold of the Dassler brothers was in soccer, which Adidas and Puma long had almost entirely to themselves. That was precisely what had drawn David Beckham to Adidas to begin with: he was determined to make it in soccer just like the heroes from his childhood, playing with Manchester United in Adidas boots.

. . . .

The link between Beckham and the three stripes came about in 1993, after an Adidas employee spotted the talented teenager on the soccer field. When he was brought to the company's English offices near Manchester shortly thereafter, the people in charge were thoroughly unimpressed. "David was the most unaffected guy you'd meet," said Steve Martin, a member of the Adidas marketing team at the time. "Unlike some of the cocky youngsters who turned up here, he was very polite and so shy that it was almost embarrassing." Beckham was soon given a contract that amounted to pocket money.

The Adidas managers more or less forgot about the quiet, skinny boy from North London for two years, until they heard that he had walked over to Nike. They tried repeatedly to get in touch with their contacts at Manchester United, but to no avail. It looked like Nike had just done it again.

The Americans had started hijacking the business in the eighties, when the sons of Adi and Rudi Dassler were spending most of their time fighting each other. Blinkered by their own devious rivalry, the two Dassler cousins ignored the rise of the hard-hitting American upstart. Once it had thrashed Adidas and Puma in the United States, Nike set out to capture the European sports business by conquering soccer pitches, luring away promising youngsters like David Beckham.

Back in Manchester, in October 1995, Adidas suddenly heard from Tony Stephens, one of the managers at the well-established SFX, a management agency for soccer players and other celebrities. Stephens had been hired to take care of Beckham's interests, and he apologized for the confusion over the Nike deal. Stephens and Beckham were promptly invited back to the Adidas offices to sign an upgraded contract.

Beckham was still wearing his impeccable blue blazer and tie, but he appeared a little more confident this time, arriving for the talks in a red BMW. He had just acquired the convertible—quite an upgrade from his battered Ford Escort—on the back of a hefty deal with Manchester United.

Paul McCaughey, then soccer manager at Adidas in England, was offering a sizable check that would tie Beckham to Adidas for at least two years. McCaughey felt that the discussion was progressing smoothly when Tony Stephens quietly pulled him aside. "Would you like to make a friend for life?" Stephens asked. The agent went on to explain that the convertible had been a little above David's budget and that he was struggling to meet the insurance payment. If Adidas helped him to keep the car, he would not forget.

It took only a few minutes for clearance to be obtained from the accounts department. Compared to existing contracts, the insurance payment had cost Adidas almost nothing, yet David Beckham beamed with excitement as Paul McCaughey gave him the complimentary check.

For a car enthusiast like Beckham, the gesture was unforgettable. It would be repaid many times over the following years, as the player turned into a sports icon of unprecedented reach. Adidas repeatedly had to upgrade his deal, which could reach more than $5 million per year, but none of the other multimillion-dollar players on the Adidas payroll could rival the sheer excitement generated by Beckham. He was the shy teenager from Leytonstone turned into "Goldenballs"—an improbably attractive soccer player with pop star friends, inventive hairstyles, and a nose for trendsetting clothes.

Unfortunately for the bickering Dasslers, they would never benefit from this phenomenon. The sudden rise of Nike and Reebok, another exploding American brand, brought both Adidas and Puma on the brink of collapse. Some of the Dassler heirs were ousted from their company, while others panicked and sold out at the least judicious of times. It was left to other investors and managers to revive the two brands and steer them through a new, multibillion-dollar sports business.

. . . .

David Beckham turned out to be a demanding customer. "He had us adjust his boots over and over again, claiming that one pair was just a tad too short and the other slightly too large," recalled Aidan Butterworth, former sports marketing manager at Adidas. "We thought he was pushing it a bit, but the prints revealed that he was right. He has a unique shoe size, eight and three-quarters."

As for the Adidas clothes to be worn by David Beckham, they systematically had to be vetted by his wife, Victoria Adams, a former Spice Girl. Thierry Weil, the Adidas international manager who dealt most intensely with the player, regularly sat at the Beckhams' kitchen table to discuss the latest designs. Given the oddity of the couple's requests, he barely raised an eyebrow when Beckham asked for a pair of velour pants studded with three stripes of false diamonds. "I could not have guessed that he intended to wear them for a meeting with the Queen," Weil said, sighing.

The repercussions were invaluable. Once he joined Real Madrid, the Spanish team clad in Adidas, Beckham was covered in three stripes. Thousands of young players badgered their parents to buy "Beckham boots." Shirts featuring his name could be sold to millions of self-declared Madrid supporters around the world.

The partnership was in line with the exploding stakes in the sports marketing business, as television deals and huge player transfers came into play. The new titans of the sports business sought a handful of players who could act as superstars in massive international campaigns, from LeBron James and Tracy McGrady in basketball to Reggie Bush in football.

Only Puma opted for another tack. Bankrolled by a Hollywood film producer, the company returned at full blast as a brand mixing sports with fashion. Yet it still had to draw attention on the playing fields with an offbeat touch, such as the tight-fitting dresses of Serena Williams and the sharkskin shoes worn by Michael Schumacher.

Beckham's switch to the Los Angeles Galaxy made all of Adidas's latest investments come together. The company had already forked out $150 million to outfit all the teams in the American Soccer League. After a two-year fight, Tim Lieweke, the Galaxy chief, convinced other franchise holders to introduce exemptions to the league's salary cap. Then he relentlessly courted the Beckhams, pursuing them from England to Spain.

The move encapsulated the drastic changes that had taken place in world sports over the previous years, egged on by the take-no-prisoners battles between Adidas, Puma, Reebok, and Nike. It was the ultimate destination of a ride that had taken sports from jolly amateurism to unapologetic greed and the slickness of multimillion-dollar marketing deals—the climax of a sports business instigated by two enemy brothers on opposite sides of a medieval Bavarian town.

part one

Two Brothers, One Feud

the dassler boys

C lutching a bulging duffel bag, a short young man walked confidently onto the Berlin Olympic training grounds. Surrounded by hundreds of spectacular athletes from all around the world, Adolf Dassler hardly caught anyone's attention. Yet the little man with the large bag was fully aware that this was his chance to shine.

"Adi" and his elder brother, Rudi, had become established as the men behind Gebrüder Dassler, a Bavarian shoe factory that made some of the country's finest sports shoes. They had persisted with such drive that their factory was drawing sports enthusiasts from all around Germany, generating unprecedented hustle and bustle in their small town of Herzogenaurach, not far from Nuremberg, in the northern part of Bavaria.

Controversial as they were, the Berlin Olympics, opening in the German capital in August 1936, would enable the Dassler brothers to spread their name much farther. It would yield formidable publicity for Gebrüder Dassler to get their spikes on the feet of any prominent athletes—and there was one whom Adi Dassler wanted to catch above all others.

When it was established in the 1920s, the brothers' shoe business put an end to their family's many years in the weaving industry. Their father, Christoph, was the last in a long line of Dassler weavers from Herzogenaurach, known until the end of the nineteenth century as a bustling mill town, employing hundreds of weavers and dyers. Yet the industrial revolution made Christoph's skills obsolete, prompting him to switch to shoe production.

While the elder Dassler learned tedious stitching methods, his wife, Paulina, complemented her husband's meager earnings by setting up a laundry at the back of their house on Hirtengraben, aided by her daughter, Marie. The clean wash was then delivered around town by her three boys, Fritz, Rudolf, and Adolf, known around town as "the laundry boys."

While the Dassler brothers were still at school, at the beginning of the twentieth century, the word *sport* barely existed. Yet Adi Dassler, the youngest of the boys, spent most of his spare time inventing games, carving sticks to make javelins, and choosing heavy stones for the shot put. Adi often dragged his best friend, Fritz Zehlein, the son of the town's blacksmith, out on long runs in the forests and meadows that surrounded the medieval town.

This insouciance came to an end in August 1914, when the two eldest Dassler boys, Fritz and Rudolf, were drawn into the war. They were among the thousands of Germans who believed they would be back in a matter of months, but who would spend four long years away from home in the muddy trenches of Flanders. Just months before the end of the war, the seventeen-year-old Adi Dassler, then a baker's apprentice, was called to join his two brothers at the front.

When the Dassler brothers returned to Herzogenaurach unharmed, the three hardened men found their mother's laundry empty. In the postwar misery there weren't many who could afford to have their clothes washed by someone else, and Paulina had given up the business. Adi rapidly made up his mind: he

The small town of Herzogenaurach, where the Dassler brothers lived.

would build up his own small shoe production unit, right there in the former laundering shed.

In the aftermath of the war's savagery, Adi spent many days scouring the countryside picking up all sorts of army utensils left behind by retreating soldiers. He scavenged any debris that could be remotely useful and hauled it back to his workshop. Strips of leather could be cut from army helmets and bread pouches, to be recycled as shoe soles. Torn parachutes and army haversacks were more useful for slippers. To make up for the lack of electricity, Adi came up with an equally clever device: among his early inventions was a leather trimmer affixed to a bicycle frame, which his friends could pedal to get the band turning.

The ingenious young man built up his trade with sturdy shoes that could be expected to last for several years, but he was still most interested in sports. Tinkering away in his shed, Adi came up with some of the earliest spiked shoes—with lethal nails that were forged and then driven through the soles by his friend Fritz.

Three years into the venture, in 1923, Rudolf stepped in. The partnership between the two brothers worked smoothly, even with their contrasting personalities. Not much of a talker, Adi relished the time spent in his workshop, which was permeated with the smell of leather and glue. Rudolf, however, with his loud and extroverted manner, was better equipped to head up the company's sales efforts.

In fact, the Dasslers could hardly have picked a worse time to get their business going. Under the harsh prescriptions of the Versailles Treaty, the war victors had seized most of Germany's resources, leaving little to rebuild the battered country. This caused huge resentment and appalling deprivation, with millions of Germans suffering from unemployment and hunger.

Yet amid this tension and misery, sports and other forms of entertainment began to attract swelling crowds. By the mid-twenties, sports clubs were springing up all around the country, and thousands of supporters thronged shaky soccer stands. The time had come for the Dasslers to launch Adi's inventive sports products on a larger scale. The shift was consecrated on July 1, 1924, with the launch of "Gebrüder Dassler, Sportschuhfabrik, Herzogenaurach."

By sending offers to sports clubs, the Dasslers raked in growing orders. They chiefly sold spikes and soccer boots, which at the time looked much like those of their English forebears—heavy contraptions with leather studs and thick protection for toes and ankles. In 1926, the growth of their company prompted them to leave the former laundry and move into much larger premises, in an empty factory on the other side of the Aurach, the river running through Herzogenaurach.

The breakthrough for the company came when a spluttering motorbike screeched to a halt in front of the Gebrüder Dassler plant. On the saddle sat Josef Waitzer, a lanky man with a crew cut and a neatly clipped moustache. The coach of the German Olympic track-and-field team, he had heard about the spikes made by the sports enthusiasts in Herzogenaurach, and he had driven all the way from Munich to check them out himself.

The unexpected visit turned into an hours-long discussion, and Josef Waitzer's motorbike soon became a regular sight at Gebrüder Dassler. He was effectively employed as an adviser for the two brothers, and closely befriended by Adi. They ran together and spent hours discussing Dassler's shoes. Trailing

The young Adi Dassler stands proudly among samples in his new factory.

behind Waitzer, Adi Dassler easily made his way into the Berlin Olympic Village.

As the Dassler brothers began to enjoy the spoils of their thriving business, the country's economic hardship and the government's perceived impotence paved the way for the rise of extremist politicians. Support was spreading fast for the radical changes advocated by Adolf Hitler and his National Socialist German Workers Party (NSDAP). Swept up by the movement, the three Dassler brothers registered for party membership on May 1, 1933, just three months after Hitler seized power.

For Gebrüder Dassler, Nazism was a formidable stimulant. Hitler's stooges implemented their theories with haste, and one of the most urgent tasks they set for themselves was to promote German sports. The Führer regarded sports as a prodigious instrument to encourage discipline and comradeship, while sports victories held high propaganda value.

Another benefit was that the widespread practice of sports would help Hitler to build up an army of athletic young men. As he explained in *Mein Kampf*, "Give the nation six million impeccably trained bodies, all impregnated with fanatical patriotism and animated with the most fervent fighting spirit. In less than two years if need be, the national State will turn them into an army."

As Nazi fervor continued to spread, the Dassler brothers unwittingly benefited from the exploding demand for sports shoes. Gebrüder Dassler expanded several times over, with additions and a tower, *der Turm*, built at the entrance of the former Weil factory. A second plant was acquired on the other side of the Aurach, on Würzburger Strasse. Among the Dasslers' bestselling products were spikes named after Josef Waitzer.

Although the Olympic Games were given to the German capital two years before the Nazis seized power, Hitler came to regard the competition as a matter of utmost priority for the Third Reich. It offered an extraordinary stage to demonstrate the superiority of the Aryan "race." At the same time, it could serve to appease other European nations, which watched the rise of the new Germany with a mixture of wonder and concern.

Some Olympic committees began to protest that, under the circumstances, the Olympics could not decently be held in Berlin. The runup to the Olympics was marred by heavy protests from American athletes and mass demonstrations in New York, demanding a boycott of the "Nazi Olympics." The debate raged for three years. Avery Brundage, president of the U.S. Olympic Committee, decided to assess the situation himself, but Josef Goebbels, Hitler's propaganda minister, took impeccable care of this American guest: when Brundage returned to the United States, he was adamant that Jews would indeed be given a fair chance to compete in German sports.

This could not have been more untrue. The segregation was made official by the Nuremberg Laws of September 1935: stripped of their civil rights, Jews and people with any Jewish blood were to be banned from sports organizations. Still, Avery Brundage had his way. He staunchly believed that Olympic Games should be held every four years no matter what—in line with the principles of Baron Pierre de Coubertin, the French aristocrat who had revived the Greek games in 1896. At a meeting of the Amateur Athletic Union in December 1935, Brundage shut up the critics, and the proposed boycott of the Berlin Games was rejected. Scores of American athletes headed for Berlin.

Back in Europe, the racist bile that rose in Germany caused further outrage. Just before the opening of the Olympics, Henri Baillet-Latour, the Belgian president of the International Olympic Committee, expressed his disgust at the anti-Semitic posters he had seen around Germany. In an uncharacteristic show of defiance, Baillet-Latour told Hitler that the slogans would have to be removed—otherwise the Olympics would be called off. Hitler barely managed to contain his anger, but he still ordered a radical cleanup.

Regardless of the concessions, the Führer was determined to turn the Olympics into a spectacle of German power. Leni Riefenstahl, his favorite filmmaker, was offered unlimited resources to film the proceedings. Hitler ordered the construction of a bombastic Olympic stadium, and still complained incessantly that everything was far too small. The Olympic Village was set in a majestic forest, with manicured lawns and artificial ponds. For several weeks, athletes from all around the world ran, jumped, and chatted in the village, oblivious to the atrocities that were brewing just outside.

Through his friend Jo Waitzer, now the Nazis' track and field coach, Adi Dassler could rest assured that many of the German athletes would be wearing his spikes, but he had set his sights on the most admired athlete of them all. The son of an Alabama cotton cropper, Jesse Owens had obtained a scholarship to practice his extraordinary running talents at Ohio State University. As they wrote in the American press, Hitler himself had asked for details about the record-breaking American Negro who threatened to undermine the German team's medal haul in Berlin.

On the road in the United States, Jesse Owens and his black teammates constantly suffered from racist insults. While white runners wolfed down their snacks in roadside diners, the coach had to smuggle sandwiches out of the restaurant for his black athletes, who sat waiting in the car. Predictably, some of Germany's reporters proved just as bigoted, printing a photograph of an ape next to Owens, and attributing his speed to "animal qualities." But the German public at large still revered Owens for his feats. To his amazement, thousands of admirers converged in Hamburg for the arrival of the American team, and the crowds excitedly chanted his name.

Equally awed by Jesse's unprecedented performances, Adi Dassler was desperate to get his shoes on the runner's feet. Regardless of politics, Owens was a stupendous runner, and there was no doubt that he would be the hero of the Berlin Olympics. Once he had found the American athlete, Adi timidly pulled out his spikes, gesturing and mimicking until Owens agreed to try them out.

Among the most poignant contests of the Berlin Olympics was the long jump. This pitted Jesse Owens against the German Carl "Lutz" Long, who could easily have featured in an advertisement for Aryan superiority. After a heated duel, Lutz Long walked down the track to prepare for his last jump. Hitler beamed as the German athlete, in an all-out effort, achieved a remarkable jump of 7.87 meters, equaling the Olympic record set by Owens just before him.

But the American was unfazed. As the packed Olympic stadium erupted in frenetic applause, he prepared for his last jump. After two long minutes of silent concentration, Owens powered toward the board at full throttle. He soared through the air with such strength that, for a moment, he appeared to be floating above the sandpit. Owens destroyed the previous record with a stunning result of 8.06 meters. Much to Hitler's distaste, Lutz Long rushed to hug and congratulate the winner.

The American's display in the running heats was marred by Hitler, who was accused of snubbing Owens by storming out of his lodge after the sprinter's spectacular triumph in the 100 meters race. But Owens ignored the commotion. Stunningly composed, he went on to take two more gold medals, for the 200 meters and the relay. Sitting among the rapturous crowd, Adi Dassler could barely contain his pride and excitement: Owens

Jesse Owens and Lutz Long give their own salutes to the German public.

was wearing dark Dassler spikes with two stripes of leather running down the sides.

The Owens coup anchored the Dasslers' reputation with the world's most prominent athletes. While traveling in Germany for international meets, athletes and coaches dropped by in Herzogenaurach to check out the shoes worn by Jesse Owens. This marked the onset of an interest that would propel the Dasslers to international fame.

By then, however, tensions had begun to simmer in the Dassler family. While Gebrüder Dassler was taking off, the opposite characters of the two brothers were causing increasingly frequent rifts. Rudolf, who drove the company's skyrocketing sales, rolled his eyes at Adi's obsessive tinkering. He regularly lost patience with his brother's aloofness when it came to business matters. As for Adi, he became increasingly disturbed by his older brother's somewhat ostentatious, loud manner. The divergences caused some unpleasant conversations at Gebrüder Dassler, yet they were much sharper in the family's shared home, fueled by tensions between the Dassler women.

A few years after they settled into the empty shoe-making plant, the Dassler brothers had begun to build their own home, adjacent to the factory. A large mansion with three floors, it became known in Herzogenaurach as the Villa. Fritz, the eldest brother, stayed behind in the family house on Hirtengraben to run a lederhosen factory, called Kraxler. The upper floor of the new house was reserved for the Dassler parents. Rudolf Dassler settled just one floor below, with his family, while Adi took the ground floor.

Rudi's bachelor years had come to an end on a train platform in Nuremberg, where he met the eighteen-year-old Friedl Strasser, her younger sister, Betti, and their cousin. The four began to chat on the platform and then sat together in the train. By the time they reached their destination, Friedl, a pretty brunette, had agreed to a date with Rudolf. "Rudolf was a bit of a peacock, but there was no doubt for Friedl that he was the man of her life," her sister Betti recalled.

Since their father had died shortly after the war, the Strasser sisters had been brought up by their mother, who ran a grocery store in Fürth, on the outskirts of Nuremberg. Friedl and Rudolf's wedding was celebrated there, with about forty guests, on May 6, 1928. Brought up in a Catholic family with hardworking and conservative values, Friedl quickly adjusted to her role as hausfrau. She became a mother with the birth of Armin Adolf, in September 1929.

As for Adi, he met his bride in Pirmasens, a small town in the hills of the Palatinate, along the Rhine. In the early 1930s he had registered at the town's highly reputed Schuhfachschule, to learn more technical shoemaking skills. One of his mentors there was Franz Martz, an established producer of lasts, the wooden molds used to shape a shoe. As Adi began to show up at his home more frequently, Martz quietly condoned the relationship between his pupil and his fifteen-year-old daughter, Käthe. Together with Rudolf Dassler, Martz was one of the witnesses at their rain-soaked wedding in Pirmasens on March 17, 1934.

A harmonious and self-effacing woman, Friedl Dassler, Rudolf's wife, won the approval of her in-laws by easily blending in with

When the brothers still spoke: Rudolf and Friedl Dassler *(left and center)* in front of the company truck, with Adi grinning *(rear, center)*.

Dassler family life. While taking care of their son, Armin, she was also always prepared to lend a hand at Gebrüder Dassler. She tolerated her husband's notorious gallivanting and put up with his curtness. By the ultraconservative standards of the Dassler parents, Friedl Dassler was a model daughter-in-law.

Adolf's wife, Käthe, on the other hand, was far more assertive. Like most German women at the time, she strove to serve her husband without complaints, waking up at four every morning just to fry his sausages. She watched him patiently as he practiced his jumps, and she packed sandwiches for his soccer matches on the weekends. However, she was an outspoken woman who liked to take charge and make her presence felt.

Warm and spontaneous, the youthful bride found it hard to deal with the suspicious and somewhat boorish ways of the Franconian Dasslers. "She was a serious person, yet she was used to the relaxed attitude of her environment in the Palatinate," wrote Hermann Utermann, the family biographer. "The Franconians seemed brusque and hard to talk to." Amplified by Käthe's hard-headed character, this unease led to recurrent clashes between Adi's wife and the rest of the family.

In a letter to his American business partners much later, Rudolf Dassler unequivocally blamed Käthe for the rift between him and his brother. "The relation to my brother was ideal from 1924 till

1933," he wrote. "Then his young wife tried to interfere in business matters, although she, with her 16 years, had no experience at all, and the warfare began."

The rise of the Nazis caused deep disagreements between the two brothers. The stranglehold that the Nazis established on all aspects of German life forced both brothers to become more deeply involved with the movement. They signed off letters with the obligatory "Heil Hitler!" They held the same, swastika-stamped membership card of the National Socialist Driver Corps, the NSKK. The two brothers, however, didn't embrace the cause with equal warmth. While Rudolf vocally expressed his approval of the government's policies, Adi usually stuck to his ordinary, hardworking decency.

Hans Zenger was among the employees who benefited from Adi Dassler's protection. After misbehaving during a visit to Herzogenaurach by a high-ranking Nazi dignitary in 1937, Zenger was barred from the *Hitlerjugend* (Hitler Youth). Adolf Dassler was then ordered to dismiss Zenger, but he consistently ignored the instruction. "It was Adi Dassler who prevented my dismissal," Zenger recalled. "He knew that if Gebrüder Dassler sacked me, I would likely end up at the Front."

Such discussions increasingly raised questions about the company's leadership. Due to Käthe's somewhat defiant attitude, Rudolf became convinced that she was hostile toward him—a pushy intruder who purposely undermined the previously close relationship between him and his brother. With the outbreak of the war, the frictions that had built up between the two couples turned into full-blown enmity.

two brothers at war

The war was trouble for Gebrüder Dassler. On the back of the Berlin Olympics, the company benefited fully from the Nazis' enthusiasm for sports. But once Hitler's priorities shifted to the battlefields, the factory was subjected to the tight regulations of the regime. After some hemming and hawing, it was decided that Gebrüder Dassler would not be shuttered, but its production was sharply curtailed.

The war came closer to the Dassler family when Adi received a dreaded letter from the Wehrmacht on August 7, 1940. He was instructed to report for training at the beginning of December as a radio technician at an intelligence regiment near Nuremberg. But he was promptly relieved of his military duties. Ranked as an officer, he was exempted on February 28, 1941, because his expertise was deemed indispensable for Gebrüder Dassler.

While German soldiers wreaked havoc throughout Europe, the small town of Herzogenaurach was relatively unperturbed. The Dasslers struggled along with a vegetable patch in their garden.

The women had turned the courtyard into a small farm, with chickens and a couple of pigs.

By then, Adi's family had expanded with the addition of three children. Käthe gave birth to their first child, Horst, in March 1936, followed by Inge in June 1938, and a second daughter, Karin, in the early days of the war, in April 1941. Rudolf and Friedl's son, Armin, now had a younger brother, Gerd, born ten years after Armin, in July 1939.

As the war progressed, the authorities continued to streamline German industries, but Gebrüder Dassler escaped several rounds of closures. Due to rampant shortages, the company scraped by to make the required pairs of shoes and it even ran short of staff: to complete his assignments, in October 1942, Adolf Dassler requested five Russian prisoners of war. While the Dassler catalogue still featured Waitzer running shoes, the soccer line was widened to include such names as "Kampf" and "Blitz."

Just like Gebrüder Dassler, several other international shoe manufacturers had been drawn into the war efforts of their respective countries. Converse, the American company that shot to fame with the All Star basketball shoe, made flying boots that were worn by the entire U.S. Army Air Corps. Gola, one of the oldest makers of soccer boots in England, turned out marching boots for British soldiers.

Meanwhile, the war entered yet another deadly stage, as Allied bombs virtually erased entire towns from Germany's map. The people of Herzogenaurach shivered in their cellars for two nights in February 1943 when an incessant stream of bombers flew overhead to destroy large parts of neighboring towns such as Nuremberg and Würzburg. Herzogenaurach itself was amazingly spared, with just five casualties due to stray bombs. Yet the opening of the eastern front claimed the lives of many more men from the town.

The heightened demands of the war began to take their toll on the entire Dassler family. Over the previous years the tensions in the family had escalated, mostly caused by Rudolf. They were aggravated by the close proximity of the family members, who spent too much of their time together. With the Dassler elders,

Nazi banners flying in Herzogenaurach during the Second World War.

two bickering couples, and five children, the Villa felt crowded. Dassler sister Marie had married and moved in with her husband, but she, too, worked at Gebrüder Dassler and spent much of her time with Adi and Käthe.

While Adi was clearly regarded as the linchpin of Gebrüder Dassler in the factory, his brother strove to impose himself as the company's leader. Marie was devastated, and Adolf apparently helpless, when Rudolf refused to employ her two sons at Gebrüder Dassler. "Rudolf bluntly rejected his sister's pleas, saying that there were enough family problems at the company," recalls Betti Strasser, Rudolf's sister-in-law. "He could be incredibly harsh and mean."

So could Fritz Dassler, the oldest brother, who tended to side with Rudolf. Established in the former family home on Hirtengraben, his own company had had to replace its production of lederhosen with leather pouches for German soldiers. When the war broke out Fritz made some arrangements with his brothers to protect some of their employees, but later he and Adolf were barely on speaking terms.

This transpired when Fritz picked Maria Ploner, one of his many adolescent employees, to be drafted as a *Flakhelferin*, one of the teenage girls used as helpers for the army at the front, with very little chance of returning home unharmed. Maria had been stitching leather for Fritz Dassler since 1938, after a four-year stint at Gebrüder Dassler. Adolf was shaken to hear that Maria was to be laid off. "He thought Fritz was unfair because my two brothers were already at the front," Maria Ploner recalled. Adolf Dassler found space for her at Gebrüder Dassler, where she stayed safely until the end of the war.

. . . .

Adolf's early release from military duties caused further skirmishes in the family. The decision identified the younger of the Dassler brothers as the most indispensable half of their leadership duo, which deeply irked Rudolf and Friedl. They became convinced that, egged on by Käthe, Adi was plotting to oust them from Gebrüder Dassler. The frictions that had been building up between the two couples soon boiled over into full-blown arguments, and Rudolf's suspicions took a paranoid turn.

One night, when Allied bombers started to drop their deadly loads on German soil, Rudolf Dassler took refuge in the family shelter with his son Armin, his wife, Friedl, and her sister Betti. They were promptly joined by Käthe and Adi, who snapped, "Here are the bloody bastards again." It was obvious to Betti that Adi was peeved about the bombers, but Rudolf jumped up angrily at the remark. "It was impossible to persuade Rudolf that the comment was not [directed at] him," Betti recalled.

The recriminations turned into hateful resentment after January 1943, when Hitler called for the complete mobilization of the German people to put a quick end to the war. As part of this all-out effort, men from age sixteen to sixty-five and women aged seventeen to forty-five could be asked to defend the Reich. While Adolf Dassler was still regarded as unavailable because of his duties at the factory, Rudolf was drafted to reinforce a regiment in Glauchau, Saxony.

He regarded this as an unbearable injustice and was certain that his brother had plotted to have him sent away. "In 1941 my brother enlisted to the army and became a soldier. His wife succeeded to make me forget everything and I could get my brother released for the factory," he later wrote to his American business partners. "As a reward I had to go to the army in 1943 within 24 hours and I heard that I had to thank my brother and his party-friends for this."

At the beginning of April 1943, Rudolf was moved to the customs department in the small town of Tuschin. On the eastern outskirts of the Reich, Tuschin belonged to the district of Litzmannstadt—the name the Nazis gave to the Polish city of Lodz and its infamous Jewish ghetto after the German invasion of Poland in 1939. Due to alleged night blindness, Rudolf was assigned to an office job.

Compared with millions of other able-bodied German men, his position was almost comfortable, but he still couldn't stand the thought that his brother had escaped the army. "I will not hesitate to seek the closure of the factory," wrote Rudolf to his brother in a spiteful letter from Tuschin, "so that you will be forced to take up an occupation that will allow you to play the leader and, as a first-class sportsman, to carry a gun."

Six months later, Rudolf apparently prevailed. A letter from Berlin informed Adi that Gebrüder Dassler was to be closed down. The factory had escaped several rounds of closures over the previous years as the Nazi regime tightened its grip on the country's production facilities, but the ongoing war called for the requisitioning of yet more workers and machinery for weapons manufacturing.

Josef Goebbels, the propaganda minister, had called for a *Totaler Krieg*, an all-out war, which ushered in an era of heightened terror for German civilians. The country's last reserves were to be thrown into the war, requiring the remaining civilians and war prisoners to work in armament factories for up to seventy hours per week. Sports shoes would no longer be needed, since the *Totaler Krieg* banned cultural and sporting events. Gebrüder

Dassler's equipment would be used to manufacture spare parts for panzers and bazookas.

Rudolf, who happened to be on leave in Herzogenaurauch when the decision was confirmed, rushed to the factory to seize stacks of leather and to paralyze the shoe production at once. He was enraged to find out that his brother had been in the storage room before him to put some leather aside as well. As the Dassler employees ignored Rudolf's angry outburst, he turned to some of his high-ranking Nazi friends at the *Kreisleitung*, the regional authorities. Adi was swiftly called to their offices. "My brother-in-law apparently had some high-placed contacts, because my husband was instructed to show up immediately and these gentlemen treated him in the most demeaning manner," Käthe Dassler later wrote.

The dust settled in Herzogenaurach when Rudolf had to return to his customs office in Tuschin. Hundreds of miles away in his Polish outpost, he still plotted incessantly to regain control of the factory. Through his contacts at the Luftwaffe, he persistently attempted to have Gebrüder Dassler's welding assignment replaced with another order to make parachuting boots, for which he personally held a patent. Rudolf figured that if he obtained such an assignment, he would be sent back to Herzogenaurach to take charge of it. His patent, however, turned out to be flawed.

. . . .

While Adolf tinkered with panzer parts, Red Army tanks advanced toward his brother in Tuschin. By the beginning of 1945 the Russians had come so close that Rudolf became jittery and decided to flee. One of his declared motives was that his unit had been integrated into the *Schutzstaffel* (SS), Heinrich Himmler's security police. "My disapproval of Himmler's police rule, the proximity of the front and the fact that the war had long been lost, prompted me to refuse any further military duties," he wrote later. When Rudolf reached Herzogenaurach, exhausted and disheveled, he headed straight to a physician, who complacently issued a medical certificate declaring him inept for service due to a frozen foot.

Several weeks later he was told that his former unit in Tuschin had been disbanded—killed or captured by the Soviet soldiers who liberated Lodz on January 19, 1945. But the Third Reich still hadn't capitulated, so Rudolf's superiors at the SS ordered him to report to another of their branches: the *Sicherheitsdienst* (SD), the infamous intelligence service. One of the most reviled units of the Nazi regime, set up by Himmler and run at the time by Ernst Kaltenbrunner, the SD worked closely with the Gestapo to smash any potential opposition. Relying on thousands of informants, it provided the intelligence required by the Gestapo to perform its murderous tasks. Rudolf wrote that he was summoned to report to the Gottsmann cell of the SD in Fürstenwalde, near Berlin, but he refused to join the intelligence service and failed to show up as ordered.

Although the Allies were closing in fast, zealous Gestapo officials apparently deemed it useful to open a file on the suspected desertion of Rudolf Dassler. As Rudi recalled, he reported to their offices in Nuremberg on March 13, 1945, and was told to remain at their disposal until they finished studying his case. In breach of these orders, Rudolf slipped out of the Gestapo offices and returned to Herzogenaurach on March 29. The Third U.S. Army, led by General Patton, had just crossed the Rhine at Oppenheim, and Rudolf had heard that his father lay dying. "I expected that, given the turbulent situation at the time, my absence would not arouse any particular interest in Nuremberg," he wrote.

The Dassler family was briefly reunited in Herzogenaurach on April 4, 1945, for the funeral of Christoph Dassler, the humble slipper maker, who died of heart failure at the age of eighty. The next day, Betti Strasser, Rudolf's sister-in-law, felt uneasy as she headed down to the Dassler home. There seemed to be some agitation. When she pushed the door open she found her sister, Friedl, in shock, wailing that Rudolf had been arrested. The Gestapo had fetched him, she explained. He was taken to the Bärenschanz prison in Nuremberg for several days, and he would not return home until early May, about two weeks after the liberation of Herzogenaurach.

Over the previous months, only die-hard supporters of the Nazi regime had failed to admit its defeat. The people of Herzogenaurach began to prepare for the arrival of the Allies by the end of March 1945, when U.S. tanks crossed the Rhine. Nazi authorities fulfilled their duty by calling for an insurrection to defend Herzogenaurach. However, the effort was less than halfhearted. On April 14, about sixty men left the town and headed west to confront the U.S. Army. A few miles down the road half of the contingent somehow vanished into ditches and roadside farms. The others called it quits and turned around after less than one day. Their less than glorious retreat took a farcical turn when the would-be fighters met a group of women who had just plundered the nearby wine cellar of Joachim von Ribbentrop, the Nazi foreign minister. They walked away with bucketsful of fine wine and generously shared it with the tired civilians of Herzogenaurach.

The two bridges over the Aurach were blown up, but when the U.S. troops entered Herzogenaurach in the early hours of April 16, they didn't have much to fear from the local insurgents. Valentin Fröhlich, the conservative prewar mayor, persuaded the town's staunchest Nazis to avoid bloodshed by surrendering immediately. Again, the people of Herzogenaurach were spared from the atrocities that accompanied the fall of many German towns.

Apparently, some U.S. tanks halted in front of the Dassler factory. They were pondering the destruction of the building, which was believed to harbor SS officers, when a young woman stepped out. The twenty-eight-year-old Käthe Dassler bravely walked toward the soldiers and pleaded with them to leave the factory intact. All that the people in there wanted to make was sports shoes, she explained. Käthe's charm probably helped, but the Americans had another motive to leave the factory and its adjacent Villa standing: the Villa was clearly one of the most comfortable houses in town, and they needed a place to stay.

Over the following weeks, chaos and uncertainty reigned in Herzogenaurach. Valentin Fröhlich was temporarily reinstated in the mayor's office, while American troops rounded up the town's worst Nazis. To purge the conscience of German citizens, the U.S.

rulers instilled guilt and shame in the citizens, bluntly confronting them with the unthinkable devastation caused by the Nazis, which many had refused to see and others had failed to condemn. The people of Herzogenaurach got their share of guilt when the Americans herded them into the local cinema and forced them to watch films that revealed the unspeakable horrors they had discovered upon the liberation of Dachau concentration camp.

It was precisely this inferno that Rudolf Dassler claimed to have escaped when he returned to Herzogenaurach, about two weeks after its liberation. Rudolf told his family, who last saw him being taken away by the Gestapo, that they had detained him for fourteen days. Then the local Gestapo chiefs rounded up some of the inmates and instructed guards to bring them to Dachau. The twenty-six men were to walk the two hundred miles to the concentration camp in chains, attached two by two.

On the way, Rudolf said, the driver who was supervising the march, Ludwig Müller, was instructed by a local officer of the *Waffen* SS to shoot the prisoners. Müller ignored the command and led the prisoners farther south, but they never reached Dachau. The convoy was halted by Americans near Pappenheim, and Müller gladly let the prisoners walk back to their homes.

By then, the animosity between Rudolf and his brother had taken on such proportions that he was convinced his brother had been glad to see him taken away by the Gestapo. "When I came back on foot on May 1, 1945, my brother and his wife were unpleasantly surprised," he wrote much later. "They had not thought that I would return."

Rudolf was determined to regain his influence at Gebrüder Dassler. But on July 25, he was arrested again. This time he was in the hands of American soldiers. It was an "automatic arrest," applying to people who had held high-ranking positions in specific Nazi organizations. In Rudolf Dassler's case, the arrest sheet stated that he was suspected of working for the SD, performing counterespionage and censorship.

Like hundreds of thousands of other women in these chaotic days, Friedl Dassler desperately looked for her husband for several weeks, together with her sister Betti. When they finally located him in Hammelburg, a camp in the northern part of Franconia, Rudolf Dassler was fuming. He had been told by the Americans that his arrest had been triggered by a denunciation, and he didn't have the slightest doubt about its source.

3

the split

For several months, the Hammelburg internment camp for German war prisoners consisted roughly of a bare field fenced off by barbed wire and heavily armed American soldiers. The sanitary conditions improved slowly, as the barracks were constructed only after the arrival of the prisoners. Internee 2597, Rudolf Dassler, repeatedly wrote to the people in charge of the camp, desperate to make himself heard and to return to Herzogenaurach. But Hammelburg was overflowing with hundreds of political prisoners, and in the immediate postwar months, the Americans were intent on studying each case thoroughly.

While his file sat waiting at the bottom of a huge stack, Rudolf Dassler prepared his defense. Detained with him in Hammelburg was his cousin Valentin Zink, the Nazi propaganda chief in Herzogenaurach, and Markus Sehring, head of the NSDAP in Herzogenaurach since 1926. More important for Rudolf, the inmates included several men who agreed to act as witnesses in his favor. One of them was Friedrich Block, his immediate superior in Tuschin, who was arrested by the Americans as head of the intelligence service for the district. The other was Ludwig Müller, the man who had supposedly escorted the convoy of twenty-six prisoners of the Gestapo, including Rudolf Dassler, from Nuremberg to Dachau.

The statement by Block appeared to confirm some of Rudolf Dassler's most paranoid suspicions about a plot to keep him away from Gebrüder Dassler. As his former superior in Tuschin wrote, Rudolf repeatedly asked for leave to take care of his shoe company. Block eventually agreed to release Dassler from his duties as soon as the local authorities gave their approval. However, Block continued, he then received an odd instruction from Nuremberg, marked "secret," that "Rudolf Dassler should not be allowed to take any leave for the purpose of checking on his factory."

The investigation conducted by the Americans uncovered other information. They established that Rudolf had joined the NSDAP in 1933 and volunteered for the Wehrmacht in 1941. At the border police station in Tuschin, he worked on records of "personal and smuggling cases," presumably helping to inculpate individuals who had been caught in unauthorized trading or other illegal activities. The crux of the file, though, was Dassler's activities for the Gestapo in Nuremberg in March 1945: Rudolf Dassler contended that he merely reported to the office on a daily basis while the Gestapo conducted investigations into his earlier unauthorized departure from Tuschin; but the Americans became convinced that he was lying.

As the U.S. officer wrote in his report: "According to his wife, interrogated this office, he actually worked there. According to Adolf Dassler, subject's brother, also interrogated this office, Dassler actually worked there." With a hint of irritation, the officer relayed Rudolf Dassler's claims that he was arrested by the Gestapo and sent to Dachau. "Dassler continuously reminds the interrogator of this fact," he noted. However, "investigation of Dassler in Herzogenaurach reveals that all informants consider this as a mere cover by the Gestapo to protect him, considering his work in Poland in the *Abwehr*, his party affiliation and political Nazi ideals."

The picture was less than flattering for Rudolf Dassler. The American investigator clearly felt that Dassler should not get away scot-free, but the chaos that reigned in internment camps had forced the U.S. authorities to alter their policies. They acknowledged that it would take decades to conscientiously clear up every single case. Just like Dassler's, hundreds of thousands of other files were made of claims and counterclaims that were almost impossible to verify, due to obvious bad faith and to the destruction of many documents. The delays were causing massive problems in the camps and frustration elsewhere, at a time when all agreed that efforts should be concentrated on reconstruction. The Americans therefore decided to release all prisoners who were not considered a security threat. With several other men from Herzogenaurach, Rudolf Dassler was freed on July 31, 1946—almost exactly one year after his arrest by the Americans.

His return caused ugly scenes, as the two brothers and their wives attempted to clear up what had happened during the war and its immediate aftermath. The rows were particularly explosive between Rudolf, who became obsessed with his brother's supposed betrayal, and Käthe, who staunchly defended her quiet husband, Adi. Rudolf was raging that he had been arrested on the back of "a malicious denunciation," as he wrote to his U.S. guards in Hammelburg. As he saw it, Käthe was a venomous hag who had wanted to oust him all along. During the war she had used the most revolting means to push him out. Käthe vehemently denied any wrongdoing, and countered that Rudolf's resentment had driven him to some disgustingly disloyal deeds.

To make matters worse, the two couples were still living under the same roof. By then, Adolf's family had had a fourth child and a third daughter, Brigitte, born in May 1946. *Der Turm*, the tower, was large enough for the Dasslers to erect partitions and organize separate homes for the two families, but the walls were too thin to protect the children's ears from the furious arguments that raged between their parents. Horst and Inge, the two eldest children of Adi and Käthe, were sent to boarding schools.

. . . .

The situation finally became untenable when Adolf Dassler had to defend his own case before the local denazification committee in July 1946. Rudolf closely followed the deliberations, because they would have a decisive influence on the control of Gebrüder Dassler. From then on, the recriminations the two couples hurled at each other in *Der Turm* were thrown into the court proceedings. Rudolf's suspicions turned into vicious accusations.

Just two weeks before Rudolf's release, on July 13, 1946, Adolf was classified as a *Belasteter*, meaning that he was believed to have actively contributed to the Nazi regime and personally profited from it. The written ruling was devastating for Adolf, because it implied that he would be barred from the shoe factory and probably dispossessed. Adolf Dassler could not deny his party membership, from 1933, or his involvement in the *Hitlerjugend*, since 1935. On the other hand, he swiftly put together a thick file to protest the judgment of some local opposition leaders, who branded him "100 percent Nazi."

One strong Adi supporter was the mayor's office. "In contrast with his brothers, D. is appreciated in the community and, contrary to his brothers, he was ready to help anyone," was their verdict. The former mayor Valentin Fröhlich, who was honored by the Americans for his impeccable wartime behavior and elected to the *Landrat*, the regional council, emphasized this point in a personal letter: "Anybody who knows Adolf Dassler would acknowledge that he is a man who is always prepared to help, regardless of status or political opinions," Fröhlich wrote.

In his plea to the committee, Adi Dassler added that only one of the sixty people who remained at the factory at the end of the war was a party member. He also referred to Hans Zenger, whom he refused to fire when Zenger was dropped from the *Hitlerjugend*, and to Jakob Ploner, who was known in town as an antifascist and whom Adi continued to employ throughout the Nazi years. The five refugees and four prisoners whom Adi had requested to work at the factory were treated as generously as the other employees, he boasted: "These nine people obtained extra rations of coffee from us every day, we often gave them extra bread and sometimes clothing."

On his ties with Nazi organizations, he argued that his membership of the NSDAP should be regarded as a sign of political ignorance. His activities in the *Hitlerjugend*, since 1935, concentrated exclusively on sports. He had conscientiously stayed away from any political rallies. Before the war, Adolf Dassler had been a member of many sports clubs, some of them affiliated with conflicting political movements, from the liberal gymnastics club to Herzogenaurach's conservative FCH soccer club and even a workers' sports club called Union. "The way I knew him, sports was the only kind of politics that counted for him. He didn't know political politics," confirmed a witness who described himself as a longtime member of the local Communist Party (KPD).

When it came to his relationship with Jews, the shoemaker's records confirmed that he continued to deal with Jewish leather traders long after this had become politically incorrect. But the most convincing piece of evidence in this respect was a letter from Hans Wormser, mayor of the adjoining village of Weisendorf, who described himself as a half-Jew. Wormser vividly recounted how Adolf Dassler had warned him of his impending arrest by the Gestapo and sheltered the mayor in his property. "A true supporter of Adolf Hitler would certainly not have done this, putting his existence and the well-being of his family on the line," Wormser wrote.

Dealing with the accusation of profiteering, Adi further contended that the increase in Gebrüder Dassler's sales was unrelated to any favors from the Nazi regime. True, the number of employees had roughly doubled to eighty between 1934 and 1938, but this was due to the fact that the demand for sports shoes had boomed after the Berlin Olympics. Since the shuttering of the shoe production in October 1943 and the switch to weapons manufacturing, the company had lost about 100,000 reichsmark—a considerable loss at the time.

None of this sufficed to clear him. On July 30, just as Rudolf was packing his few belongings in Hammelburg, Adi received another letter from the denazification committee, informing him that it had changed its verdict: Adolf Dassler was to be classified as a *Minderbelasteter*, a lighter charge than the previous ruling but one that still meant he was deemed guilty. He would have to pay a fine of 30,000 reichsmark and, most damagingly, would be on probation for two years. In other words, Gebrüder Dassler would be placed in the hands of a curator. For two years, Adolf Dassler would not be allowed to own or run his shoe factory. Somewhat panicked, Adi hired a lawyer, who appealed the decision.

When the freshly liberated Rudolf Dassler was questioned about the wartime activities of Gebrüder Dassler, he leapt at the opportunity to bad-mouth his brother. Rudolf apparently told the denazification committee that the production of panzer parts at the factory had been organized solely by Adolf, that he knew nothing about such assignments, and that he would have firmly opposed them.

This blatant lie infuriated Käthe Dassler. It was on this occasion that she wrote her own account of the wartime quarrels between the two brothers. Evidently exasperated, she insisted that Adolf had consistently gone out of his way to help his brother, in spite of Rudolf's openly malevolent attitude. "Rudolf Dassler further accuses my husband of having denounced him," she wrote. "I certify that this is untrue. My husband did everything that he could to exonerate his brother." Käthe was equally livid that Rudolf accused her husband of holding political speeches at the Dassler factory. "The speeches held inside and outside the factory should be attributed to Rudolf Dassler, as any factory employee could confirm," she concluded.

Käthe's statement, written on November 11, 1946, was duly added to the denazification committee's files. Before the end of the month, it reversed its earlier verdict on Adolf Dassler, classifying him as a *Mitläufer*—one of the millions of Germans who became party members without actively contributing to the Nazi regime. For Adi Dassler, this was akin to a clearance. As a *Mitläufer*, he was allowed to pursue his activities at Gebrüder Dassler, which was being solicited from all sides to step up production.

From then on, the cohabitation in *Der Turm* became unbearable. After all the rows and mudslinging, the two brothers resolved to split. Rudolf Dassler gathered his belongings and moved to the other side of the Aurach River with his wife and two children, Armin and Gerd. Convinced that Gebrüder Dassler would sink without him, he agreed to take over the small factory the brothers owned on the Würzburger Strasse, leaving the larger plant near the railway station to his brother. Rudolf further agreed to leave the requisitioned Villa to Adolf and Käthe. The rest of the brothers' assets, from the equipment to the patents, was painstakingly divided between them.

Adolf and Rudolf let their employees decide for which side they wanted to work. Predictably, most of the sales staff opted for the Würzburger Strasse, while the technicians sided with Adolf. Their sister, Marie Körner, supported Adolf and Käthe. She could not forgive Rudolf for refusing to employ her two boys, who never returned from the war. Their mother, Paulina, sided with Rudolf and his wife, Friedl. They took gentle care of Paulina until she died under dreadful conditions from a skin disease.

After many months of wrangles regarding the distribution of assets, the separation between the two brothers was completed in April 1948. It paved the way for the registration of two separate companies over the following months. Adolf filed a registration for a company called Addas, but this was promptly turned down due to the objections of a German children's shoe company with a similar name. The youngest of the two brothers then contracted his name and surname to form "Adidas." Rudolf did the same, registering "Ruda" soon after the split. However, that name was deemed inelegant and plump. Rudolf then took on another suggestion and registered the much sleeker "Puma."

. . . .

The rift between the two Dassler brothers tore apart their family, setting the scene for yet more feuding over the coming decades. At the same time, it deeply divided Herzogenaurach, with the

Aurach River acting as a liquid partition between Rudolf's supporters on one bank and Adolf's on the other. Herzogenaurach soon became known as the city where people always looked down, because they were careful to see what shoes others were wearing before they started a conversation.

On either side of the Aurach, the split left the Dassler brothers half-stranded. Rudolf was joined by nearly all of Gebrüder Dassler's administrative and sales staff, but since all of the technical staff had picked Adolf's side, Rudolf's men didn't have anything to sell. Conversely, Adolf quickly restarted production but lacked any sales force to speak of. In his late forties, Adi Dassler had to crank up his business yet again.

To make up for Rudolf's abrupt departure, the rest of Adi's family was drawn into his company more intensely than intended. Käthe began to handle all sorts of small tasks, filling out orders and supervising dispatches. Her sister, Marianne, became another influential member of the Adidas family. Shortly after the separation, Adi called up the two women to inspect some samples. They watched curiously as several employees ran around the grounds of the Dassler factory. Their dark leather shoes were adorned with white stripes running down the sides, from two to six on each side.

Stripes had long been used by the Dasslers and other shoemakers to strengthen the sides of their shoes, but most of the time they weren't visible because they were made of the same leather as the rest of the upper, nearly always black or dark brown. This made it hard for the Dasslers to back up their claims that some outstanding athletes had been wearing their spikes. On most pictures, even experts were unable to tell which brand of spikes the runners had on their feet. Advertising material and catalogues therefore contained quotes from the athletes or their trainers extolling the virtues of Dassler shoes. But Adi Dassler figured that, if the stripes were painted white, they could be used to make his spikes stand out from afar.

A two-stripe design was rapidly discarded because it had been used by Gebrüder Dassler. They might as well avoid another

Rudolf Dassler (with glasses) endeared himself to many employees with a joyous and paternalistic touch.

bustup with Rudolf. Four stripes looked somewhat too busy. But three stripes seemed an excellent compromise: the sign, easily spotted from a distance, that would cleanly distinguish Adidas from competing brands of shoes. The trademark was registered in Germany in March 1949, at the same time as the company, now called "Adolf Dassler adidas Schuhfabrik."

On the other side of the Aurach, Rudolf Dassler quickly hired technicians who once worked for competing companies to run his share of Gebrüder Dassler's machines, often turning out obvious copies of his brother's designs. After all, there were still plenty of unemployed shoemakers in Herzogenaurach. Due to the address books that Rudolf's aides had taken from Gebrüder Dassler, Puma sales rapidly took off.

The earliest form of the Puma logo—a square and rapacious-looking beast jumping through a *D*—was registered along with the brand name in October 1948. Just like his brother, Rudolf hit upon the thought of using white stripes on the side of his shoes, but his early version was one wide chunk of leather across the side of the foot. This later evolved into the "Formstripe," a single broad stripe that started from the same place along the side of the shoe but then became thinner as it curved toward the heel.

When it came to soccer, Rudolf Dassler held some of the best cards. Until the end of the war, German boots were inspired by their British ancestors—the sort of heavy clodhoppers that would have gone unnoticed on a building site. The much lighter Puma boots were remarkably sleek, and they could have conquered international soccer pitches much faster than those of Adidas. But unfortunately for Puma, Rudolf Dassler picked a fight with the wrong man.

. . . .

A short man with a crumpled face, Sepp Herberger, Germany's soccer coach, had long worked with the Dassler brothers, a relationship built up by Rudolf Dassler. But now the elder brother blew it. Full of himself, he apparently felt that Herberger was not treating him with sufficient deference. "You're a small king," Rudolf reportedly told Herberger. "And if you don't suit us, we'll just pick another guy." This turned out to be one of his most damaging outbursts.

After Rudolf's rebuff, the German trainer cultivated a close relationship with Adi. Both men of few words, they formed a quiet couple, understanding each other with merely a short sentence and a nod. Herberger appreciated the boot-maker's devotion to detail, and Adi soon became a familiar sight in the small entourage of the German national team— with a modest grin and a toolbox, he'd sit next to Herberger, always at the ready to get the boots precisely right for each of the players, tightening a screw here, adjusting some padding there.

The English and their ungainly boots still ruled over international pitches in 1950, when Brazil hosted the first soccer World Cup since the war. However, the tournament would mark one of the worst humiliations for the British, and the most unexpected triumph of U.S. soccer. The American team had qualified with a ragtag assemblage of amateurs, most of them from Saint Louis, and three of them not even U.S. citizens. The team members had hardly ever trained together before they took off for Brazil, where they faced the mighty English team of Stanley Matthews and Stan Mortensen.

The American team was deemed so hopeless, and the tournament attracted so little interest in the United States, that only one reporter was there to witness the game in Belo Horizonte—and he had paid for the trip out of his own pocket. But the U.S. team went on to mortify the English by defeating them with one lucky goal from Joe Gaetjens, a student from Haïti. The American victory would rank as one of the most shocking upsets ever in international soccer.

While the game in Belo Horizonte put an end to the undisputed supremacy of the English on the pitch, it was the following World Cup, in 1954, that heralded the demise of British boots. This time the Germans, who were barred from most international sporting events in the postwar years, would be allowed to take part again. The competition would take place just around the corner, in Switzerland, and Adi Dassler had a mighty trick up his sleeve.

. . . .

Sepp Herberger needed all the help he could get from his friend in Herzogenaurach. His squad's prospects seemed uncertain, in line with the mood that prevailed around the country at the time. The West Germans had the dèutschemark, their own constitution, and an economy that was recovering at a staggering pace, yet all of this had failed to lift the veil of humiliation and grief that still shrouded the country.

After some unexplained ups and downs, Herberger's squad made it to the finals, which would pit them against the Hungarians. Led by Ferenc Puskas, the heroic Hungarian striker, the Mighty Magyars had not conceded a single international defeat in more than four and a half years. The prognosis for the game, scheduled for July 4 at Bern's Wankdorf Stadium, was near-unanimous: the Germans, who had already been battered 8 to 3 by Puskas and his teammates in the preliminary rounds, didn't stand a chance.

On that fateful day, Adi Dassler and Sepp Herberger scanned the skies that hung over their balcony at the Belvedere Hotel, overlooking Lake Thun. They were hoping for some rain because the German team's captain, Fritz Walter, was known to favor heavy pitches. There was not a cloud in sight that morning. But by the time the players departed for the stadium, they were delighted to feel the first drops of a steady downpour.

The time had come for Adi Dassler to do his trick. As he revealed to his friend Herberger before the start of the World Cup, the boot-maker had come up with an invention that would become known as adjustable cleats, or studs—to be screwed on or off, to varying lengths, depending on the state of the pitch. If it was dry, the players could keep short studs to give them traction. But if the grass turned to mud, the studs could easily be lengthened to increase the grip of the boots on the slippery surface. "Adi, screw them on!" Sepp Herberger instructed when it became clear that the Wankdorf Stadium would soon be soaked.

At halftime, Herberger's squad unexpectedly managed to remain level with the Hungarians, with both teams having scored two goals. But just six minutes before the end of the game, with the pitch turned to mud, the stadium came alive again. There to provide a calm, matter-of-fact description to the millions of people glued to their radios, a German reporter flipped. "Schäfer delivers a cross into the box. Header, cleared," commented Herbert Zimmermann, still calmly. But then he saw the ball landing on the feet of Helmut Rahn, a thickset striker from Essen. "Rahn should take a deep shot, Rahn shoots. Goal, goal, goal!" Zimmermann shrieked. After a moment of stunned silence, the reporter tried to capture the madness of it all. "Germany leads three to two, five minutes before full-time! Call me mad, call me crazy!"

Zimmermann's voice betrayed his nerves over the next few minutes, willing the whistle to blow. Hundreds of jubilant fans then ran onto the field and scenes of boisterous elation erupted all across Germany. The exhausted players lifted Herberger onto their shoulders. He tugged at Adi Dassler, insisting that the boot-maker be included in the victory snapshot.

On the other side of the Aurach, the compliments stung badly. Rudolf Dassler was entirely sidelined in Switzerland. The technicians at Puma angrily claimed that they had also introduced lightweight boots with screw-in studs several months before the Bern game, but their protests were drowned in the euphoria of the German victory.

The unlikely triumph in Bern would be celebrated as the unof-

Adi Dassler with Sepp Herberger at Wankdorf Stadium after "The Miracle of Bern."

ficial rebirth of German democracy—a founding moment for the Bundesrepublik. On paper, the country had regained its economic standing and earned its democratic credentials. Yet for millions of people, it was Helmut Rahn's shot that ended the dark years of shame and shortages suffered by many Germans after the defeat of the Nazi regime. For the first time in many years, Germans could innocently rejoice together and affirm their pride in something German. Due to the amazing outcome of the game, as well as its repercussions, the 1954 final was heralded as *Das Wunder von Bern*, the Miracle of Bern.

Along with the tired soccer heroes and their deadpan coach, Adi Dassler was widely acclaimed as an instrument of the triumph. The Bern boots were given such exposure that Adidas was suddenly bombarded with requests from other countries. With the Swiss miracle, the three stripes established an international advance with which rivals would never manage to catch up.

. . . .

With his bullying brother on the other side of the Aurach, Adolf imposed himself as *Der Chef* at Adidas. Quiet and withdrawn, he gladly entrusted business relationships to his wife, who began to dispatch three-striped boots and spikes all around the world. Adi was still most at ease behind his desk, poring over technical drawings. Employees at the factory appreciated the little man's down-to-earth attitude.

The only things that Adi did not tolerate were sloppiness and ignorance. "If Adi felt that somebody was not completely up to scratch, just because he held up a shoe in the wrong way, the poor guy was out," recalled Horst Widmann, Adi's longtime personal assistant. "The same went for anybody who spoke up at meetings for the sake of it. Adi just didn't have time for these kinds of people."

Adi's own office was littered with strips of leather, rubber samples, and scores of little notes. "He was particularly prolific at night," said Heinrich Schwegler, one of Adi's early assistants. "In the morning he would do the rounds with his scribblings and hand them out. That was the way he organized his business." The heavy pieces of machinery sometimes filled Adi with fear, however, since he had inadvertently injured himself with one of them in the late forties. He was using the sharp leather punch and forgot that it often recoiled. The machine cleanly severed the index finger of his left hand.

On the other side of the Aurach, Rudolf ruled over his company more brazenly. He burst into meetings with resounding laughter, brimming with enthusiasm. Prone to paternalistic chats with the workers, Rudolf wouldn't hesitate to sit down and share a packed lunch with them. When his mood swung, however, which occurred quickly and recurrently, the employees soon became aware of it, too. Rudolf made his presence felt loudly under any circumstances, cheering one minute and booming with anger the next.

The problem was that, for all his impulsiveness, Rudolf often had the reflexes of a small-time family businessman: "tight and generous at the same time." "Sometimes we made mistakes because Rudolf didn't have a real entrepreneurial attitude," said Peter Janssen, former Puma production manager. "He was often exceedingly thrifty and even more risk-averse. For me it was always a struggle to convince him when we needed to buy upgraded machines."

In the tug-of-war between the Dassler brothers, the women had to pull their weight. They were meant to support their husbands, to lend a hand here and there, and to contribute to the family atmosphere at the company. They were always at the ready to welcome the guests, athletes, and retailers who dropped by to pick up some spikes or to have a chat with the Dasslers. Forging such friendly relationships was critical at a time when money hardly played a role in sports: back then, athletes picked the shoes that fit best or the ones that were recommended by their trainers; but a friendly touch could still make all the difference.

Käthe was one of Adolf's most precious weapons. Although she had given birth to a fifth child, Sigrid, in 1953, Adi's wife kept a close eye on the business. With her forceful personality and diplomatic charm, she more than made up for her husband's withdrawn attitude. With Käthe, distributors and other guests felt instantly at ease. She enthusiastically ushered them into the kitchen, immediately setting a warm plate on the table.

As the callers began to stream in from afar, it was Käthe who dealt with the company's international partners. One of the most interesting requests came from Ray Schiele, a German who had moved to Canada in the early fifties and took on all sorts of sales assignments, peddling anything from marmalade to locomotives. A soccer enthusiast, Schiele pleaded with Käthe to send him some Adidas soccer boots to sell in Canada. The three pairs he received didn't suffice to build up a business there, but Schiele persisted and soon broke through when he obtained the endorsement of the Edmonton Eskimos, a Canadian football league team.

Others just knocked on Käthe's door because they had heard about Adidas through coaches and runners. Simeon Dietrich, owner of a small hardware business in Michigan, turned up in 1955 while running an errand for a friend, a track coach who needed spikes. Dietrich left the Villa with exclusive rights to distribute three-striped products in the entire United States. Just like many other Adidas partnerships at the time, the agreement was sealed with a handshake. It was later confirmed in a written contract that contained just two paragraphs.

On the other side of the Aurach, Friedl Dassler bent over backward to support her husband. Her gentle attentions were appreciated by the employees, too, who called her "die Puma-Mutter," the Puma mother. Friedl put up with the mood swings of her husband, who was becoming increasingly gruff, but she still couldn't compete with Käthe's ebullient, spontaneous charm.

By the mid-fifties, both feuding Dassler brothers ruled over respected sports companies. While Puma was most firmly established in German soccer clubs, Adidas had achieved much stronger recognition in the international scene, and it would continue to outfit the German national team for several decades. Nearing retirement age, the two brothers weren't prepared to relinquish the leadership of their companies. But they could rest assured that their sons would drive Adidas and Puma with equal obstinacy.

olympic handouts

A lean twenty-year-old with intense eyes and a hawkish nose, Horst Dassler landed in Australia with a couple of summer suits and the address of an Adidas retailer in Melbourne. His parents, Adi and Käthe, had sent him over to peddle Adidas spikes at the 1956 Olympics, but the outing would have far deeper repercussions than they had foreseen.

When Horst landed, the spikes sent by his parents were still blocked at the docks, alongside a Puma consignment. The young German tackled the problem with characteristic shrewdness: he pleaded with well-known athletes to write letters to the customs officials to explain that they needed the Adidas shoes for the Olympics. At the same time, Horst made sure that the Puma consignment would remain blocked at the docks.

To some extent, Horst Dassler had been groomed for this assignment from the moment he began to walk. On both sides of the Dassler family, all of Adolf's and Rudolf's children were drawn into the business, beginning with menial tasks during their school holidays and graduating to full-time jobs. But for Horst

Dassler, the Melbourne Olympics were much more than a student job. They marked the onset of a career that would reshape the world of sports.

Horst was the eldest of Adolf and Käthe's five children, and their only son. He'd spent much of his childhood in the Villa with his cousins Armin and Gerd. In spite of the war's deprivations, the Dassler children were among the most privileged in Herzogenaurach. Yet the childhood of the two sets of cousins was deeply affected by the war and the rift between their parents.

None of the boys dared to enquire about the motives behind the split. Once their fathers had settled on opposite sides of the Aurach, the children barely needed telling that they should not mingle with their cousins. Like the rest of the village, they had to stick to their own side—at a safe distance from the cousins and playmates with whom they had shared a house since their birth.

On the weekends, Horst was often dragged along with Adi for lengthy runs in the forest. The young man relished the shared sports activities, which gave him time to forge silent bonds with his father. "My father wasn't exactly bubbly in terms of conversation. His words tended to be pragmatic," Horst told a German reporter much later. When it came to his mother, Horst Dassler's biographer noted that "he respected her highly and, to some extent, even appreciated her," but "he didn't have such a close relationship to his mother."

Horst spent part of the war years at the Bavarian monastery of Ettal, and returned to attend the Fridericianum college in Erlangen, which provided general education with a humanist slant. A quiet and unpretentious youngster, Horst went on to spend two years in a Nuremberg school of commerce before he was sent to Pirmasens to take the same shoe-making course as his father. But in Melbourne, the young Dassler heir demonstrated skills that could not be acquired anywhere.

Amid the excitement of the Olympic preparations, Horst Dassler drove to the Melbourne Sports Depot, a sports retailer that had just begun to sell some Adidas spikes. Once he met up with its owner, Frank Hartley, he unveiled a startling project: instead of selling Adidas shoes, Horst would hand them out for free. At a time when money was still a dirty word in international athletics, this was a completely unheard-of proposal. Until then, athletes had always turned up with their own spikes. In some of the wealthiest countries, they might be given a pair by their federation, but in many other cases they had to find the money for them themselves.

Under the Olympic rules, the athletes were still meant to be strictly amateur. They were not to accept any money or other forms of compensation that could be traced directly to their accomplishments as athletes. Likewise, the shoe companies were not supposed to exploit the commercial worth of the athletes: when advertising, they were forced to disguise the identity of any runners pictured by blurring their faces or placing a black band across their eyes. Avery Brundage, the American chairman of the International Olympic Committee since 1952, watched over these rules with near-fanatical devotion, which earned him the unflattering nickname of "Slavery Avery."

Yet Horst Dassler bet that he would not be reprimanded for offering athletes free spikes, because they could be regarded as technical equipment. Spikes were an indispensable piece of equipment for runners at a time when races were still held on cinder tracks in which athletes dug their own starting holes with a little shovel. Since spikes were expensive, runners wore them and fiddled with them until they fell apart.

When Horst Dassler explained that he wanted to hand out free shoes, Frank Hartley at the Melbourne Sports Depot was not impressed. He regarded the Olympics as a splendid opportunity to boost his sales, but there was little hope of selling shoes if the son of the owner of Adidas was giving them away. Still, Horst convinced Hartley that the gifts would be a smart investment. He couldn't think of any better publicity for his business than a throng of athletes hitting the tape in three-striped shoes. The retailer let Horst fill his store with boxes of "Melbourne" spikes, designed for the Olympics, with three green stripes and a cross on the heel. Entire delegations of athletes were invited to take their pick.

By then Adidas had made such headway that many other athletes were turning up in Melbourne with their German spikes. Al Oerter, the American discus thrower, had worn Adidas since the early 1950s, when his father, a plumber, found a pair for him at the back of a store for electrical appliances in New York. "None of the American companies made a size fourteen shoe for throwing," Oerter explained.

American track and field coaches had gotten to know the German brand through the Severn brothers in California. Longtime importers of cricket equipment, the Severns had heard about Adidas spikes and begged the Dasslers to send them a consignment. They excitedly stored the boxes in their garage in North Hollywood but quickly realised that unloading them would be an uphill struggle. After the war, California had adopted a "buy American" policy, which meant that retailers were reluctant to take Adidas, and it could not be sold to high schools. The only thing the Severns could do was to drive from one college campus to another and painstakingly build the brand's reputation among up-and-coming athletes.

Mingling with the athletics team at the University of California at Los Angeles (UCLA), Clifford Severn easily gained entrance to the university tracks. He badgered the coaches until they agreed to blow their whistle and gather the athletes on the bleachers. Yet many of them were still reluctant to try Adidas because they didn't look anything like the ordinary spikes worn by U.S. athletes. "It was a blessing and a problem," said Chris Severn. "The athletes had always worn black spikes, and here we were with blue kangaroo leather and three white stripes."

As they continued to hang around campuses, Chris, Cliff, and Ernie Severn became friendly with such coaches as Oliver Jackson, who headed the track team at Abilene Christian in Texas. Their star sprinter was Bobby Morrow, a farmer's son who had become known as the San Benito Bullet. Some of the other coaches who watched Morrow run described him as the greatest sprinter they had ever seen. With his relaxed and graceful style, they said, Morrow could have run with a beer float on his head and never spilled a drop. Once the phenomenal sprinter had tried Adidas, he would not return to anything else. "They were just the only good spikes around at the time," said Morrow; and many others thought as much. Although the American track and field federation supplied its Olympic athletes with Wilson shoes, many refused to wear them and ordered Adidas instead.

While such athletes had rallied to the Adidas cause, Horst Dassler relentlessly pursued his quest to convince others. The friendly Adidas man toting his large holdall became a familiar sight at the Melbourne Olympic Village.

Meanwhile, Horst's cousin Armin, who had begun to work for Puma, was busying himself around the Cricket Ground, too. However, he chiefly had to appease athletes, as some of the Puma spikes appeared to be falling apart. Dick Bank, a West Coast real estate developer and athletics reporter who accompanied the American team in Melbourne, watched with a mixture of amusement and pity. "It was a huge embarrassment for Puma," Bank said. "The spikes kept coming unglued, and here was poor fat Armin running around to pick them up."

Among Horst Dassler's less familiar rivals was a brand called Onitsuka Tiger, established after the war in Kobe, by Kihachiro Onitsuka, as a means to keep youth off the streets and encourage them to practice sports. Leaning on Kobe's huge rubber factories, Onitsuka set up his own plant and started off with basketball shoes. But the company broke through in long-distance running, supplying marathon runners from Japan and elsewhere. Tiger shoes made their first high-profile appearance in international sports on the feet of Japanese athletes at the opening ceremony of the Melbourne Games.

Yet it was Adidas that truly dominated the Melbourne tracks, leaving both Puma and Tiger sidelined. When the medals were counted, Horst Dassler proudly informed his parents that more than seventy of them had been won in three-striped shoes. The athletes had received their free Adidas spikes with such eagerness

An all-Adidas finish line, with Bobby Morrow breaking the tape.

that the brand seemed ubiquitous at the Melbourne Games. The snapshots of many finishes were dotted with Melbourne spikes, yielding unbeatable publicity for Adidas.

Among the winners, Bobby Morrow lived up to expectations by taking two gold medals for the 100 and 200 meters, then another one for the 4-by-100 meter relay. The Severns could not believe their luck. "There he was on the cover of *Life* magazine with his three-striped spikes," Chris Severn said. "It caused quite a stir, and all of a sudden retailers became interested." Orders picked up so rapidly that the Severns no longer had enough storage space in their garage.

Beyond the track, the Melbourne Olympics enabled Horst Dassler to establish himself in the sports business. Many of the athletes who competed in Australia remained involved in international sports, and some of them went on to become high-profile executives in sports-related organizations. Horst Dassler made sure that they would remember him as the easygoing twenty-year-old who gave them free Adidas spikes. Melbourne had provided him with an unbeatable array of grateful contacts.

· · · ·

When athletes turned up for the next Olympics, held in Rome in 1960, they scoured the track in search of the nice German with his large duffel bag. But in the intervening years, the Puma Dasslers had caught on. They also began to cultivate contacts with leading athletes and give away their own spikes. And to beat Adidas, they dedcided to give something more.

From the late 1950s, Rudolf Dassler shared the company's leadership with Armin, his eldest son. Rudolf himself continued to occupy Puma's largest office and to make his voice heard at all times. His eldest son was encouraged to increasingly take over contacts with athletes and international partners, but the relationship between the two men was heavily strained.

Throughout his youth, Armin suffered from his father's harshness. Rudolf Dassler made it clear that he held high ambitions for his son, and that he had been disappointed. "Rudolf wanted a child with athletic gifts and supreme intelligence," recalled Betti Strasser, Armin's aunt. "He constantly belittled Armin, often in public." Armin pleaded with his father to let him leave and study electronics, but Rudolf wouldn't hear of it: Armin was to learn the tricks of the shoe business as soon as he left college.

This was all the more appalling since Rudolf displayed apparently unjustified indulgence toward his second son, Gerd, born ten years after Armin. By openly favoring Gerd, he stimulated an aggressive and sometimes unhealthy form of competition between his two sons. The disputes crushed Friedl, mother of the two children. She often begged her husband to put an end to this injustice, but he consistently brushed her pleas aside. Once a joyous and courageous woman, Friedl crumbled under the relationship with her despotic husband.

The problems later appeared at Puma, where the tensions between Rudolf and his eldest son caused embarrassing scenes. "The relationship was not easy," said Peter Janssen, one of Armin's former schoolmates and later a Puma board member. "Young Armin was eager to climb the ladder, but his father consistently

pushed him down." Once he committed himself to Puma, however, Armin displayed the same eagerness as his father to per-
petuate the feud with Adidas.

By then, word had spread among athletes. Some of them con-
spicuously hung around the training grounds, waiting for the
shoe peddlers to make their move, while others didn't hesitate to
beg for a pair. But Horst Dassler himself had become a little more
selective than he was in Melbourne: he meticulously followed
athletics news and saved his spikes for the contenders who stood
the strongest chances to reap medals.

Armin Hary, a controversial German sprinter, was the first athlete who blatantly exploited the Adidas-Puma rivalry. Ahead of
the Rome Olympics, Hary had repeatedly demonstrated that he
was the fastest man in the world. He could even claim that he
was the first man ever to run 100 meters in precisely ten seconds:
the time was clocked in Zurich in June 1960, just weeks before
the opening of the Rome Olympics.

Adolf Dassler was elated. Armin Hary had been a regular guest
in Herzogenaurach, and Adi had eagerly followed his progress
and appreciated the feedback from the tall runner. Adi spent
many hours crafting Hary's spikes. If he stayed in shape, Adidas
looked certain to feature prominently on the podium of the 100
meters at the forthcoming Olympics.

As Adi observed, Hary's performance had improved substan-
tially since he spent some time in the United States. However,
along with the latest techniques on fitness training, Hary had
learned that performers deserved to be rewarded financially.
While this still didn't officially apply to athletes, Hary appreciated this part of the American ethos and firmly intended to apply
it to his own athletic career.

The sprinter apparently turned to Alfred Bente, the husband of Inge, the eldest of Adi Dassler's daughters. Since Alf
had been fully adopted by the Dasslers, the Bentes moved into
another house in the Adidas compound and took over much
of the company's German business. Handling production, Alf
gradually imposed himself as the second-in-command in Her-

zogenaurach, while Inge was in charge of promotion among German athletes.

In his chat with Bente, Hary bluntly enquired what Adidas would be prepared to offer for his commitment. Flabbergasted by this highly unusual request, Bente flatly refused to hand over cash. On the other hand, he agreed to consult Adi Dassler on Hary's alternative proposal: that Adidas appoint Hary as a distributor in the United States, with ten thousand pairs of shoes as an interest-free beginners' credit. As Bente had expected, Dassler angrily refused.

By then, Armin Hary had made some friends on the other side of the Aurach. The contacts had been laid by Werner von Moltke, a German and later European decathlon champion who began wearing Puma in 1958. Von Moltke accepted some free Puma shoes and agreed to act as an intermediary for the brand at international track meets. With Armin Hary it was easy: they were teammates. "I gave him shoes from Puma and we had a little bit of money so I could invite him for lunch," Von Moltke recalled. Over the months the relationship deepened, and Hary soon commuted between the two banks of the Aurach.

When he took his seat in the Stadio Olimpico for the final of the 100 meters, Adolf Dassler was still convinced that Armin Hary would have forgotten about the money nonsense and that he would turn up in his Adidas spikes. He was utterly dismayed, therefore, when the German sprinter emerged from the tunnel in a pair of Pumas. While all of the other four contestants had the three stripes, Hary's Formstripe was clearly visible from the stands.

The Puma clan beamed as Armin Hary raced to his gold medal in 10.2 seconds. As Von Moltke admitted, the sprinter's choice was at least partly motivated by a thick brown envelope. Hary was offered a bonus of an estimated 10,000 German marks for winning the gold medal, a substantial sum at the time. But a few minutes later, the faces dropped on the Puma side. They watched with consternation as Hary turned up at the medal ceremony in Adidas shoes. "It was truly hurtful for Rudolf and Friedl Dassler, who had welcomed him with open arms," Werner Von Moltke said, sighing.

An avid businessman, Armin Hary apparently figured that the trick would enable him to collect money from both companies. But Adi Dassler was so disgusted that he barred Hary from his side of the Aurach. The German sprinter continued to collaborate with Puma, but the company's managers could not forget the Rome incident and consistently referred to Hary as "a chap who eats on both sides." After the Rome Olympics they all knew that athletics, and the shoe business that came with it, would never be the same again.

. . . .

Some of the Japanese guests who turned up at the Rome Olympics anxiously watched these developments: the organizers of the Tokyo Olympics, to be held four years later, didn't want to see their Games marred by undignified shoe dealings around the track. The Tokyo Olympics were to herald Japan's return among the world's most respected nations, putting an end to the anguish and isolation of the postwar years.

On that count, the 1964 Games were a formidable success. In the runup to the Games the Japanese capital was entirely transformed, with new expressways and train lines crisscrossing the town and spectacular sports facilities built in the Komazawa Olympic Park. The National Stadium designed by Kenzo Tange was an avant-garde monument to Japan's reconstruction.

The opening ceremony, attended by Emperor Hirohito in a packed stadium, had been arranged in the same spirit, placing much emphasis on the message of peace that Baron de Coubertin had sought to propagate. One of the highlights was the entry of the Olympic flame, with Yoshinori Sakai as a last torchbearer: born on August 6, 1945, the day the atomic bomb exploded in Hiroshima, the young student had been picked in homage to the victims of that day and as a call for peace.

Yet all this high-minded symbolism still couldn't prevent the shoemakers from using the Tokyo Olympics as another opportunity to further their more prosaic business. Since the Hary precedent, the Dassler brothers' rivalry had intensified, and many more athletes were receptive to the advances of shoe companies.

The largest investments were committed by Onitsuka Tiger, which poured about thirty billion yen into promotion for the event—"an outrageous sum back then," as Kihachiro Onitsuka observed. Among the events targeted by the Japanese brand was the marathon: although Tiger had started off as a basketball shoe, Onitsuka had since shifted the emphasis to running. But much to his dismay, the previous Olympic marathon had been won by Abebe Bikila, an Ethiopian runner who had covered the distance barefoot. Onistuka regarded this as a "shocking incident." "If running barefooted became popular, I would be out of business," he remarked.

The next time Bikila was in Japan, for the Mainichi Marathon, Onistuka went out of his way to meet the runner at his hotel. He was allowed to examine Bikila's feet and found them "soft as silk." He pleaded with the Ethiopian to try out a pair of ultralight Tiger shoes, made specially for him, convincing Bikila that they would feel just like bare feet—except that they would protect him from broken glass on the road. When Bikila turned up for the Tokyo marathon, however, Onitsuka was confronted with another shocking sight: the runner was wearing a brand-new pair of Pumas.

Both of the Dassler cousins turned up in Japan, and this time they didn't shy away from blunt monetary offers. But since it was still strictly illegal for Olympic athletes to take any money, at the risk of exclusion, they had to tread very carefully. On both sides, the Dasslers quickly learned to lurk around corridors and to whisper the word *bonus* in many languages.

The American sprinter Henry Carr, winner of the 200 meters race, recalled precisely how it was done. "I remember—like in the James Bond or mystery movies. In Tokyo, a shoe agent goes into the bathroom and leaves an envelope under the stall, and I go into the stall after him," Carr recounted much later. "You get an envelope that had six, seven hundred or a couple of thousand dollars in fives and tens. You thought you were rich." In his case, it was apparently Adidas that placed the largest envelope under the stall.

But in Tokyo, the Adidas men taught their Puma counterparts another trick. They were upset to discover that Bob Hayes, the most promising sprinter of the Olympics, turned up for training with a brand-new pair of Pumas. Horst Dassler's aides immediately caught up with Hayes and offered him more cash to switch back to the three stripes. At the same time, they insisted that he continue to wear Puma until the beginning of the races: that way Armin Dassler would discover the loss only at the last minute, and he wouldn't get a chance to up the ante.

Among the influential men in Tokyo was Dick Bank, the athletics reporter who had accompanied the American team in Melbourne. He had heard that Adidas was offering free spikes to American athletes, to be picked up at the store opened by the Severns in North Hollywood. Much to his dismay, however, Bank discovered that the Severns were merely reducing the prices of spikes intended for athletes, instead of giving them away.

Therefore, Bank was all ears when he bumped into Kurt Baechler, a Puma representative, at a track meet in Hanover in 1963. Always eager to help out athletes, Bank provided a list of names and shoe sizes, and Baechler excitedly promised to deliver the goods before the Tokyo Olympics. Rudolf Dassler took such a personal interest in the matter that he invited Bank for dinner at his home in Herzogenaurach."

But over the next few months, Bank became frustrated with Puma as the free spikes failed to arrive. Bank therefore turned to Horst Dassler, who had approached him in New York in February 1964. With that, Adidas gained invaluable contacts and insights into American athletics.

For the Tokyo Games, Bank had obtained a broadcasting assignment, but he still spent much of his time at the Adidas booth. While there, he heard a commotion and saw Billy Mills, a long-distance runner on the American team, stomping away. He had come to ask for a pair of spikes and had been turned away, because some of the Adidas aides had never heard of him. But Bank had closely watched Mills over the previous months, and he was certain that the young man was about to break through. He hurried to catch up with the furious Mills and persuaded him to accept a pair of the latest Adidas "Tokyo" spikes.

Bank was behind his microphone again when the runners lined up for the final of the 10,000 meters races, which featured an impressive cast. Ron Clarke, who happened to be the Adidas importer in Australia, looked certain to win a gold medal at last, after an unbelievable string of misfortunes at the two previous Games. Two laps before the finish, the Australian was ahead with just two followers, Mohammed Gammoudi and Billy Mills. Since neither of them had ever come close to Clarke's world record, it seemed only a matter of time before Clarke surged ahead.

However, tensions flared in the last laps as the three front-runners had to elbow their way between the stragglers. As Clarke described it, the last lap was "like a dash for a train in a peak-hour crowd." When Mills refused to move aside to be passed, Clarke gave him a shove that sent the American reeling on the outside. Gammoudi lunged into the gap, with Clarke on his heels. At the beginning of the last stretch, the Australian was in front again after a heated duel with the Tunisian, with the crowd roaring with excitement all around them.

But all of a sudden Billy Mills kicked in with a final sprint that left the two others stunned. Sitting next to the NBC commentator, who was concentrating on the two front-runners, Dick Bank went wild. "Look at him! Look at Mills! Look at Mills!" he yelled hysterically over the running commentary, bursting out in joyous laughter as the American steamed across the finishing line, several yards ahead of Clarke and Gammoudi.

The winner was immediately surrounded by bewildered journalists, who all seemed to be asking the same question: "Who is Billy Mills?" It turned out that he came from South Dakota, was an Oglala Lakota Sioux who had been orphaned at twelve, and had gone to a school for native Americans in Kansas before attending the University of Kansas on an athletic scholarship. Royal blue suede with white stripes, the spikes Mills had obtained from Bank, could be seen from any corner of the stadium as Mills savored his victory—the first and last American ever to win for this distance.

Yet again, Horst Dassler and his team proved by far the most efficient of all the shoe peddlers in Tokyo. While the Olympics were meant to be a showcase for the Japanese brands, Onitsuka Tiger and Mizuno, ninety-nine medals were won by athletes wearing Adidas. Among the hundreds of athletes who wore the three stripes were an overwhelming majority of the medal winners in track and field. To all who had watched the rise of Horst Dassler at the Olympics, there was no doubt that the Adidas heir would quickly grab power.

the alsatian plot

In the middle of the night, a group of young men sat huddled around a large table in a coquettish Alsatian restaurant. Sipping vintage cognac, these excited managers were fomenting bold and elaborate plans. They were plotting to take over the sports business.

The young men went into conclave at the Auberge du Kochersberg almost every day. A former hunting lodge, the Auberge had been refurbished at considerable expense, and converted into a plush hotel with a gourmet restaurant and a formidable wine cellar. Guests were entertained there until late in the evening. Then the French managers gathered around their youthful chief, Horst Dassler.

His parents had dropped him off in the Alsace when he was still in his early twenties. Since his return from the Melbourne Olympics, Horst had become restless. He had inherited the drive of his father, as well as his mother's persistent and hardheaded character. He wheedled his parents to get more leeway and influence in the company, but his pleas were met with reluctance. His mother insisted that all of the children be given equal chances to prove themselves at the company. The discussions increasingly ended in acrimonious run-ins between Horst and his mother.

The friction was further aggravated by Monika Schäfer. Horst Dassler saw her as a charming young woman with whom he would consider sharing his life. But his parents, who had set their sights on the daughter of a well-established family, were not impressed. They cringed when they heard that Monika, a talented gymnast, once had a trapeze act in a local circus. To make matters worse, she was a Protestant, while the Dasslers had been brought up as Catholics.

Adolf and Käthe Dassler decided that they would be better off sending their impetuous son away from Herzogenaurach, but they realized that it would be foolish to deprive the family business of this talented heir. The solution was to place Horst in charge of a separate plant. The move would have the dual benefits of putting some distance between him and his parents, while helping Adidas cope with growing demand.

The Dasslers chose the Alsace. Just across the French border, the region was conveniently located more than four hours' drive away from Herzogenaurach. Its shoe industry was in trouble, with scores of plant owners desperately looking for buyers. The Dasslers' choice fell on the decrepit Vogel plant, in the small village of Dettwiller.

Enjoying the independence, Horst gladly settled in the Alsace, residing in an apartment above the factory. Much to his parents' chagrin, this drab setting did not deter Monika Schäfer from joining Horst there. A quiet celebration was held for their wedding at the Auberge du Haut-Barr, in Saverne.

By the late sixties, less than ten years after his Alsatian exile, Horst Dassler had turned the smelly Vogel factory into a hard-hitting production plant. But his aspirations went far beyond Dettwiller, and Horst had spotted exactly the right place to build the sort of business that he had in mind: nestled in the hills of Landersheim, the Auberge du Kochersberg would become the re-treat of his personal team.

While the hunting lodge was renovated, a block of offices was erected behind it, along with some tennis courts and a soccer pitch. On paper, the French business was just a subsidiary that had to take its instructions from Herzogenaurach. Yet with Horst at the helm, Landersheim and its Auberge du Kochersberg turned into the nerve center of Adidas.

. . . .

Once he had spotted an opening, Horst Dassler bulldozed ahead. Ignoring obstacles, he prodded his aides into immediate action. Alain Ronc, one of Horst's most intrepid managers, was among the trusted aides whom Horst sent out with tricky instructions. "[Horst] just didn't care about consultation, weighing problems and costs. He took bold decisions, then it was up to us to find the means to implement them," said Ronc, who joined the company as an assistant in the export department. "He was racing at two hundred miles an hour, and we were puffing behind, struggling to keep up."

Horst made his employees sweat hard. Most of them worked indecent hours and gave up most of their private lives to follow him. They started early in the morning and usually finished late at night, after a long dinner meeting at the Auberge, followed by a nightcap with Horst. Although contracts didn't stipulate that employees work on Saturdays, the offices were usually full that day. On Sundays the discussions often took place in more comfortable settings, at the Auberge or at Horst's house in Eckartswiller.

"Le Patron," as Horst was known in Alsace, worked hardest of all. A workaholic by any standards, he always looked for ways to exploit his time as efficiently as possible. One of his most bizarre ploys was known as the revolving dinner. "Three groups of people would be set up in three separate rooms, with one leading executive at each table," one witness recalled. "Horst would have drinks with one group. Sit at the table. Then, as planned, he would be called away for an urgent meeting. He would then move on to the next group, eat an appetizer, then be called away. And on to the next group for dessert. At the end of the evening all of those guests would feel they had dined with Horst Dassler."

Horst barely needed sleep. Those who worked closely with him routinely received phone calls in the middle of the night. Fully awake, Horst would have just been hit by another idea that he urgently wanted to discuss. The American girlfriend of one employee became so annoyed by the nightly intrusions that she once picked up the phone herself. "Horst, you are interfering with my sex life," she told him angrily. For the next weeks her hapless partner was asked daily about the state of his intimate affairs.

The insomnia was worse for those who traveled with Horst. With him, meetings would last usually until the wee hours of the morning, but that didn't prevent him from calling a few hours later. "You weren't sleeping, were you?" Horst would tease. At breakfast he would then casually ask his co-travelers what they thought of the bobsleigh competition that had been broadcast during the night.

Shortly after their wedding, Monika Dassler had given birth to two children, Adi and Suzanne. But Horst rarely saw them, and he didn't expect his employees to feel much need for a family life, either. Alain Ronc was confronted with a tough dilemma when Horst asked him to take part in a conference in Malta. Ronc explained that he couldn't because he was getting married on that day, but that didn't seem to bother Horst very much. "He asked if my prospective wife had ever been to Malta," Ronc said. "When I replied that she hadn't, he suggested that I could take her along. I would then spend three days at the conference and three days with her. That's how our honeymoon turned into a business trip."

To obtain such selfless commitment, Horst Dassler treated his employees with the same consideration he deployed for his guests at the Auberge. Although he rarely discussed private matters with other Adidas executives, he was always prepared to lend a hand. At least two employees felt indebted to Horst because he got them out of police custody when they were caught drunk-driving. Another acknowledged, with a mixture of embarrassment and affection, that Horst had helped one of his family members out of a dire financial situation. Horst came to see another in the hospital, where he was recovering from a minor injury. "Of course there was a manipulative touch to it," one employee later admitted.

But most of the youthful Adidas managers were entranced by Horst. They were in awe of his drive and mesmerized by his stamina, his persuasive powers, and the incessant activity of his mind. Horst was surprisingly a shy person, a weak orator who avoided the limelight. Yet he oozed a charm that captivated most of the people he met. His followers felt that he had embarked on an extraordinary adventure, and they would do almost anything to stay on board. "It was exhilarating," said Johan van den Bossche, a company lawyer at the time. "We all wanted to be a part of it, even if that meant that we had to run like hell."

. . . .

Because of his technical studies in Pirmasens, Horst deftly supervised operations in Dettwiller. His father, who turned up to advise the Alsatians from time to time, had to admit that their boots were worthy of the three stripes. As the demand for Adidas boots continued to swell, Horst Dassler quickly acquired several other decaying plants in Alsace. Yet the hungry young man hardly regarded himself as a plant manager.

To begin with, Horst launched an onslaught on the French market. For about two years, most of the products from the Alsatian plants were sent straight to Herzogenaurach, for the German market and some foreign distributors. Horst Dassler then turned Adidas France into a full-fledged subsidiary, surrounding himself with equally youthful sidekicks, who relentlessly peddled the French-made Adidas wares around the country.

At the beginning, Adidas received only piecemeal orders from French clubs and athletes. The company chiefly competed against Hungaria and Raymond Kopa, one of France's most revered soccer players in the 1950s, who later set up his own sports company. Kopa could open many doors in French soccer, but Horst Dassler picked resourceful players—the kind who would scour the country on match days to hand out Adidas boots and spend many more hours cultivating friendships at the bar. Extra rounds were bought for photographers if they promised to shoot close-ups of Adidas boots.

Unlike other athletes, soccer players were entitled to rake in extra money while they were still playing by selling sports gear. Once they retired, Horst sometimes hired them outright. They represented prestige and precious contacts, but Dassler could also be certain that they would have the required drive and persistence. It was easy enough to teach them the ropes of the sports trade.

Then Horst decided to conquer the sports ball business, and it was in Spain that he spotted an opening. When he was still a teenager, his parents had sent him out to spend some time with the Garcias, a Spanish family in Oviedo. He had learned to speak fluent Spanish, felt at ease in the country, and gladly returned there from time to time.

On one of these occasions he was walking along the streets of Murcia with the export manager of Adidas France, Günther Morbitzer, when they spotted a sports store. Called Deportes Martin, the store featured all the latest soccer gear, including leather balls with tags that read "Made in Spain." Immediately intrigued, Horst entered the store and enquired about the provenance of the balls. He was told that they came from Fabara, a small village at the other end of the country, not far away from Caspe, in Aragon.

Dassler and Morbitzer hurried back to their car and drove off to Fabara. The German sedan made quite an impression on the locals as it cruised through the village. The two men were equally astonished to watch people sitting in their doorways quietly sewing balls.

Horst managed to strike up conversation with one of them and found out that the sewing was organized by a man of mixed Spanish and French origin, Pedro Albiac. Albiac had scores of olive and almond farmers sewing balls for him to complement their often meager earnings. The balls were made of up to thirty-two pieces of leather, and it took about two and a half hours to stitch them together. Before Horst returned to France, he had struck a deal with Albiac. From then on, most of the balls sewn in Fabara would be sent straight to the Adidas warehouse in France.

Other balls were promptly squeezed out of the market. François Remetter, the French national team's goalkeeper, was well known for sneaking into the changing rooms and placing Adidas balls in the referee's locker. "Otherwise he asked befriended players who were on the pitch that day to kick the ball above the bleachers," recalled Jean-Claude Schupp, in charge of promotion at the time. "François would stand there at the side of the pitch and casually roll an Adidas ball towards the players."

While endorsement deals were still meaningless, Horst Dassler taught his employees to hook sports people by weaving together personal relationships. One of the crew was gruffly rebuked when he lamented to Horst that some of the players on a team contracted by Adidas had trotted onto the pitch in other brands of shoes. "Were you in the locker rooms with them?" Horst snapped. "Do you know the names of their wives? Did you have lunch with them beforehand? Well, then, what do you expect?"

Horst himself excelled at this discipline. His phenomenal memory stored the names and faces of countless athletes and officials. Le Patron would never close a conversation without enquiring about the welfare of the other person's family. The interest was flattering enough, but it often turned out that Horst genuinely listened to the reply, too. One business relation who vaguely spoke of his son's enthusiasm for a soccer team was stunned to receive, shortly afterward, a package for his son with autographed shirts from some of the team's players. Such attentions were perfectly in line with Horst Dassler's motto, "Business is about relationships."

To cement these relationships, the ultimate tool was the Auberge du Kochersberg. When they arrived in Landersheim to discuss their contracts, soccer coaches and players could spend several days at the Auberge, where they were wined and dined at length before the Adidas men began to discuss business.

With his indefatigable team and his personal brand of hospitality, Horst Dassler cultivated a style of his own in the sports busi-

The Auberge du Kochersberg, a former hunting lodge in the Alsatian village of Landersheim, which turned into a favored haunt for international sports supremos.

ness. This required heavy personal investments, but Horst was certain that they would pay off. Meanwhile, back in Herzogenaurach, his older cousin still had to find his place at his father's company.

. . . .

Armin Dassler left Herzogenaurach in a huff. After yet another row with Rudolf, his irascible father, he had decided to call it quits. He angrily packed his bags and set up his own company in Salzburg.

The relationship between Rudolf and his eldest son had always been strained. It deteriorated further when Armin, having become more self-assured, began to question his father's conservative methods. Watching Horst, Armin acknowledged that the sports world was undergoing rapid changes. And unless he was allowed to steer Puma in the right direction, the company would be entirely left out.

At the time, Armin had just separated from Gilberte, the mother of his two elder children, Frank and Jörg. When he stormed out of Herzogenaurach in 1961, it was Irene Braun who moved with him. A former employee in the Puma export department, Irene settled in Salzburg with Armin and Jörg, the youngest of the two boys, while Frank stayed with his mother.

Under a hasty agreement between him and his father, Armin

obtained the funds to buy up a plant in Salzburg and to cover the Austrian market. From then on, however, Armin was entirely on his own. His father stubbornly refused to provide any guarantees for Austrian bankers or any other form of support. "The old man sure made things difficult for us," Irene recalled.

To make matters worse, the couple soon discovered that the Austrian sports market was highly seasonal. From the beginning of November, the Austrians spent most of their weekends on the ski slopes. For nearly six months after that, there was no point in trying to sell them trainers. Puma Austria quickly ran into financial troubles, and it certainly couldn't rely on the parent company to lend a hand.

Armin then resolved to complement his Puma business with a few sales on the side. While his father strictly forbade him from selling the Austrian products in any other markets, Armin discreetly explored openings to sell Puma in the United States. He had already been sent out there by his father shortly after the war, and the visit had made a very strong impression on him. He saw that Puma would be at a huge advantage if it managed to make its mark in that country. From his hideout in Salzburg, the banished Puma heir therefore teamed up with Beconta, a distribution company based in New York.

Beconta had been set up in Berlin before the war and was taken over in the thirties by a Jewish businessman named Walter Blaskower. As a specialist in the distribution of Scandinavian javelins and discuses, Blaskower was assigned by the Nazi regime to deliver the track and field equipment for the 1936 Olympic Games. But as soon as all the foreign dignitaries had left, Blaskower's friends at the German Olympic Committee firmly advised him to leave the country at once.

After a harrowing journey, he arrived in the United States, with empty hands and a new name, Walter Blascoe. He resumed his imports of Scandinavian sporting goods after the war, and was quickly approached by Adidas to sell their products in the United States. However, Blascoe furiously refused. As a supplier of the Nazi Games, he had watched the close relationship between

Adi Dassler and the Nazi sports hierarchy. He couldn't even consider working with Dassler.

In the late fifties, Beconta was taken over by two younger businessmen, Karl Wallach and Jim Woolner. They already sold an improbable array of sporting goods, from javelins to ski pullovers, but felt that they should complement their offering with an athletic shoe brand. Through an agent in Austria, they arranged to meet with Armin Dassler in Salzburg and struck a deal to import his shoes, starting with just one model of cleated boots, under the brand "Puma Austria."

Although the two Americans were not privy to the details of the relationship between Armin and his father, they could not fail to notice that there was something badly amiss there. Their contract had been signed by Puma of Austria, yet Armin never suggested that they be introduced to his father in Herzogenaurach.

For several years, the relationship between Rudolf and his son remained so distant that the old man turned down an invitation to attend Armin's second wedding. The celebration was scheduled for September 1964, at the same time as Rudolf's annual holiday in Bad-Wörishofen. "We offered to have him chauffeured back and forth for the day," said Irene, "but he replied with a letter saying that he would not interrupt his break for our wedding."

Yet three years after his Austrian exile, Armin was drawn back to Herzogenaurach. Although they never fully reconciled, Rudolf Dassler had sheepishly asked his son to return. He was well into his sixties, he no longer had the stamina to drive Puma forward, and he needed Armin to reaffirm the family's grip on the company.

Among the assets Armin brought back with him to Herzogenaurach was his contract with Beconta in the United States. Karl Wallach and Jim Woolner had patiently built up the brand in that country and they could even claim to be well ahead of Adidas in American team sports. Still, the temporary reconciliation of the Puma Dasslers would certainly make things easier for them.

Too young to share the leadership in Herzogenaurach, Gerd

Dassler, Rudolf's second son, then in his early thirties, was sent to establish a subsidiary for Puma in France. As if the Dasslers consciously chased each other, this operation was established in Soufflenheim, just a few miles away from Horst's offices in Landersheim.

Inevitably, the cousins bumped into each other from time to time. The rivalry between them wasn't as visceral as it had been between their fathers, but the Dassler cousins remained deeply suspicious of each other. And in Mexico, Armin Dassler discovered exactly what he was up against.

dirty tricks in mexico

Long before their opening, it had become clear that the Mexico City Olympics would be mired in controversy. They formed another stage for the virulent protest mood of the times, buffeted by the Vietnam War, the assassination of Martin Luther King, Jr., and the Soviet invasion of Czechoslovakia, which had put a brutal end to the Prague Spring. The Mexico Olympic Games also provided the backdrop for the most devious quarrels between the Dasslers—leading to the collapse of the amateur athletics world.

At the center of the tumult around the Mexico City Olympics was a group of vocal black American athletes from California. Embodying the refractory spirit of 1968, they were determined to stand up for their political rights, and to shake off the legacy of the alleged bigots who ruled track and field.

Until the last weeks before the opening of the Games, on October 12, 1968, it remained uncertain whether any of the protagonists would make it to Mexico at all. Tommie Smith, John Carlos, and Lee Evans, the most promising runners on the U.S.

team, were also at the forefront of the Olympic Project for Human Rights, an organization that was rallying support for a proposed boycott of the Games. "It's time for black people to stand up and refuse to be utilized as performance animals for a little extra dog food," they thundered.

Among the targets of the Project's scorn were the Olympic rules that still forbade payments to athletes—although brown envelopes littered the locker rooms. The black American athletes were among those who sharply denounced the hypocrisy of it all. If officials nailed all the leading athletes who dealt with shoe companies, they argued, the Mexico City Olympics would turn into a second-rate track meet.

The dogged rivalry between the Dassler cousins was a boon for those who were determined to cash in on their performances, like one group of American runners who honored an invitation by Adidas in Landersheim a few months ahead of the Mexico City Olympics. Although two of them were longtime Puma wearers, they were wined and dined at the plush lodge for an entire week. As they groused about their lack of money, an Adidas executive offered them a contract to wear Adidas spikes, in exchange for five hundred dollars. Horst Dassler was away during the stay of the U.S. athletes, but he found out precisely what happened. "They got the money, signed the paper, and then received a copy of the paper they had signed. I would not have given them the copy," Horst said, sighing. "They took it straight to Puma."

Armin Dassler's trump card was Art Simburg, a former student at San José State University. While working as a sports writer, Simburg rounded off his earnings by peddling Puma shoes. A likeable young fellow, he was the butt of many jokes among other shoe companies and was regularly left stranded at U.S. track meets when Adidas people called hotels and car hire companies to cancel Simburg's reservations. The lonely silhouette of poor Art Simburg lugging his bags from one hotel to the next in the hopes of finding a spare room became a familiar sight in U.S. athletics.

Despite such hiccups, the Puma agent built up an impressive list of contacts, which was relatively easy due to his personal situation: he was engaged to Wyomia Tyus, a black sprinter who had won gold in the 100 meters race at the previous Olympic Games. She had been training for another set of medals with some of the most promising athletes on the American track team, such as Tommie Smith, Lee Evans, and John Carlos.

Beconta, Puma's American distribution firm, had unwittingly recruited Carlos shortly before the Mexico City Olympics, upon a recommendation by a coach in New York City. "He will either become part of the Olympic team or end up in serious trouble," the coach put it less politely. The Beconta managers readily agreed to hire Carlos in their New York warehouse.

Simburg's opponent at Adidas was Dick Bank, the sports broadcaster and real estate developer from Beverly Hills. Bank still eagerly followed athletics, but he was reluctant to take any part in the payoffs that proliferated around international tracks. At a meet at Mt. San Antonio College, Horst Dassler watched in dismay as half of the American athletes strode onto the track in Puma spikes. While displaying understanding for Bank's attitude, Horst recruited slicker aides to beat his cousin.

Staged high above Lake Tahoe in September 1968 (to replicate the atmospheric conditions in Mexico City), the U.S. Olympic trials constituted a full-dress rehearsal for the runners, and for the officials and shoe companies—and once again spikes were stuffed with banknotes. As the cynics joked, the true losers at Lake Tahoe weren't the athletes who failed to qualify for the Olympic team but those who walked away with empty wallets.

Among the most impressive performances was the one by Lee Evans in the 400-meter dash. Evans smashed the previous world record for the distance in 44.06 seconds. However, Horst Dassler remarked aloud that the black athlete was wearing the latest running shoe from Puma, known as the "brush shoe." Instead of the customary nail-like spikes, the shoe was fitted with scores of much smaller steel spikes—while track rules prohibited shoes with more than six spikes. The rubber bits under the Puma shoes could hardly be described as spikes, but Horst Dassler, alerted by Dick Bank, had more persuasive arguments to swing around the athletics federation. To the consternation of the San José clan, Lee Evans's record was promptly disallowed.

As the opening of the Games neared, Simburg settled down in Mexico with a group of Puma managers and eagerly waited for the arrival of the container of Puma shoes that had been sent over by Armin Dassler. Yet Armin's shrewd cousin, Horst Dassler, had already made special arrangements for the Puma container.

. . . .

Three years earlier, Horst had struck a deal with some mustachioed friends in the Olympic establishment. In blatant violation of the most elementary fair trade rules, Adidas would obtain exclusive rights for shoe sales in the Olympic Village. Most of the shoes would be manufactured by a Mexican company, but Adidas would get a special license to import another allotment of shoes from Germany for free. Puma, on the other hand, would be taxed at a stiff rate of about ten dollars per pair to get its German-made shoes into Mexico.

Exasperated by his conniving cousin, Armin apparently plotted a little trick of his own to eschew the import duty. The shipment of Puma shoes that reached Mexico in the last days of September looked intriguingly like a container of tax-free Adidas shoes. A telegram from Air France even identified the incoming shipment as urgent Adidas business, and the boxes were marked "AD, Mexico."

But Horst Dassler had instructed the customs officials thoroughly. When the Puma men headed for the customs storage center to pick up their shoes, smirking guards shook their heads. "The whole container had been impounded," recalled Peter Janssen, a former Puma board member. "Just days ahead of the opening we were all sitting there in Mexico City unable to get any shoes out of the customs office."

Armin Dassler was in for another shock when uniformed men burst into his hotel room. "They came to fetch us in the middle of the night and accused Armin of handing over forged papers to the customs authorities," Janssen recalled. Interrogated for several hours, Armin argued vehemently. He couldn't help it that Air France had made a mistake and that his initials were AD, the customary code prefix for Adidas shipments. But his protests fell on deaf ears. He was firmly advised to leave the country.

The problem was partly fixed through an envelope. "I placed it in my handbag, then took a cab for a long ride from our hotel to the airport and handed it over to Sepp Dittrich, our sports promotion manager, who found the right man to bribe," said Irene Dassler, Armin's wife. "It cost us several thousand dollars to get just fifty pairs of shoes out of the customs depot."

However, a group of British athletes agreed to smuggle more spikes out. "They walked over to the customs with empty shoe boxes, insisting that they should be let into the depot because the spikes didn't fit and they had to fetch another pair," explained Irene Dassler. Once inside, they stuffed each box with several pairs of Puma spikes. "If any guard had bothered to look at the contents of the boxes, we would have been in an awful lot of trouble."

Several days later, Art Simburg was walking around the Olympic Village in Mexico City clutching a bag full of Puma shoes when two men grabbed him by the arms. The undercover policemen ignored Simburg's pleas and drove him away without any further explanations. Wyomia Tyus frantically searched for her fiancé. Given the political climate in Mexico City that year, when scores of students had been shot dead in a demonstration just days before the opening of the Games, there was no telling what might have happened to Simburg. "She cried her eyes out, thinking that I was dead," Simburg recalled later. "I just disappeared from the face of the earth."

Detained in a Mexican cell, Simburg was not given any motives for his arrest and was not allowed to make any telephone calls. "The detention was dreadful," Simburg said. "One day there was a guy next to me who was suffering from acute stomach cramps. They just pushed him into a corner until he stopped yelling."

Karl Wallach and Lee Stock, two Beconta managers, were just preparing to leave for Mexico themselves when they received a call informing them of Simburg's detention. Wallach immediately alerted an attorney who had strong connections in Washington. "Just two hours later, I got a call from the White House," Wallach recalled.

When the American officials located Simburg, they were apparently told that he had been arrested for doing business while traveling with a tourist visa. It took a vigorous intervention from the State Department to get Simburg released after five days of detention.

To get the remaining shoes released from customs, Karl Wallach was advised to bring along a hefty check. He would then formally buy the consignment from Puma: while the German company had no Mexican import rights, Beconta, as an American company, would be authorized to get the shoes out of their container.

Wallach and Stock swiftly left for the airport. But in the meantime, the State Department had apparently looked further into the situation. As he was preparing to embark, Wallach heard his name being called over the airport's loudspeaker. The State Department was on the line. "They firmly advised us not to board the plane," he recalled.

Still, Wallach and Stock felt that they had no choice. To make sure they would be safe, the State Department sent a limousine to pick them up at the Mexico airport. They were placed in the same hotel as American officials and remained under guard throughout the Olympics. The shoes were finally released when Wallach wrote out a check for $20,000 to Puma, officially acquiring the shoes.

This didn't put an end to the distribution of traveler's checks. American reporters spotted athletes lined up in front of Armin's room to collect their money, and the queue was just as long at Horst Dassler's hotel. There was a commotion when one of the athletes attempted to cash in his hefty traveler's check from Puma at a bank in the Olympic Village. For fear of frequent holdups, local banks didn't have that kind of money in their tills.

Among the most enduring Olympic memories was the final 200-meter dash. Tommie Smith and John Carlos had both broken world records in previous heats. Carlos seemed to have the strongest chances, since Smith had apparently suffered a small tear in his groin during his last dash, but Smith ran a near-perfect race. He covered the distance in yet another world record time, 19.8 seconds, leaving John Carlos in third place behind the Australian Peter Norman.

As the three men headed for the podium later that day, on October 16, 1968, a gasp rippled across the packed stadium. Smith and Carlos were wearing black socks, with black scarves draped around their necks. As "The Star-Spangled Banner" resounded across the stadium, each man dropped his head and raised one arm to the sky, his clenched fist covered in a black glove.

Pointing to the glaring injustice and poverty suffered by many blacks in the United States, the gesture shocked the establishment and got Tommie Smith banned from athletics. Much later his raised fist would be pictured in history schoolbooks as a poignant symbol of black emancipation—a gutsy expression of Black Power. However, as Smith walked out for the awards ceremony, he brought along a single Puma spike, which he neatly laid down on the podium.

In the excitement of the competition, other deals were struck in the catacombs of the Olympic stadium. A spectacular about-face took place on the rainy day when long jumpers turned up for their final attempts. Bob Beamon, a black athlete from New York who spent part of his adolescence in jail, was among the athletes whom Simburg had won over for Puma. The fourth out of seventeen jumpers in the finals, Beamon tore down the runway toward the takeoff board, hit it perfectly, and sailed through the air at what seemed an improbable height. He hit the sand so hard that he bounced back and landed outside the pit.

His was such an awesome jump that the optical measuring device could not reach the point of impact. Stupefied judges had to call for an old-fashioned measuring tape. The verdict was 8.90 meters, a figure that pulverized the previous record and set another one that would hold for more than twenty years. When Beamon realized what he had done, he was felled by a cataleptic seizure.

Tommie Smith and John Carlos make a stand for the rights of black Americans in the United States at the Mexico City Olympics in 1968—still remembering to bring along a Puma shoe.

Arguably the most extraordinary athletic achievement of all time, Beamon's jump transfixed millions of viewers, over and over again. Much to Armin Dassler's chagrin, however, the three stripes on Bob Beamon's shoes were clearly visible from every angle.

Not all athletes were receptive to the Dasslers' cash appeal. An upcoming American athlete, Dick Fosbury, had his shoes hand-crafted by Adolf Dassler himself. A keen high jumper, Adi had heard in amazement that a part-time engineer from Idaho had come up with a new technique. While others jumped from their inside leg and curled the other over the bar, Fosbury rolled over the bar head first, with his back to the bar. When Fosbury inaugurated his weird flop, he was derided by other athletes and officials, but Adi Dassler immediately picked up his phone.

Several weeks later Fosbury was thrilled to receive a package from Germany containing handmade shoes that were exactly right for him, with distinct colors for each foot. They were the ones he wore in Mexico City, when he stunned onlookers with a jump that propelled him over a bar set at 2.24 meters. The Siberian-born Valery Brumel had done slightly better, but at Mexico City the 2.24-meter feat was enough to earn Fosbury a gold medal. "It was just amazing that this German cobbler would spend hours on spikes just for me," said the high jumper. "I was extremely grateful and certainly wouldn't dream of accepting cash to wear them." Fosbury's jump has since been adopted as a standard technique for high jumpers, known as the Fosbury Flop.

But the bundles of dollars that were handed out to many other athletes at the Mexico City Olympics deeply upset the supporters of the amateur rules, and they easily identified the culprits. To end the corruption, one of them suggested "the entire Dassler family would have to be deported to Siberia." Many others acknowledged that the outdated rules should be abolished.

As traumatic as the Mexico City Olympics turned out to be for the Puma team, they could leave the country with their heads held high. Their unbeatable contacts in the United States had enabled them to outfit many of the most remarked-upon athletes of the Games, in spite of all the devious tricks that were played on them. The contacts would prove even more rewarding in American sports, where Puma reached for the stars.

the puma swinger

Since Armin Dassler returned to Herzogenaurach, Puma had redoubled its efforts to crack the American market, and the brand's distributors in New York were making remarkable headway. Yet Puma really caught the eye of millions of Americans when a defiant football player trotted onto the field in a pair of swanky white sneakers.

Joe Namath had risen to prominence over the previous years as an outstandingly gifted athlete. While growing up in Beaver Falls, Pennsylvania, in a family of Hungarian emigrants, he caught the eye of both football and baseball coaches. He ended up with the University of Alabama's Crimson Tide, which he led to a football championship title in 1964. He then obtained the stunning sum of $427,000 to join the New York Jets, which was part of the American Football League (AFL).

Namath hit the headlines not only for his shotgun arm but for his exuberant lifestyle as well. A handsome football star, he was among the most wanted bachelors in New York and didn't hesitate to enjoy this status. The pleasures of the hippie years didn't pass him by, either. Asked about his preferred surface, he once answered, "I don't know whether I prefer Astroturf to grass. I never smoked Astroturf."

Most judiciously for Beconta, one of their owners, Karl Wallach, had become very chummy with Bill Mathis, a halfback for the New York Jets. Although he wasn't on the Beconta payroll, Mathis acted for all intents and purposes as a Puma representative in American football. When Joe Namath joined the New York Jets, he briefly shared a flat with Mathis. Later they lived just a block away from each other on New York's East Side and spent many of their evenings hanging out together.

Bill Mathis duly brought his new friend along to Beconta, but this athlete would come at a price. Namath's agent obtained an unprecedented deal worth $25,000 per year, paired with a payment of twenty-five cents for each Namath shoe sold by Puma. "It was most unusual, to say the least," chuckled Karl Wallach.

The deal proved most rewarding for both sides, as Namath enraptured the football crowds in impeccable white Puma boots. Inspired by the stupendous Jets quarterback, players on many other teams, from the Pittsburgh Steelers to the Miami Dolphins, began to wear the Formstripe. Beconta was selling Namath shoes by the hundreds of thousands.

Some of the Beconta men were slightly disturbed by Namath's attitude and liberal manners, which earned him the nickname of "Broadway Joe." Then again, Namath and his behavior also guaranteed headlines. The company therefore opted to play on the situation by having Namath pictured in full playboy attributes, with fur coat and Puma shoes, for an ad with the tagline "The Puma Swinger." "Sure, he was a swinger, always," said Karl Wallach. "But we were doing so well that it never bothered me."

The crowning moment of the relationship came as the Jets were preparing to face the Colts in the World Championship Game, later renamed Super Bowl III. The country's football business was then divided between the National Football League (NFL), to which the Colts belonged, and the AFL, which featured the New York Jets. The NFL teams were regarded as vastly superior, and they were so self-assured that they didn't hesitate to belittle their opponent.

The game came at a time when there was talk of a merger between the two leagues, but some writers contended that it would take several years for the AFL to compete with the NFL. A former NFL coach even chirped that the match would be the first professional game for Joe Namath. The two previous editions had ended with resounding victories for the Green Bay Packers, on the NFL side.

Yet three days before the game, Joe Namath could no longer contain his own confidence. "The Jets will win on Sunday," he shouted to a heckler. "I guarantee it!" Since such boasts were highly unusual at the time, his words made headlines around the country. But what was much more remarkable was that the Jets then proceeded to make the boast come true, with a stunning display by Joe Namath.

Although the forerunner of the Super Bowl wasn't quite the gigantic affair that it would become, the bravado of Joe Namath secured unprecedented exposure for Puma in the United States. That year alone, Beconta sold an estimated four hundred thousand pairs of Namath shoes. Unfortunately for Puma, the relationship would peter out soon thereafter, as Namath suffered from multiple injuries.

Still, the publicity gained through Namath had taken the Puma brand way beyond the confines of the track and placed it squarely on American football fields. It could rightly claim leadership of the game for several years, as Adidas struggled to come up with an adequate football boot.

. . . .

The Namath hit confirmed Armin Dassler's thinking. While his cousin apparently wanted as much exposure for the three stripes as he could get, the Puma heir had another tack. He figured that he would be better off by concentrating on a handful of international and charismatic players, the ones that grabbed all the headlines.

The strategy was partly dictated by necessity. Adidas had such means at its disposal that it could give away shoes to almost any athlete skillful enough to tie his own laces. Armin Dassler acknowledged that Adidas would always outspend him, and he therefore had to take a few bets.

A little ahead of his time in this respect, Armin Dassler sought to exploit the rise of a sports business in which the media avidly zoomed in on a handful of personalities. The endorsement of such heroes was risky, but it could still achieve much better returns than a spate of smaller players who never made it to the front pages.

While the rise of sports personalities occurred a little earlier in American sports than elsewhere, the same culture began to pervade international soccer in the late sixties. Soccer players in most countries had long become professionals, and the smartest of them eagerly sought to capitalize on their exposure.

As the stakes rose in the soccer business, Horst and Armin Dassler strove to avoid a repeat of the Mexico City episode. After all, their rivalry had served only to stimulate demands, which had cost them both dearly. Alf Bente, Adi's son-in-law, was therefore dispatched to the other side of the Aurach on several occasions to discuss with Armin Dassler informal arrangements regarding German soccer. Meanwhile, Horst Dassler and his cousin Gerd, established just down the road from Landersheim as head of Puma France, each agreed to stay away from at least some of the other's players.

But there was one astonishing deal that was sealed directly between Horst and Armin Dassler. It came about a few months before the 1970 soccer World Cup that would see the Dasslers return to Mexico. There was one soccer player, the enemy cousins jointly decided, who would remain entirely out of bounds for both companies: a bidding war for Pelé, the unique Brazilian player, would certainly have triggered a money explosion that neither of them could have afforded. They called it "the Pelé pact."

The Brazilian burst to prominence in 1958, when he made his international debut as a seventeen-year-old at the World Cup in Sweden. He stunned other players with his deftness and agility, helping Brazil to win its first World Cup. Wealthy European clubs offered huge sums to buy the young Brazilian, but to prevent his transfer out of the country, the Brazilian government declared Pelé a national treasure. He stayed true to his club in the Brazilian seaport of Santos, which cashed in on Pelé's fame by organizing regular exhibition tours and handing over a large share of the revenues to the player.

Pelé exited the next two World Cups early, injured by particularly brutal tackles. That didn't take anything away from the adulation he enjoyed in Brazil and elsewhere: as leading soccer players began to be treated as celebrities, "King Pelé" was a living myth. Watching him in action, one broadcaster suggested a new spelling for the word *God*: "P-e-l-e." As the world's greatest players prepared to congregate in Mexico, all eyes were on the Brazilian again.

A few months ahead of the 1970 World Cup, Puma decided to work with a plucky German journalist who could bring them into closer contact with the Brazilian team. Hans Henningsen had long covered Brazilian soccer for an array of international newspapers. He regularly shared a beer with the players and he could easily deliver most of them for Puma. But to his amazement, Henningsen was firmly instructed to ignore Pelé.

The situation was deeply embarrassing for Henningsen, who knew the player well. Pelé kept nagging the journalist, clamoring for an offer from Puma. He had obtained a small contract with Stylo, an English company, but he was puzzled that he couldn't get a juicier offer from the Germans, while all the other Brazilian players had long since signed their deals. Just days before the start of the competition, its most spectacular contender was still contract-less. Henningsen felt that "the situation was just too ridiculous." He resolved to ignore "El Pacto," offering Pelé $25,000 for Mexico and another $100,000 for the next four years, with royalties of 10 percent on Puma boots to be sold under the Pelé name.

For Armin Dassler, the opportunity was irresistible. He knew that his cousin's wrath would be devastating, but the prospect wasn't scary enough to make him pass on the deal concocted by Henningsen. The two personally delivered the cash to Pelé in Santos. As the journalist recalled, they were "quite astonished to watch him throw the thousands of dollars into his safe."

The tie-in had an awesome impact for Puma. Before one of the end games, Henningsen and Pelé came up with a trick to get some extra exposure. It was agreed that just before kickoff, the player would have a chat with the referee and ask him to hold on for a moment. Pelé would then kneel down and slowly tie up his laces. For several seconds, Pelé's boot filled millions of television screens around the world.

The publicity was unique, as Pelé helped Brazil to another World Cup triumph in Mexico. Tarcisio Burgnich, the Italian defender who marked Pelé during the finals, didn't understand what was going on. "I told myself before the game, 'he's made of skin and bones just like everyone.' But I was wrong," the Italian said after his team's 4–1 defeat. Puma would exploit the tie-in to the full: although their deal with Pelé lasted for only four years, the boots they made with him, such as the King and the Black Pearl, secured orders for several decades.

Predictably, Horst Dassler was not amused. Before he left Mexico, Hans Henningsen got caught in a most unpleasant meeting. There he was, stuck between an embarrassed Armin Dassler and an irate Horst Dassler, and flanked by three square-shouldered aides who clearly hadn't tagged along for a friendly chat. From there on, all peace agreements between the competing Dassler cousins were off.

. . . .

While Pelé sent soccer enthusiasts into ecstasy, American spectators were still more interested in their own sports. In American football as well as basketball and baseball, the rise of national leagues, paired with abundant glitz and media coverage, placed the heroes of these games squarely in the middle of popular culture.

In New York, one of the hubs for the sports crowd was Duncan's, a restaurant and bar on Manhattan's East Side. In the sev-

As part of a unique peace agreement, Horst and Armin Dassler agreed to stay away from Pelé, but Armin couldn't resist the Brazilian player.

enties it turned into a meeting point for assorted sports stars, accompanied by a posse of journalists, announcers, and other media types. Duncan's was owned by Bill Mathis, former halfback with the New York Jets, and Tucker Frederickson, a former running back with the New York Giants.

An upscale steakhouse with a stupendous piano bar, Duncan's had its walls covered with Leroy Neiman prints. Among the many regulars was Howard Cosell, then regarded as America's prime sports announcer, surrounded by athletes of all stripes. "Whether you were a basketball player or a quarterback, it didn't matter," said the Beconta manager Karl Wallach. "It was a real hangout for the sports society in New York."

Wallach himself didn't mind spending the evening at Duncan's, as he remained in close contact with his friend Bill Mathis. But any rounds of drinks Wallach might have offered at the bar were repaid many times over by a short phone call from Mathis. "How would you like to sign Clyde?" Wallach's friend asked.

Otherwise known as Walt Frazier, "Clyde" had earned his nickname from a coach at the New York Knicks who had made him their first draft in 1967. Frazier's sudden steals reminded the coach of the robber Clyde Barrow. Frazier enraptured basketball pundits with his speed and sharp passes. One opponent was baffled by Frazier's hands, which seemed "faster than a lizard's tongue."

Walt Frazier had grown up as the eldest of nine children in the segregated South, and had learned basketball on a dirt playground with rusted fences. He was such a remarkable sportsman that he was offered scholarships for football as well as basketball. However, he could not help noticing that there weren't any black quarterbacks at the time and therefore took up the basketball offer from Southern Illinois University. There he drew the attention of the Knicks scout when his relatively obscure school went on to win the National Invitation Tournament in 1967, with Frazier playing as point guard.

Perhaps his finest hour on the court came at the seventh game of the NBA finals in 1970 against the Los Angeles Lakers at Madison Square Garden in New York. In a dramatic start, center Willis Reed, who had suffered an ankle injury, hobbled on the court to score the two opening baskets of the game. Frazier then took over and electrified the audience with a dazzling display, to celebrate the Knicks' first NBA win.

However, there was more to Frazier than sheer talent. He distinguished himself also through his unflappable cool, exuding such calm that it even seemed as if he sweated less than his opponents. One sports writer marveled at the elegance of it all: "Frazier's smooth, sultry style of play was the physical equivalent of a Southern drawl," he wrote.

Off the court, Frazier was more likely to stand out for his style and eccentric dress sense. He routinely walked around in long fur coats and fedora hats with feathers, and he owned an improbably large collection of dress shoes. In his own way, he embodied a new generation of supremely stylish and self-confident black sportsmen. The Beconta men even saw Frazier driving a Rolls Royce. "He was the epitome of cool," as Jim Woolner summed it up.

At the time, Converse still ruled almighty on American basketball courts. Puma had made some headway in the basketball business by handing out its trademark suede shoes, but the sales weren't anything to write home about. That's why Karl Wallach couldn't believe his ears when Mathis let him know that Clyde would be interested in signing with Puma. "Do it," he replied.

Just a few days after the call, Walt Frazier and his agent dropped by the offices of Beconta, which had since moved to Elmsford, New York. Frazier and his agent didn't even bother to negotiate Beconta's opening offer. They gladly signed exactly the same deal as Joe Namath had a few years earlier: $25,000 per year and a royalty of twenty-five cents for each pair of signature shoes.

Yet Walt Frazier still ended up with a much larger check than Namath, because his shoe turned into a huge hit. While Elvis Presley had been rocking around the world with his "Blue Suede Shoes," Walt Frazier strutted on the court with his own blue suedes (and white Formstripe), with his signature printed on the shoe in gold lettering.

As the Beconta managers recalled, sales of the Puma "Clyde" reached well over one million pairs throughout the seventies. The shoe consisted of just one model, but it was produced in many different color combinations. The Clyde was often bought by youngsters who admired Frazier for his stylish flair as much as for his steals, and they wore their Clydes on the street rather than the basketball court. With the Clyde, Puma sneakers had made their first steps in the realm of fashion.

Such hits enabled Armin Dassler to deftly build up the Puma business outside Germany. But in the meantime, his cousin Horst had attained an altogether different stature. No longer was he the affable young German with the holdall full of spikes. Instead, he had turned into a respected entrepreneur, the international face of Adidas. From his French hideout, Horst Dassler was seizing control of his parents' brand.

8

stars and stripes

ack in Herzogenaurach, Adolf and Käthe Dassler watched their impetuous son with growing unease. While they contentedly filled out orders, Horst pushed ahead with increasingly bold moves. The contrasting attitudes led to rancorous discussions between Horst and his parents, but he staunchly refused to be held back by their conservative ways.

Although Horst deeply respected his father, he was often at odds with his mother and he was altogether exasperated by the pretensions of his four sisters. They were all still living in the compound and meddling with the business, with varying degrees of seriousness. Yet none of them could match the commitment of her brother, and many employees felt that the Dassler daughters would never have attained their position if they had been subjected to normal job interviews.

Given his drive and achievements, it seemed obvious that Horst was best equipped to take charge of the business one day, but his family was not in a hurry to admit this, and Horst didn't have the patience to sit around waiting. He felt that his parents were wasting precious time while the sports market was changing at breathtaking speed. Permanently on the lookout, Horst saw opportunities for the three stripes everywhere, and he could not bear to let them lie around.

To wrest control of the company Horst needed to spread his influence beyond the French borders. Adidas was mostly sold in other countries through distributors, who bought their products from the company in Herzogenaurach. But Horst figured that if he could persuade these partners to buy more products from his French operation, his turnover would take off.

Horst effectively resolved to compete against his parents. To this end he transformed Landersheim into a parallel organization with its own development, production, marketing, and export units. They would produce their own lines of Adidas trainers and offer them alongside the German lines. The arrangement caused many awkward exchanges, as the French and German managers assiduously courted the distributors and unashamedly competed for their orders.

Predictably, distributors in the French-speaking countries placed most of their orders in Landersheim. Then Horst more or less annexed Spain, where he forged many personal and business ties. Yet the French and the Germans competed head on for orders from other countries, which were open to offers from both sides.

The most heated discussions centered on the United States. It had become the weightiest market in the sports business, both in size and international influence. Neither of the two Adidas companies could decently claim international leadership if they didn't command a large share of sales in the United States.

By the late sixties, the American market had been carved up among four distributors. Simeon Dietrich, the Michigan businessman who obtained the deal to cover the United States while running an errand for a friend in Herzogenaurach in the fifties, had since passed the business on to his nephew, Gary. While he continued to cover the Midwest from Lansing, Michigan, Gary Dietrich agreed to share the rest of the country with three other distributors.

To the West, the Severn brothers were replaced with Bill Closs. The tall Texan had graduated from Rice University to play basketball for the Philadelphia Warriors and the Fort Wayne Pistons, before landing a job as a sales representative for Converse. Then he set up his own distribution company in Palo Alto, and in 1968 he obtained the deal to sell Adidas on the entire West Coast.

To the east, the Adidas distribution deal had been entrusted to a small-time New York City businessman, Dave Murray of Carlson Sports on Broadway. However, it quickly became apparent that Murray didn't have the resources to cope with the growth of Adidas. In 1970 he was replaced by the hard-charging Ralph Libonati, who built up the brand on the East Coast.

The South was covered by a cigar-chomping Texan. H. B. "Doc" Hughes had started peddling sporting goods in the twenties. He later set up his own company in Dallas and bumped up his sales by importing track shoes made by Puma, which he sold under his own Jaguar brand. But the deal that Hughes obtained with Adidas in 1966 transformed his business: "I hit the jackpot," he wrote.

After a few years of strenuous brand-building in the United States, the four Adidas distributors enjoyed soaring sales. As they conceded, the three stripes were almost selling themselves. "The growth was exponential," recalled Gary Dietrich. "For several years I spent most of my evenings at the office, just filling orders."

The distributors relished their gatherings with Adi and Käthe Dassler in Herzogenaurach. They flew to Bavaria at least twice per year to discuss business, to review upcoming products, and to write out their orders for the next season. To the four Americans and their partners, the meetings often felt like family reunions. They reveled in the warmth of Käthe's welcome and thoroughly enjoyed the convivial aspects of the entertainment that was arranged for them.

However, they were still receptive to Horst Dassler's approaches, because they were becoming increasingly frustrated by the shortages of Adidas products delivered by Herzogenaurach. The problem was that Adidas was submerged: Käthe Dassler had signed agreements with scores of international distributors, and once the demand for the three stripes began to run away, the company could no longer follow. It was swamped with orders that just could not be fulfilled.

The shortages drove the Americans and other distributors to despair. "We were ordering one year in advance and the products would still come in late," said Gary Dietrich. "It was constant. It was hell." The U.S. distributors were bombarded with phone calls from irate retailers, who had to turn away customers.

"I once requested an entire container and sat waiting for months," recalled Bill Closs. "Our contact person at the export department eventually admitted that it had gone missing. They simply could not locate it. I suspect that they just decided to divert it to someone else."

His son, Bill Closs, Jr., was intensely groomed by the Dasslers themselves as he spent several months living on the third floor of their home in Herzogenaurach. Yet even he could not get it across to them that late deliveries were disastrous for business. "Based on a commitment from Adidas we would take orders four or five months in advance," he said. "Sometimes they were for a team order: they're going to start at the beginning of the season, they're depending on a dealer in this little town in Washington to sell them the shoes. And we don't ship."

The American distributors complained incessantly and often felt that the Germans weren't tackling the problem as vigorously as they should. Horst Dassler rightly saw that if his business in Landersheim could make up for some of the German shortages with more timely and adequate French products, these distributors would gladly turn to him.

To grab the American orders, the French sealed production deals with plants in Hungary and in Czechoslovakia, at a time when such agreements still required much diplomatic palaver. The Germans retaliated by setting up production in Yugoslavia, but this badly backfired when the inaugural batches of Yugoslav boots fell apart. By and large, the French boots were much cheaper than their German counterparts, and the deliveries of them proved more reliable.

Since the production organized by Horst Dassler somewhat eased the shortages, his parents allowed him to offer his lines to the distributors at their meetings in Herzogenaurach—on the condition that French products could not make up more than half of the export orders. But Horst was far too hungry to abide by this rule.

The distributors began to feel uneasy at their meetings in Herzogenaurach, when German and French managers openly fought about their orders. Some of them eagerly exploited the rivalry, by pitting the Germans against the French. After their regular get-together in Herzogenaurach, they would sneak off to Landersheim to take a closer look at the entire French line, and to negotiate purchasing prices.

"Once we had finished in Herzogenaurach, we would drive them to the Nuremberg airport for their return flight," said a former export manager in Herzogenaurach. "But as soon as we turned our backs, they'd walk out of the airport again and head straight for Landersheim."

While the Germans fiercely defended their patch, the more ingenious French managers still snatched large chunks of American business from Herzogenaurach. Along with the more aggressive prices, their decisive advantage was that Horst Dassler was an abundant traveler, and he listened very carefully to the demands of the distributors.

. . . .

When Gerhard Prochaska, the French marketing manager, drove to Herzogenaurach for the regular meetings with international distributors, his German colleagues eyed his large hold-all with suspicion. The chances were that it would contain yet another nasty surprise for the Germans.

Prochaska played out the act many times over. "Horst thoroughly prepared for the meetings. From his talks with the distributors, he knew precisely what they wanted," he recalled. "When we started reviewing products, the Germans would display a few models which weren't exactly right. Then I'd fumble in my bag, hesitantly pull out a sample, and say, 'Oh look, we just happen to be working on the kind of shoe you're describing. Would that be all right for you?'"

The most startling invention to come out of the French marketing manager's bags was the Superstar. Until then, basketball had been more or less owned by Converse, the American shoe company of All Star fame. Like all the other basketball shoes on the market at the time, Converse high-tops were all canvas. With the launch of the leather Superstar, in 1969, Converse was almost squeezed out of the American basketball business.

The move was inspired by Chris Severn, whom Horst had retained as a consultant when the distribution deal for the West Coast was transferred to Bill Closs. As Severn observed, basketball shoes had barely changed over the previous decades. Due to their abrupt moves on the court, and the poor grip of their canvas shoes, players regularly hurt their ankles and knees. With an upper made entirely of leather, the Adidas shoes would provide a much firmer hold. To protect the shoe's nose, Severn devised a weird-looking shell toe. Another distinctive feature was the outsole: lined with thin grooves, it soon became a reference in the shoe business, known as the herringbone.

When Chris Severn proudly turned up in the locker rooms with his Superstars, the players weren't too sure if they should take him seriously. "They had played in canvas all their lives; the Superstar looked completely alien to them," explained Severn. "They weren't even getting paid by Converse; it was just a habit." While Converse was working with an entire army of salesmen, often former players, Severn was hawking his shoes all by himself, with just a few introductions and no budget at all.

Horst's special envoy was getting discouraged when he met up with Jack McMahon, then manager of the San Diego Rockets. McMahon was more than receptive to Severn's pitch because three of his players were suffering from slip injuries. He convinced nearly all of the players to give the leather Superstars a try. At the opening of the season, Chris Severn was sitting in the bleachers with his fingers crossed. He had heard that a Converse man had made the trip to San Diego and that the players had been offered some money to stick with the canvas shoes. "When they ran into the arena, lo and behold, they were all wearing three-striped shoes," said Severn. "It was a real thrill and it caused quite a stir among the public."

The Converse men still weren't shaking in their canvas shoes, though. After all, the San Diego Rockets were the lowest-ranked team in the league. What Converse failed to grasp was that, in spite of their start-up performance, the Rockets still had to play every single team in the country. By the end of the season, each professional player in the United States had been confronted with the startling sight of leather shoes on the feet of the Rockets. Chris Severn began to receive phone calls from players in other teams.

The second year after the shoe's introduction, word has spread to such an extent that the Superstar was worn by most of the Boston Celtics. Their victory of the American championship that same year opened the floodgates for the Superstar. The tide was phenomenal: less than four years after the launch of the leather shoes, about 85 percent of all professional basketball players in the United States had switched to Adidas.

Converse retaliated with player contracts, giving rise to a multi-million-dollar endorsement business. Some of the players grabbed the dollars and reverted to their canvas shoes. Chris Severn then convinced Horst Dassler to sign some emblematic players for Adidas. Towering over them was Kareem Abdul-Jabbar, a seven-foot-two player who had ascended to fame at the Los Angeles Lakers. The Dasslers reluctantly agreed to cough up $25,000 per year for Abdul-Jabbar, the first basketball player to be contracted by Adidas.

Just as Horst intended, the Superstar massively inflated the orders posted by the American distributors in Landersheim. By the early seventies, basketball made up more than 10 percent of Adidas sales—sales entirely in the hands of Adidas France. But with his next volley, Horst swept his German rivals off the court.

. . . .

Kareem Abdul-Jabbar signs an unprecedented endorsement deal for the Superstar. He is flanked by Horst Dassler and Chris Severn, the man behind the best-selling basketball shoe.

As Horst Dassler observed in the second half of the sixties, tennis was undergoing a radical change. No longer monopolized by the upper crust, posh men in pressed trousers and women in frocks, tennis courts had been taken over by a more diverse cast of players. It didn't take long before Horst and his managers decided to hijack the market, ushering in the white sneaker.

Until the sixties, tennis was reserved for well-heeled amateurs who safely locked the gates of their country clubs to players of less distinguished descent. They organized the major tournaments that could be entered only by fellow amateurs—players who were wealthy enough to train hard without any prospects of a financial reward.

Once they retired, some of the amateur players still sought to cash in by affixing their names to tennis clothing lines, such as René Lacoste and Fred Perry. But the segregation between amateurs and professionals became largely artificial in the sixties, as the major tournaments were infiltrated by supposedly amateur players who had found ways to earn a living on their performances: if they could not earn money by winning tournaments, they could at least pay the rent by lending their names to a shoe.

Until then, tennis shoes had been chiefly inspired by the plim-solls worn by English strollers, with canvas uppers and rubber soles. They could be regarded as the ancestors of such brands as Dunlop and Uniroyal, which turned out court shoes as a sideline to their rubber tire business. Yet rising enthusiasm for tennis prompted other companies to invest in the sport, unof-ficially paying players to promote their products. From then on, the whole principle of amateurism became known as "shamateur-ism."

The technicians in Landersheim set out to launch a tennis shoe along the same lines as the Superstar: it would be made of leather. To introduce it, Horst Dassler leaned on Robert Haillet, one of just two French tennis professionals at the time. When the "Robert Haillet" was introduced in 1965, the small cast of emerging tennis professionals widely agreed that it was by far the best tennis shoe on the market. As with the Superstar in basketball, the shoe's leather provided more support, which prevented twisted ankles and other slip injuries.

In the meantime, tennis continued to draw swelling crowds. The changes became most apparent in 1968, when Wimbledon gave up its exclusively amateur status. It ushered in the Open era, allowing self-declared professionals to take over the game. The all-white decorum was partly abandoned, tennis became more egalitarian, and players could openly seek sponsorship deals.

However, Robert Haillet had retired from the game, to become a sales representative for Adidas in the south of France. His pro-file was no longer in line with Horst Dassler's searing ambitions. The hungry heir therefore decided to launch roughly the same shoe under the name of a more prominent player, who could gen-erate publicity throughout the tennis world.

Donald Dell, a former player himself and the most influen-tial agent in the tennis business, offered Stan Smith. Due to his huge, Viking-style frame, the American champion was sometimes dubbed Godzilla. He rarely smiled on court and refused to provide any entertainment other than his game. Yet Smith topped the international tennis charts for most of the early seventies, repeatedly leading the American team to Davis Cup victories.

Smith had previously worn canvas shoes by Converse and by Uniroyal, an unpretentious American brand, which contracted him as part of an entire team. With Adidas it was another story: they promised Smith a separate contract and pledged to back it up with generous marketing investments. They were eyeing a large slice of the appetizing American tennis market, and Smith was thrilled to obtain royalties on a shoe with his own name.

While the "Robert Haillet" had been hobbling along, Stan Smith catapulted it to another dimension. Sales started ballooning shortly after the name switch, in 1971. The player himself was somewhat baffled to see many of his opponents adopt the "Stan Smith." "I got really annoyed the first time that I lost a match against a guy who was wearing my shoes," he said.

The "Stan Smith" was worn by an entire generation of tennis players, but its sales went much further as students began to match their jeans with tennis shoes. Entirely white, with stripes represented only in the shape of ventilation holes, the Stan Smith was particularly suitable for this habit.

Nowhere did it take off with such speed as in the United States. When she appeared at her campus wearing her Stan Smiths, Kathy Closs, the wife of Bill Closs Jr., was nearly mobbed. Shortly thereafter, entire Californian campuses appeared to be populated with tennis players. The Adidas distributors were tearing their hair out again as they struggled to deliver, and even celebrities had to be placed on long waiting lists.

Mike Larrabee, a former runner on the American Olympic team, quickly realized that something had changed. Larrabee had been spotted by Horst Dassler at the Tokyo Olympics, where he ran the 400 meters of his life: at the final curve he trailed in fifth position, but his opponents seemed paralyzed as he burst past them all to take the gold medal.

When Larrabee retired from athletics four years later, Horst Dassler immediately hired him to weave contacts with other

American athletes and to hand out Adidas spikes at track meets. Larrabee stored the shoes in his Santa Monica garage, which became a meeting point for athletes from all around the region. But by the early seventies Adidas had become such a coveted brand that Mike's wife, Margaret, once found herself opening the front door of their house to find members of the Jackson family, of the Jackson Five, standing there. They had just dropped by to pick up a pair of sneakers.

. . . .

From its cheaper cleats to the basketball and tennis shoes, the French export business assumed such proportions that the Adidas heir pleaded with his managers to truncate their figures. "Horst asked us to disguise the fact that our exports were growing much faster than the business in Herzogenaurach," said Günter Sachsenmaier, former export manager in Landersheim. "He was always afraid that his parents would freak out."

As the French operation continued to spread, Käthe Dassler went to humiliating lengths to keep the situation under control. She tolerated some of the rivalry between the French and German organizations, because it evidently stimulated the company. However, she firmly intended to rule over international operations at Adidas, which provoked increasingly frequent and public clashes.

The tensions between Käthe and Horst began to taint relationships with distributors. When Käthe held little speeches to welcome them to Herzogenaurach, she rarely failed to point out, with thinly veiled bitterness, that Germany was to be regarded as the point of reference for the company's international business. The distributors, who had often planned for extensive stays in the Auberge du Kochersberg afterward, fidgeted uncomfortably in their chairs.

The situation was particularly unpleasant for the Americans, who had always professed loyalty to Käthe and Adi Dassler. With the rise of the basketball and tennis business, they were placing increasing orders with Landersheim, and there was no denying that it had served them all very well. Horst Dassler himself tightened the relationship by regularly traveling to the United States, which Adi Dassler never did.

Back in Herzogenaurach, Adi watched the business with increasing detachment. Now in his early seventies, he was tired of the relentless complaints from his managers, his wife, and his daughters. One of his assistants recalled that, to avoid responding, he sometimes drove his car from the entrance of the factory to his home. The distance was less than one hundred meters, but it spared him unwanted encounters. Still, there were some affronts that even Adi Dassler was not prepared to tolerate.

from rags to riches

For the 1972 Munich Olympics, the Adidas Dasslers had a mighty card up their sleeve. They could rest assured that the three stripes would again be worn by many of the most prominent athletes. But this time, they had struck a masterful deal with the organizers: Adidas would not only cover the feet of the athletes but would feature on their chests as well.

By moving into clothing, Adidas turned the sports business on its head. From then on, the Dasslers could chase comprehensive deals with sports federations that secured the endorsement of entire teams. And the exposure would be unprecedented: while the shoes of the athletes just appeared from time to time, their garments were permanently on-screen.

The move had been long delayed by Adi Dassler's reluctance to deal with clothing. "I'm not interested in rags," he used to grumble. At the insistent request of German soccer coaches, he just about agreed to order some sweat pants, and had them fitted with three stripes running down the pipes. But once the soccer players at Bayern Munich began to wear the suits, in the early sixties, many other clubs and federations ordered their own batches.

Adi Dassler would gladly have kept it at that, but Käthe convinced him that garments would neatly complement the Adidas spikes and boots. When it came to soccer, they could make three-striped jerseys that would tighten their relationship with soccer clubs. But for Olympic track and field, due to the strict amateur rules that still prevailed, such prominent branding was out of the question. Hans Fick, a small design studio in Nuremberg, had another suggestion: they came up with three leaves striped horizontally at the bottom. This logo became known as the Trefoil.

Until then, running shirts and other garments had been provided by sports clothing specialists, from Umbro to Mizuno, but they were allowed to print their name only on the collar label. Under pressure from the Dasslers, the organizers of the Munich Olympics proved somewhat more flexible. After drawn-out negotiations, it was agreed that Adidas would be entitled to decorate its Olympic shirts with the Trefoil.

Once they had shaken hands on the agreement, the Dasslers convinced some of the most prominent sports federations to endorse the Trefoil for the Munich Olympics. The logo appeared everywhere, from the chests of the athletes to the tunics of the gymnasts to the stretch suits of the wrestlers.

The brand was yet more visible outside the track, where athletes gladly walked around in three-striped tracksuits supplied by Adidas—green for the women and lavender-blue for the men. In a frenetic effort to curb the presence of large companies at the event, Avery Brundage, still head of the IOC, sent his aides around the Olympic Village to seize airport bags featuring the Lufthansa logo. However, he overlooked the ubiquitous three stripes.

Adi and Käthe Dassler invested most generously in the Munich Olympics. They realized that they would not be able to deal with the influx of athletes who showed up on their doorstep in Herzogenaurach, and therefore ordered the construction of an entire hotel for their guests. The Sportshotel was built on the hills above the Adidas factory. Initially laid out as a dormitory, an annex to the Olympic Village, it was later upgraded to welcome worthy guests from all around the world.

Horst Dassler still upstaged his parents at the Olympic Village, where he arranged to set up an Adidas store. Under the Olympic rules, it was officially forbidden to sell or hand out any three-striped shoes on the grounds, but the enforcement of these regulations was becoming increasingly farcical. "Every athlete in Munich knew that there was a special room at the back of our tent where we just handed out spikes," said an Adidas aide.

The Puma Dasslers watched enviously. They barely had any clothing to offer and were still concentrating entirely on wooing athletes to wear their shoes. Armin Dassler had rented out an entire villa on the Starnberger Lake, south of Munich, to entertain Puma athletes. Among his few memorable catches was Mary Peters, the Ulster woman who beat the German crowd favorite to win the gold medal for the pentathlon.

. . . .

Another contender that threatened to upset the almighty Dasslers at the Munich Olympics was a small American company called Blue Ribbon Sports. It had been set up by Philip Knight, a lanky middle-distance runner and graduate of Stanford Business School. Then known as "Buck," Knight had always run in Adidas, but he thought it outrageous that American students should be more or less condemned to buy expensive German spikes. In his Stanford paper he outlined a business plan to launch a competing brand: "Can Japanese sports shoes do to German sports shoes what Japanese cameras did to German cameras?" he asked.

The question was still at the back of Knight's mind when he left Stanford and began to work as an accountant. On his travels in Japan in 1962, he obtained an interview with Kihachiro Onitsuka, owner of the Tiger brand, which still specialized in running shoes. Although he didn't have any business to his name, Knight cheekily introduced himself as an American distributor, instantly making up Blue Ribbon Sports as a company name. He bluffed so convincingly that Onitsuka gave him an exclusive deal to sell Tiger in the United States.

But Knight quickly figured that if he sealed production agreements with the same manufacturers as Onitsuka, he could introduce a brand of his own. In 1972, he began to sell shoes that looked remarkably like Tiger shoes under another name. Knight intended to call his brand Dimension Six, but a former running mate and employee came up with Nike, the goddess of victory. A design student earned thirty-five dollars to draw a logo that looked like an inverted comma, later dubbed the Swoosh.

The other person behind Nike was Bill Bowerman, former coach of the track and field team at the University of Oregon, a training ground for many of the country's most remarkable runners and jumpers. Tinkering in his garage, like Adolf Dassler in his mother's laundry, Bowerman came up with astonishing novelties. One of them was known as The Vagina (looking scary but feeling wonderful inside). Another startling invention was the Waffle trainer, so called after the kitchen appliance Bowerman had used to mold its soles.

Knight and Bowerman repeatedly stated that they had entered the business for one single purpose: to beat Adidas. As he traveled to the Munich Olympics, his arch-enemy's home turf, Bowerman was in a combative mood. He had been appointed as coach of the American track and field team, and this was his chance to show the Germans a few tricks. He bitterly complained about the marathon route laid out by the organization, which included an uncomfortable section of gravel. Asked why he should have a say in this, he reportedly held up two fingers and replied, "World War One and World War Two."

But disappointingly for Bowerman, one of his protégés had declined to wear Nike. Knight and Bowerman both regarded Steve Prefontaine, an American long-distance runner, as an emblematic athlete for their brand. With his dashing good looks and outspoken ways, "Pre" was a crowd favorite who set multiple records as a student. But Prefontaine had been assiduously courted by Mike Larrabee, the man in charge of Adidas promotion among American athletes.

Larrabee went about his job with such dedication that he personally befriended many American athletes. He steadfastly refused to give them cash to wear Adidas, but he often offered personal services and paid rounds of drinks from his own pocket. Steve Prefontaine was just enjoying one of those, shortly before the Munich Olympics, when Larrabee brought up the subject of Adidas.

Pre was caught between two loyalties: he hated to disappoint his friend Larrabee but he didn't fancy upsetting his coach, either. It was therefore agreed that the issue would be solved through a guzzling contest. If Prefontaine downed his glass of bubbly Portuguese wine faster than Larrabee, he would wear Nike. Otherwise, it would be Adidas. Two rounds were deemed invalid because Prefontaine and Larrabee slammed their glasses on the counter so hard that they broke them. The third round sealed an Adidas victory.

As things turned out, Prefontaine finished fourth in the 5,000 meters, behind three runners who all wore three-striped shoes. When the medals were counted, the company boasted that about 80 percent of the athletes at the Munich Olympics had been competing in Adidas. Between the shoes and the clothing, Adidas crushed all of its competitors.

Adi Dassler could not deny that the move into clothing had hugely benefited Adidas. He didn't have a problem with that, as long as the garments remained strictly functional. But all hell broke loose when Horst Dassler decided to ignore such restrictions.

. . . .

While Munich's Olympic stadium witnessed some thrilling events, the most stunning feat took place in the swimming pool: the man of the Games was Mark Spitz, a handsome American swimmer who made a record haul of seven gold medals.

Remarkably self-confident, Spitz himself had predicted that he would return from Germany with a sackful of medals. He was disliked by some of his teammates, who resented his incessant bragging, and he had fallen flat on his nose in Mexico, when he felt certain to thrash his opponents in at least six races and failed to win a single gold medal in an individual event. But in Munich, Spitz was in unbeatable shape. That became apparent from the start, when he won the 200-meter butterfly with a comfortable lead, setting a new world record.

The American swimmer looked set to make waves, and Horst Dassler was eager to exploit the phenomenon. After a chat in the Olympic village, he persuaded Spitz to turn up at the medal ceremonies wearing Adidas shoes. The problem was that swimmers often wear sweat pants with very wide bottoms, to be removed more easily. Dassler therefore suggested that Spitz carry the shoes in his hands.

That was precisely what Spitz did after his second world-record victory in the 200-meter freestyle. He arrived for the medal ceremony barefoot, with a pair of Adidas in his hand. As "The Star Spangled Banner" echoed around the pool, he dropped the shoes on the podium. But once the anthem ended, he picked them up again and enthusiastically waved at the crowds with the three-striped shoes in his hands. Enraged by the publicity, the watchdogs of the Olympic Committee threatened to investigate the matter. The swimmer's manager was in tears. It took all of Horst Dassler's appeasement skills to settle the matter.

An American Jew, Mark Spitz was flown out of West Germany under a tight security escort before the end of the Games. His entourage feared more attacks from the Palestinian terrorists who had sneaked into the Olympic Village in the early hours of September 5, killing two members of the Israeli delegation and taking another nine hostage. Spitz, who had won the last of his seven medals just hours before, lay asleep nearby.

Upon winning his medals, the swimmer immediately announced that he would retire, which enabled him to sign personal contracts. Endorsements of individual swimmers were strictly prohibited at the time, but there was nothing that prevented retired champions from promoting the brands of their choice. While the drama unfolded in Munich, leading to the death of all nine Israeli hostages in a botched rescue attempt, Spitz flew to London with his agent to hold talks with a host of sponsors.

Among them were managers from Adidas France, on private assignment by Horst Dassler. As the young man saw it, the excitement generated by Mark Spitz formed a stupendous opportunity for Adidas to enter the swimwear market.

Horst had been plotting this for several months, meeting up with designers and looking for suitable fabrics. But when he heard the suggestion, Adi Dassler was not exactly thrilled. "Horst, you won't spare me anything!" he burst out indignantly. "Sure enough, you have done well for us. But bathing suits, never! You have gone completely mad. Never under the Adidas brand!" Adidas was about shoes, and swimmers didn't wear any, therefore swimwear was out of the question.

When they floated the thought at an internal meeting in Herzo-genaurach, before the Munich Games, the French managers were treated to another dose of sarcasm by their German counterparts. "You must be out of your mind," they told Günter Sachsenmaier, the export manager. "Next thing, you'll be flogging Adidas bras and pajamas!" At the receiving end of these furious tirades, Horst Dassler retained his cool. It didn't matter, he replied calmly: if his parents refused to launch swimwear under the Adidas brand, he would launch it under a brand called Arena.

Horst had been using this name for several years in Spain. The production of leather balls by Spanish farmers and later prisoners had been set up under a company called Arena España—to escape the scrutiny of the Dasslers in Herzogenaurach. Horst later used the Arena brand name to flog cheap sneakers in the French market.

Adidas France designed Arena's three-diamonds logo, which was printed on the sneakers along with two stripes. Arena had become a small and unglamorous part of the French company. For Horst, however, it was an escape route that would enable him to develop his business without his family's consent. The swimwear line was the first large-scale opportunity for him to set up a business of his own.

The task was entrusted to Alain Ronc, a dedicated manager in the export department. Called into Horst Dassler's office, he furiously scribbled notes as Dassler went through his plans for Arena swimwear. "He had it all in his head, down to the most practical details, production, marketing, partnerships, and everything," Ronc recalled. "He sat there talking for two hours. He had given me work for the next three years."

With Arena, Horst Dassler envisioned a raid on the swimwear business. Mark Spitz, who had been wearing Speedo in Munich due to a contract between the brand and the American Swimming Federation, was to be persuaded to switch to a French label that didn't officially exist. Almost single-handedly, Alain Ronc was to set up distribution deals in as many countries as possible. And most important, he was to keep his Arena files well away from any nosy German visitors.

When Mark Spitz said that he would retire, Horst Dassler was ready to strike. Right after the Munich Olympics, the swimmer agreed to pose in samples of Arena trunks. Horst Dassler spread the pictures so widely among befriended reporters that the shots were often used in conjunction with articles about Spitz's medal haul in Munich. "This gave the impression that Mark Spitz had won his medals in Arena," chuckled Georges Kiehl, in charge of international promotion for Arena.

With Arena, Horst Dassler demonstrated just how hard-hitting his French team had become. Barely one year after the confrontation with his father, Arena swimwear duly made its debut at the European championships in Berlin, in August 1973. Two years later, at the World Championships in Cali, Colombia, roughly two thirds of the swimmers wore Arena. Horst Dassler invested $100,000 in the championships, a substantial sum at the time. The money was spent on team sponsorship deals and an agreement with the organizers: the entire pool seemed covered with Arena diamonds. Speedo, the Australian brand that had previously held a virtual monopoly on the swimwear market, appeared completely dumbstruck by the advances of its French rival.

Due to the virulent objections of Horst Dassler's parents, the development of Arena required strenuous contortions. Some of the costs were indirectly borne by Adidas. After all, Alain Ronc

Horst Dassler *(second from left)* establishes Arena, endorsed by Mark Spitz *(center)*, the swimmer who won seven gold medals at the 1972 Olympics.

was on the payroll of Adidas France. But the managers behind Arena didn't have separate budgets for the company at their disposal and therefore had to deploy improvisational skills. The snapshots for the first catalogues were taken in the office of Alain Ronc, where a group of Adidas executives gladly stripped off to pose in Arena trunks.

On other occasions, Horst Dassler had to scrape for money. The situation once became so tight that he requested a personal loan of at least $1 million from Bill Closs, the Adidas distributor for the American West Coast. The call was deeply humiliating for Dassler and just as embarrassing for Closs. Horst made it clear that he needed the money for his own purposes, and that the loan should not be disclosed to his parents. "They were putting the squeeze on Horst, and he had been a personal friend for a long time. I went to our bank and sent the money to him," Bill Closs recalled. "But I didn't think this through clearly, because it couldn't please Germany at all." Given the relatively small size of the Closs business at the time, $1 million was a substantial sum.

Horst was in such a hurry to build up his brand that he sealed deals with almost anyone else who came along. One of the chosen partners was a small-time Canadian coach who claimed to have a sizeable distribution company. Horst Dassler entrusted him with the exclusive distribution rights for Arena in all of Canada and the United States.

Alain Ronc, who sat in on the dinner, was somewhat worried about this rash decision. His concerns appeared more than justified when it turned out that the operation of the Canadian coach consisted of a few boxes of goggles in his California garage. "In our frenetic drive to expand Arena, we regularly fell flat on our noses," said Ronc. "But the whole sports market was still so fresh that we still progressed at incredible speed."

Irked by Arena's fast expansion, the German side of the company resolved to retaliate by setting up Adidas swimwear. "The situation was crazy enough for us to launch a swimwear line when we didn't have the slightest competence in this business," conceded Peter Rduch, then export manager in Herzogenaurach. "The Germans felt they had to have this, just because Horst had it, too."

. . . .

For all of Adi Dassler's disdain, clothing promptly made up nearly half of Adidas sales in Germany. The explosion occurred at a time when the distinction between leisure and sports clothing was becoming increasingly blurred. There was such huge demand for Adidas clothing that the company's managers hardly bothered to take orders; the retailers would have accepted almost anything.

Unencumbered by his father's hang-ups, Horst eagerly delved into the clothing market. Just like their neighbors in Germany, the French managers sold millions of three-striped shorts and tracksuits. But this was merely the skeleton of a bustling apparel business that beat the German equivalent many times over.

The French clothing operation owed its edge largely to Ventex, a former supplier that Adidas France had gobbled up. Previously owned by a chemical company, the Ventex laboratory soon became the envy of the industry. "When German managers asked to be shown around at Ventex," said Jean Wendling, then textile manager at Adidas France, "I made sure that the lab remained tightly sealed."

The vastly superior French offering in sports clothes turned into another strength for Landersheim in its stalemate with Herzogenaurach. At the same time, it entirely redefined the game of the sports gear business, as the leading brands no longer battled for athletes alone to wear their shoes. All of a sudden they could compete for the favors of entire teams as well, vying for the right to affix their brands on the shirts of the athletes and players. This endorsement business would take on ludicrous proportions over the next decades, requiring Adidas to turn out many thousands of clothing items for the Olympic Games.

Devoid of any clothing business, Puma just could not retaliate. More than ever, Armin Dassler stuck to his strategy of targeting a handful of dazzling players. Yet he would have to summon all his wits to uphold Puma's standing in the 1970s, as unashamed demands proliferated around the playing fields.

10

soccer punch

As in the rest of society, the early seventies marked a clear switch of generations among soccer players. The loyal and unpretentious men befriended by Adi Dassler had nearly all retired, to make way for a cast of emancipated and assertive young players.

The demands of the long-haired youngsters placed increasing strain on the Dasslers. Since Puma had reneged on the Pelé pact, Horst and Armin Dassler had engaged in an all-out fight around the soccer pitches, which still constituted the largest chunk of their business and generated by far the widest international exposure.

The clashes came to a head in the run-up to the 1974 soccer World Cup, to be held in West Germany. The fact that Adidas was now providing soccer shirts to many of the teams would spice up the battle between the Dasslers, and both of the cousins devised some new tricks to profit from the publicity around the up-and-coming soccer stars.

Puma's most promising catch was a scrawny Dutch player called Johan Cruijff. He had been hawked by Jaap and Cor du Buy, the

Dutch brothers who held the distribution rights for Puma in the Netherlands. Under the deal, signed by Cruijff's mother in January 1967, the twenty-year-old player was to earn fifteen hundred Dutch guilders ($420) to wear Puma boots at each game and training session. As part of the agreement, the athlete would allow Puma to sell boots called "Puma Cruijffie," his nickname at the time.

Unfortunately the relationship suddenly turned sour as Johan Cruijff insisted that the Puma boots hurt his feet. He began to turn up at games in Adidas and demanded that his deal with Cor du Buy be rescinded. Du Buy derided the claim as "complete codswallop." Johan Cruijff's feet were very special indeed, but surely Puma could still find suitable boots for him.

After several failed attempts at mediation, Cor du Buy filed a complaint for breach of contract. Cruijff was ordered to pay a fine of 24,500 guilders ($6,800), a considerable sum at the time, amounting to 250 guilders ($70) for each of the games and training sessions he had attended in Adidas. When Cruijff refused to pay up, Du Buy obtained the seizure of his earnings from his soccer club, Ajax Amsterdam.

The case landed before the judges in Amsterdam. Unimpressed by the player's allegations, they confirmed the Du Buys' rights. "The truth of the matter is that [Cruijff] wants more money," the presiding judge summed up at the hearing, held on September 3, 1968. Johan Cruijff lost the case but, by the end of the year, he had obtained a vastly upgraded deal with Cor du Buy. The contract guaranteed him at least 25,000 guilders ($6,940) each year for the next three years.

Intriguingly, Johan Cruijff still seemed to prefer Adidas boots. Just weeks after he signed the fresh deal, one of the Du Buys' aides peered at a picture in *De Telegraaf*, the Dutch newspaper, and with an expert eye noticed that Cruijff's left boot was an Adidas, as evident from the special white cushioning on the heel. "We would be grateful if you agreed to disguise this element, for example by painting it over in black," the Puma distributor wrote to Cruijff. "Of course it would be even better," he added sheepishly, "if you also wore a Puma boot on your left foot."

The squabbles between Cruijff and Puma were perfectly in line with the overall perception of the player as a quick-witted soccer genius but also a nitpicker who permanently watched out for his personal interests. In contrast with players before him, Cruijff openly argued that soccer was his job and that he should be properly rewarded for it. He was ardently backed up by Cor Coster, his agent and father-in-law. A feisty wheeler-dealer, Coster used hardball tactics that terrified the most hardheaded soccer club managers.

As Puma's upgraded contract with Cruijff came to an end, Cor Coster kept all his son-in-law's options open. He gladly accepted an invitation to Landersheim, where he was wined and dined extensively. Shortly afterward, in April 1972, Horst wrote a personal letter to Coster with an unbeatable offer of 1.2 million guilders ($375,000) for an Adidas tie-in with Cruijff over the next five years. A shrewd businessman, Cor Coster knew exactly what to do with the proposal: four days later, the copy of the Adidas offer landed on the desk of Gerd Dassler, then in charge of international affairs at Puma.

Gerd Dassler rushed to his typewriter. "Dear Horst," he wrote. "We understand that you approached Johan Cruijff's father-in-law, Herr Coster, to obtain a contract with Cruijff." As Gerd Dassler explained, however, Puma had the Dutchman cornered. As part of his contract with Cor du Buy, Cruijff had unwittingly given the Dutch agents exclusive and unlimited rights on the use of his name. Cor du Buy had duly registered Cruijff and a flurry of derivatives as its own trademarks. "We are therefore convinced that you have attempted consciously, or at least negligently, to influence the player Johan Cruijff, encouraging him to breach his contract," Gerd angrily wrote to his cousin.

"Dear Gerd," came the reply. Horst Dassler confirmed that he had "privately befriended" Johan Cruijff. He argued that the Du Buys' registration of the Cruijff name would not prevent the player from wearing Adidas boots, "especially since he has always preferred our boots, out of technical reasons and due to our friendship." Since Puma had breached the Pelé pact in

Mexico, Horst wrote, he could not be expected to abide by any informal rules.

Just as Horst intended, the exchange forced Puma to improve its contract with Cruijff again. Horst had just played out a well-worn business trick: he knew that he could not get a deal with Cruijff, but he could at least weaken his competitor by driving the prices up and thus forcing him to punch a large hole in his budget. In a combined deal with Le Coq Sportif, French producers of soccer clothing, Puma offered Cruijff minimal earnings of 150,000 guilders ($46,875) each year. From then on, the hardheaded Dutchman professed unstinting loyalty to his partners at Puma.

This caused splitting headaches over the next years, as the Dutch prepared for the 1974 World Cup, to be held in Germany. By the early seventies they could align a stunning team, with some of the most coveted players in the world. The team would lean most strongly on the Ajax squad that had dazzled soccer amateurs with its fast and unpredictable game, known as Total Football.

The problem was that the Dutch soccer federation had signed with Adidas. Under the agreement, Cruijff and all the other players were meant to walk onto the pitch in three-striped tracksuits and orange shirts. But Cor Coster insisted that, due to his lucrative deal with Puma, Johan Cruijff should be exempted from this. He could not be expected to wear a three-striped shirt while his contract with Puma explicitly stated that he should refrain from promoting any other sports brand.

Much to the relief of the Dutch soccer federation, Adidas agreed to strike a deal. They could easily picture the furor if it turned out that they had caused the loss of Johan Cruijff, the linchpin of an extraordinary Dutch team. The compromise was an orange shirt emblazoned with the Dutch lion—and just two stripes running down the sleeves.

Adidas got a small revenge when the Dutch team was called up for its official team snapshot. Henny Warmenhoven, the man in charge of soccer promotion for Adidas in Netherlands, was so well connected with the Dutch officials that he could easily mingle with them on the team bench. While the team was being set up for the photograph, Warmenhoven, while chatting with one of the players, discreetly dropped an Adidas bag right in front of Johan Cruijff's Puma boots.

. . . .

The Dutch clash was in tune with the upheavals that were taking place elsewhere. Even the otherwise obedient German side was not immune to these changes. They were no longer prepared to take small hand-outs by the national league while their opponents in other European countries were being pampered and generously rewarded. They wanted a sizeable bonus to score and to wear branded boots.

The German soccer squad in the early seventies contained a cast of remarkable players. Günter Netzer and Franz Beckenbauer stood out as rival team leaders, but there was an embarrassment of talent for the supporting cast as well. While German teams often leaned on discipline and defense, this team was uncharacteristically praised for its "elegance," "inventiveness," and "genius." The players, however, were interested in more than compliments.

In order to avoid any distracting talk about payments, the German soccer federation turned to Adidas. They wanted an exclusive deal, reportedly worth 175,000 German marks ($54,900), that would oblige all German players to wear Adidas shirts as well as boots when competing with their national team. Predictably, Puma turned to the judges. In August 1972, the case was brought to the Federal Cartel Office in Berlin, the country's antitrust court, where Puma sued for "suspected abuse of a dominant market position."

The verdict was unequivocal: the judges deemed the agreement unacceptable. The Cartel Office suggested that each of the German players be given the choice of their boot brand; otherwise, they should all be equipped with black boots without any distinctive signs. The Puma and Adidas representatives at the rowdy hearing agreed on at least one thing: black boots would turn the Germans into the laughingstock of the soccer scene. The ruling therefore paved the way for more open competition at the forthcoming World Cup.

Intriguingly, the two most prominent players on the German side stood for antagonistic styles. Güntzer Netzer was regarded as a renegade, a long-haired attacker who reveled in the controversy of his fast lifestyle. Long before this became the norm for soccer players, Netzer enjoyed gallivanting with long-legged blondes in flashy sports cars or at his tacky discotheque, called Lover's Lane. He obtained a whopping deal with Puma and couldn't really complain when they asked him to wear turquoise-and-yellow boots.

The dashing rebel from Mönchengladbach, in the west of Germany, regularly snubbed the German soccer federation and superbly ignored the recommendation of Helmut Schön, the national team trainer, that all international players play for German clubs. Just before the world championships, the Puma star sneaked off to sign a deal with Real Madrid.

Franz Beckenbauer wasn't exactly shy, either. Just like most of his teammates at Bayern Munich, he grew longish hair and relished fast cars and discos. But compared with Netzer, Beckenbauer seemed almost bland. "Der Kaiser" polished his reputation as a smart player who was destined to shine long after his career was over. He built up business interests and bought season tickets to the opera.

Established several decades earlier, the ties between Adidas and Beckenbauer had further deepened over the years. In the early seventies, the relationship was cemented through a groundbreaking contract. Beckenbauer earned a sizeable commission on boots, shirts, and shorts that were named after him. The shiny Beckenbauer shorts sold in the millions, and the payments to the athlete reached such proportions that Käthe Dassler began to protest.

She was even more appalled when Robert Schwan, Beckenbauer's longtime manager, came forward with more demands. According to Horst Widmann, Adi Dassler's personal assistant, due to pressure from Schwan, Adidas had to arrange at least two large under-the-table payments to avoid losing Beckenbauer. But

Widmann made sure that the dealings would not reach his boss's ears. "He didn't want to know anything about such things," said Widmann.

Adi Dassler was therefore shocked when players bluntly demanded brown envelopes to wear Adidas. Since the Bern triumph, Dassler had taken part in nearly all of the national side's training camps in Germany. It seemed natural that he should be invited to Malente, a resort close to the Baltic Sea, where the German squad congregated ahead of the 1974 World Cup. But for the first time, Adi Dassler felt out of place. The players no longer cared about his boots. Everything seemed to revolve around money.

The unprecedented demands of the German players led to a full-fledged revolt. It was only a few years earlier that their league had begun to accept professionals, several decades later than their European counterparts. The time had come to catch up. Through Franz Beckenbauer, the players demanded a payment of at least 100,000 German marks ($38,730) per player from the federation.

After an entire night of haggling, they ended up settling on 75,000 German marks ($29,050). The incident left Helmut Schön on the verge of a nervous breakdown. The coach was so appalled by the players' attitude that he packed his bags. It took all of Beckenbauer's powers of persuasion to convince the trainer to stay.

Adi Dassler was equally dismayed. The players no longer had any obligation to wear the three stripes, and they made sure to impress this point on Dassler. Just days before the competition started, some of the players were still threatening to cover the stripes on their boots with black polish unless they obtained a bonus for wearing Adidas. Just like Helmut Schön, Adi Dassler was so disgusted that he packed his bags—and he could not be held back.

The championships provided the Germans with their second World Cup triumph, twenty years after the Miracle of Bern. The superior Dutch had become complacent, and the Germans had beaten them to the trophy, with a decisive goal by Gerd Müller. But for Adi Dassler, the finals marked the end of a personal relationship that had propelled Adidas to its overwhelming leadership of the soccer business.

Back in Herzogenaurach, his aging brother was equally disillusioned.

. . . .

While Germany basked in the euphoria of Gerd Müller's blasting shot, Rudolf Dassler had become an angry old man. His behavior was increasingly erratic. He continuously berated his eldest son and repeatedly made amendments to his will. As Rudolf's family learned later that year, he was beginning to suffer from lung cancer.

Rudolf Dassler had long faded from Puma's management, but he was still updated regularly on his company's dealings. One of the problems that tormented him in his last months was Puma's French subsidiary. It had always been a struggle for Gerd Dassler, Rudolf's youngest son, to establish the brand in the French market. Wherever he turned up, Gerd discovered that Horst had been there before him, with Adidas. And whatever Gerd offered, it could never match the reputation of the Auberge du Kochersberg. "It was phenomenal, and people talked about it all the time," he said.

With a mix of frustration and curiosity, Gerd Dassler once accepted an invitation to check out Landersheim for himself. He felt even worse when he left: glad to plant a little intrigue, Horst whispered in Gerd's ear that his brother, Armin, was hatching a plot to undermine him.

As things turned out, Gerd Dassler soon ran into deep troubles. The French subsidiary sank into losses from weak sales and disproportionate expenses, allegedly caused by the lavish lifestyle of the Dasslers. Rudolf agreed to cover the debts of the French subsidiary, but the French banks demanded that his son be removed from the company's management. "It was a thorny matter," said Irene Dassler, Armin's wife. "The rescue of the French business placed the whole company under financial strain, and my husband basically had to fire his own brother."

Rudolf Dassler relaxing in the early 1970s.

The incident occurred just as Rudolf Dassler was beginning to feel unwell. In September 1974, it became clear that the illness was serious. Rudolf hurriedly returned from a break to change his will yet again. Under the statutes of the company, a limited partnership (a "KG" in Germany), it had long been established that, upon his father's death, Armin would inherit 60 percent of Puma's shares, against 40 percent of the shares and all the remaining assets of the family for Gerd. But in the grip of his illness, Rudolf suddenly felt that this split was wrong.

In the last hours of Rudolf's life, a zealous chaplain attempted to put the dying man's agitated mind at rest by forcing a reconciliation with his brother. The two brothers had continued to pester each other long after their split. In the aftermath of the Mexico City Olympics, Rudolf received a restraining order, which had apparently been filed by Adolf, precisely on his seventieth birthday. Since then, however, unbeknownst to most other family members and employees, Adolf and Rudolf had met up several times. Horst Widmann, Adi Dassler's assistant, arranged four lengthy discussions between the two men in the early seventies, at the Grand Hotel in Nuremberg and at Frankfurt Airport.

The night of Rudolf's death, the chaplain placed the call to the Villa himself. Adolf declined to cross the river and embrace his brother one last time, but he conveyed his forgiveness. Rudolf Dassler passed away shortly afterward, on October 27, 1974.

In line with its haughty attitude toward its smaller rival, Adidas issued a sarcastic statement: "Out of pity, the family of Adolf Dassler will not comment on the death of Rudolf Dassler," it read. Yet Adi and Käthe Dassler sent their eldest daughter, Inge Bente, to attend the funeral service.

Several days later, Armin and Gerd sat down at the notary's office for the opening of their father's will. The clerk sighed heavily as he struggled to decipher all the scribbles and amendments. But long before he had finished, Rudolf's intentions had become perfectly clear: the ownership of Puma had been entrusted to Gerd, and Armin had been entirely left out of the will. "My husband was devastated," Irene Dassler recalled.

Since Gerd Dassler refused to settle, Armin and his wife consulted several lawyers, enquiring under which conditions the last-minute amendments could be declared void. They were told bluntly that they would have to respect Rudolf's will. But in January 1975, they obtained an appointment with a Düsseldorf-based lawyer, Jürgen Waldowksi, who had recently hit the headlines in a high-profile case involving a pharmaceuticals company.

With a reassuring grin, the lawyer pulled out a copy of a supreme court verdict. "You don't need to worry at all," he told Armin and Irene Dassler, because the ruling dictated that the statutes of a limited partnership prevailed over a will. "That was the end of the story," Irene Dassler said. In line with the unamended statutes, Armin was appointed *Komplementär* (partner with limited liability), with 60 percent of Puma's shares, while Gerd was a *Kommanditist* (partner with unlimited liability), with the remaining 40 percent, along with all of the family's other belongings.

After this bitter dispute, Armin could run the company as he pleased, without interference from his bullying father. This marked the beginning of a remarkable run for Puma, with sales multiplying fivefold in about ten years. Yet Armin still couldn't measure up with his cousin Horst, who was worming his way into the most influential spheres of the sports business.

part two

Champions of
the World

under the influence

As he built up his business, Horst Dassler acquired some startling habits. John Boulter, in charge of international promotion in Landersheim, began to notice them in the mid-seventies when he traveled to London with Horst for Wimbledon. A former Olympic runner, Boulter was trotting out for a jog in Hyde Park when he spotted his boss sitting alone in the lobby of their hotel. Upon Boulter's return, Horst was in exactly the same position, right across from the exit of the elevator. "I'm fine, John," Dassler explained. "I'm just sitting here in case someone important walks by."

Wherever he was, Horst Dassler seized every opportunity to reinforce his friendships among sports officials or to seal new ones. While others regarded schmoozing as a tiresome obligation, Horst complied with almost fanatical zeal. This was perfectly in line with one of his adages, "Everything is a matter of relationships." Indeed he had the right skills to make friends all around the world: he was fluent in five languages, displayed an affable manner, never asked any awkward questions, and was amazingly considerate.

To begin with, the rationale behind this tireless lobbying was to obtain favorable treatment for Adidas. The rewards could be most concrete with national sports federations: among many other things, they picked the shirts and other equipment to be worn by their national team. Unfortunately for Horst Dassler, shoes were exempted from most of such agreements because they were regarded as technical equipment, for which the athletes should be allowed to make their own choice. Yet by dealing with federations, Adidas saved all the hassle of cajoling athletes and satisfying their escalating demands. An agreement with an entire federation could be much more interesting for Adidas in terms of exposure than a deal with a single player, which could require several weeks of negotiations and might even be worthless if the athlete was injured or underperformed.

At a time when sports federations were still run with the same ethos as local billiards clubs, Horst's dedication made a huge impression. "There were these general secretaries, who were often retired and toiled away for nothing," recalled Gerhard Prochaska, former Adidas marketing manager. "All of a sudden they were propelled to the front of the stage, pampered and respected. Horst grasped such things much earlier than others."

Auberge du Kochersberg turned into the nerve center of this operation. Gault Millau rated the restaurant's cuisine with two chef's toques, while the Michelin guide expressed its appreciation with one star. Bill Siebenschuh, the sommelier, had one of the most enviable jobs in the region. With up to thirty thousand bottles, his wine cellar was regularly rated as the richest private cellar in the Alsace. After a while he had to rent out a second cellar nearby, which stored up to sixty thousand more bottles.

The French managers in Landersheim precisely budgeted the stays of their guests. A team of rugby players would get the standard treatment, a couple of nights at the lodge, hearty food, and abundant supplies of local beer. The worthiest guests, however, would be ushered into the magnificent suites on the upper floor of the Auberge. For meals they would be seated in a separate room, and they would dine on gold-decorated plates. "The gold service put quite a strain on our budget," recalled Prochaska. Such stays sometimes came with a full weekend reception, complete with hunting excursions.

Horst Dassler's most intimate guests would be taken down to the cellar, where they could savor anything from Château d'Yquem and Petrus to the finest Armagnac. On particularly intense nights, Horst enjoyed sharing the bench in the cellar to smoke a cigar, accompanied by a glass of wine or cognac. While the racks contained the most prestigious wines, his personal treat was the relatively obscure Château de la Chaise, from southern Burgundy. One of the neatest touches was to offer guests a bottle of wine from the year of their birth.

To take care of all the arrangements, Adidas France had established a full-fledged travel agency on the ground floor of its offices in Landersheim. They had an entire fleet of limousines at their disposal, to pick up guests at the local airport and chauffeur them around the Alsatian hills.

A stay at the Auberge became an inevitable rite of passage for anybody with ambitions in the sports business. "Those who had never been invited to Landersheim were nobodies," said one of Dassler's former guests. Along with the predictable sports people, guests included aspiring members of international sports federations, Olympic committees, and politicians who gravitated around sports.

Another option for international guests was a stay at the Adidas premises in Paris. The company's French managers held offices on the Rue du Louvre, where there was a small restaurant on the ground floor. Its menu could not compete with the delicacies at some of the adjoining eateries, but had there been a guestbook at the bar, its late-night entries would have read like a directory of the world's leading sports executives.

For those who stayed overnight, there was the Terrasse Hotel, where Adidas kept a running account. At the foot of Montmartre, the hotel boasted relatively modest rooms, but its roof restaurant offered a stunning view of the capital. Most important, Horst Dassler took on the services of a dedicated barman, called

Jacky. While the hotel bar officially closed at midnight, Jacky kept a backroom with a bar open for the Adidas crew and their guests. He would turn away other potential customers while continuing to serve drinks until Horst Dassler had finished his meetings—often in the early hours of the morning. Conveniently, the Terrasse Hotel was located a stone's throw from several temples of adult entertainment in Paris, particularly Le Moulin Rouge.

With guests from all cultures, the trickiest part was to find the right balance for each individual—which happened to be Horst's forte. "He had the amazing ability of always knowing what would influence an individual," observed Patrick Nally, one of Dassler's partners. "He was an absolutely charming person who would be up until the early hours of the morning, drinking, talking, to get to know and understand people. It was a matter of getting to know what was right and what was wrong and never to cause offence. If it was right for the person to give him a bit of cash, or a lot of cash, then it was right for that person."

Just in case his phenomenal memory failed him, Horst Dassler created detailed files for each of his contacts. Meticulously updated, they contained the names of that person's closest family members and their ages, clothes measurements, special likes and dislikes; the subjects discussed during the latest meeting; and the presents they received. Horst Dassler's aides were taught to keep track of their contacts in the same way. "At the end of an evening, when you'd think we'd keel over comatose, we would still keep a pretty good diary of notes," said Nally. "All these people were trained to take notes; they were very disciplined in giving Horst complete information."

Horst reveled in his reputation as the supreme businessman who knew everything. To begin with, the purpose of this intelligence remained innocent. The strategy was to make as many friends as possible, across the entire spectrum of sports and on all continents. But as time went by, these investments acquired a manipulative color.

. . . .

Yearning for yet more influence, Horst Dassler resolved to build up an unofficial team dedicated to international sports relations. While all of his disciples were taught to make friends, the sports politics squad, patched together in the seventies, went much further. Their activities were geared entirely toward the infiltration of leading sports organizations.

The venture was based on the premise that in the most influential sports organizations each country had one vote, regardless of its weight or size. Decisions that mattered to Adidas could hinge on the votes of a handful of delegates from puny and far-flung countries. Horst Dassler's sports diplomats therefore strove to cover the entire world—offering plane tickets and other resources to make sure that their friends in the remotest countries could take part in crucial deliberations.

The most accomplished lobbyist hired by Dassler was Christian Jannette, who joined Adidas in 1972, right after the Munich Olympics. As chief of protocol for the Munich Games, dealing with all the arrangements for officials, Jannette had been courted by countless Olympic friends. Since he was in charge of allotting tickets, some of them had groveled shamelessly to invite their extended family and friends. Jannette was owed more favors than the Auberge could ever have dispensed. His leading assignment was to strengthen Horst Dassler's ties with his Soviet friends.

The Adidas chief had exceptional entrées in the otherwise impenetrable Soviet Union. Adidas France executives boasted that a white bear rug in one of the suites in Landersheim had been offered to Horst by Leonid Brezhnev, then comrade-in-chief of the Soviet Union. Horst had hired a Russian-speaking assistant, Huguette Clergironnet, who accompanied him on many of his trips. He cherished a private collection of Russian icons, and he genuinely enjoyed the company of his Russian friends. But the most interesting aspect of the Soviets to him was that they provided reliable votes, dictating policies for delegates from the entire communist bloc.

The only problem that haunted Horst Dassler as regarded the Soviet Union was that his family in Herzogenaurach had earmarked the Soviet Union as its own territory. While his two eldest sisters concentrated on sports promotion and advertising, Brigitte Baenkler, the third of Adolf and Käthe's daughters, pleaded with her parents to let her learn Russian. She was fascinated by Eastern Europe, with a particular affinity for Hungary and Russia.

While Horst Dassler made personal friends in the Kremlin, Brigitte established herself as the official envoy of the Dassler family in the Soviet Union. She regularly traveled to Moscow on behalf of Adidas—never failing to bring along trolleys full of Western equipment. In the early eighties, Brigitte's efforts would help Adidas to set up one of the first factories in the Soviet Union that was at least partly controlled by a Western company.

This shared interest forged a bond between Horst and Brigitte that came much closer to respect than his relationship with any of his three other sisters. Still, the involvement of the German Dasslers in Eastern Europe sometimes caused huge frustration in Landersheim. Horst went ballistic when Brigitte was caught at a Soviet airport attempting to bring home some icons in her luggage. To avoid a diplomatic incident and get his sister safely out of the Soviet customs office, Horst Dassler used up many favors.

His relationship with Soviet officials was generally costly. As the company's sports diplomats acknowledged, Soviet sports dignitaries were among the greediest. Christian Jannette distinctly remembered walking around the Place Vendôme in Paris holding a thick purse while a Soviet delegation raided the square's most refined jewelry stores.

Through their production and equipment contracts, the Dasslers cultivated close contacts with many other East European dignitaries. Erich Honecker, head of the East German state, personally signed a totalitarian deal with Adidas, with the three stripes becoming a distinctive sign for the country's international athletes—set against the two stripes of Zeha, the regime's own sports shoe brand. The deal consisted mostly of equipment supplies, but it was still very precious for the East Germans, who invested massively in the prestige of their sports team. Sports were regarded as an integral part of East German education, and the regime pumped unparalleled resources into sports-related studies and medical science. As the East German rulers saw it, buying Adidas was just another way to make sure that their athletes would be best equipped to perform. Adidas was of such undeniably superior quality that the East Germans were prepared to turn a blind eye to its capitalist origins. One of the advantages of this all-encompassing deal was that Adidas executives could rest assured: the East Germans themselves would see to it that the commitment to wear Adidas was respected.

The ties between Adidas and the East German regime did not prevent the Stasi from closely watching Horst Dassler. One of their most prolific sources was IM Möwe. As things turned out much later, the man behind this code name, meaning "Informant Seagull," was Karl-Heinz Wehr. A relatively obscure East German sports official, Wehr regularly updated the Stasi on the dealings of Horst Dassler's aides for more than two decades. "My opinion is that this sports political department, led by Dassler personally, is also the most important unit of sports espionage in the capitalist foreign world," Wehr wrote.

As Wehr recalled, Horst Dassler began to cultivate closer contacts with the East Germans in the seventies, when communist representatives conquered some leading positions in international organizations. Sports had become another stage of world politics, in which the two superpowers of the cold war kept each other in check. The communist countries were keen to make their voice heard, and international federations were careful to preserve a representative balance of power on their boards.

Horst regularly held talks with Manfred Ewald and Günther Heinze, the two most influential dignitaries in East German sports. In an apparent effort to please the two men, Horst favored Karl-Heinz Wehr's appointment as general secretary of AIBA, the international boxing federation.

From this position, IM Möwe closely observed Dassler's crew. He thoroughly described their modus operandi, from the delegates of international organizations being "softened" by Adidas to the "drink orgies" organized by the company. "We are faced with the fact that, in the current sports world, nothing happens without this company—and that, in my eyes, many things happen under the influence of this group," IM Möwe wrote.

The Puma Dasslers watched in frustration. As reported by Wehr, the East Germans were once approached by the company's public relations manager. This man stated that Puma would be "immediately prepared" to match or improve on the contract with Adidas, which apparently earned the East Germans about 700,000 German marks ($386,740) each year. However, the Puma Dasslers could never get a foot in Honecker's door. "There was nothing we could do," said Gerd Dassler. "Horst Dassler had it all sewn up."

Among Horst's most intimate communist friends were the Hungarians. In line with his insidious approach, the interests of Adidas and the sports leaders in Budapest were intertwined. Through its production assignments to Hungarian shoe factories, Adidas provided the government with badly needed currency. In return, the Hungarian regime gladly signed with Adidas and saw to it that its leading athletes sported the three stripes.

The Adidas chief commanded such influence in Budapest that he obtained the release of an Adidas executive who had been arrested for driving under the influence. His reckless driving had killed at least one person. Any other West German citizen arrested under such circumstances might have expected to spend the rest of his life in a Hungarian cell. But after a few phone calls by Horst Dassler, the culprit was back in Germany.

To facilitate travels to Eastern Europe and beyond, Horst and some of his closest lieutenants had two passports: one containing all their visas for the East, and the other, void of communist stamps, enabling them to travel around the rest of the world unimpeded.

. . . .

Among the other most likely targets of the Adidas diplomats' largesse were African sports delegates. In many of that continent's emerging nations, with their faltering economies, there was no way that the average citizen could afford a pair of Adidas shoes.

There were only a handful of African countries that could be regarded as markets. However, Horst Dassler invested heavily to spread the three stripes and exert more influence in Africa.

His interest there stemmed partly from the fact that the continent produced stupendous athletes. To some extent, the Adidas diplomats assisted in the development of sports in the emerging nations of Africa, persuading politicians to invest in sports by arguing that sports victories unleashed more popular fervor than any political projects. To affirm their political standing, nations needed high-performance athletes. Adidas was there to help them: although there weren't many African sports federations that could pay for an endorsement deal, Horst Dassler showered them with three-striped equipment.

Many of Horst's aides were convinced that, in many cases, he acted out of sheer philanthropy. Yet in the long term, the grateful contacts he built up were certain to pay off, as Africans began to take seats in international organizations. "When a sports official has received unfailing support from Adidas for many years, and Horst Dassler advises them to back this or that person, is there any way they could refuse?" asked Gerhard Prochaska, former Adidas marketing manager.

Blago Vidinic, the coach of the Moroccan soccer team, was among the beneficiaries of Horst's special attention. Tall and square-shouldered, Vidinic started his career as a remarkable goalkeeper for Yugoslavia, occasionally quoted in the same breath as Lev Yashin of the Soviet Union. Vidinic then moved on to coaching. His first assignment brought him to Morocco, which had wrested its independence from France in 1956. Vidinic was asked to form a decent squad ahead of the 1970 World Championship in Mexico. During that year, he was startled to receive scores of Adidas boxes filled with shirts and boots. Although the federation couldn't afford such classy equipment, the boxes kept coming right up until the World Championship in Mexico, where even more boots were waiting for the Moroccans.

After the squad's predictable elimination in the first round, Vidinic and his team hung around Mexico City for a few more days to watch other games. While Vidinic was sitting in his team bus in front of the Maria Isabel Hotel, waiting to leave for the hour-long drive to Azteca Stadium, a man asked if he could hop on. Vidinic agreed, and the two started chatting. It had been tough for Morocco to patch together a proper team in time for the championships, Vidinic conceded. "Fortunately we received unbelievable support from Adidas," he added. "Throughout the tournament they gave us boots and tracksuits. I don't know what we would have done without them." The man next to Vidinic held out his hand. "That's an extraordinary compliment," he said. "I'm Horst Dassler. From now on, your family and mine shall be friends." The handshake provided Horst with a devoted African informant.

Admittedly, it was hard to tell how much of the equipment donated by Adidas reached the athletes themselves. This came to mind when Thomas Sankara, former president of Burkina Faso, in West Africa, asked for a container of soccer balls to be delivered to his palace. Although the request seemed odd, even by Adidas standards, the company duly sent the balls to the Burkina Faso embassy in Paris. They couldn't help chuckling in Landersheim a few years later when newspapers reported the circumstances of Sankara's murder. The presidential palace had been ransacked and, to their delight, the rebels had found three thousand Adidas balls in the cellar.

The company's high-ranking African friends were unashamedly flattered in a publication called *Champion d'Afrique*. Launched by English-speaking journalists in 1974, the magazine covered African sports with incisive reporting. In the late seventies, the banner was taken over by the Tunisian colonel Hassine Hamouda. Hamouda had met Horst Dassler at the Melbourne Olympics and later become involved as an official in one of the competing bodies that ruled over the tumultuous boxing scene. With *Champion d'Afrique*, he became an integral part of Dassler's diplomatic team.

At Horst Dassler's direction, the magazine was transformed into an Adidas pamphlet to the glory of Horst Dassler and African sports officials. Most of the space was taken up by photographs of African dignitaries shaking hands with Dassler and other sports supremos. It contained barely any stories on actual sports but all the more editorials congratulating African friends for their supposed vision.

These African contacts would prove most useful for Horst Dassler when he sought to influence the decisions of international sports organizations. Much like the rest of the world at the time, these were often split between the communist bloc and the capitalist forces of the West. In many cases, the African vote could tip the balance either way.

Another style was required in the United States, where Horst Dassler relied on the resourcefulness of John Bragg. He was getting bored with his small family business when his longtime friend Mike Larrabee, the former runner, suggested that Bragg team up with him as an informal Adidas agent.

While Larrabee dealt mostly with athletics, Bragg often handled other tricky issues. He caught Horst Dassler's eye when a crisis emerged with Muhammad Ali in December 1970, on the eve of a fight with the Argentine boxer Oscar Bonavena in New York's Madison Square Garden. For several years Ali had been wearing boots made by Adi Dassler himself. But suddenly he decided to wear all-black boots, in line with his spiritual credo.

When Adi Dassler dispatched one of his German envoys to sort out the problem in New York, Ali sent him packing. Sent to the rescue, John Bragg tried another tack. "Adi Dassler would like to design the greatest boxing boot in the world," he told Ali at his New York hotel. "We need the advice of the greatest boxer in the world."

After a pause, Muhammad Ali talked of the female dancers he had watched the previous night in a New York club. They had been wearing short skirts with tassels, which moved elegantly as they shuffled. For his fight against Bonavena, he wanted Adidas boots with tassels. Over the next hours, Bragg frantically scoured the backstreets of New York to find tassels and a sewing machine. Ali was delighted when he unpacked the boots at his hotel that night, but he firmly instructed Bragg to keep them under wraps. At the weigh-in, "The Greatest" refused to answer the questions of the assembled reporters about the upcoming fight. All he would talk about was the "secret weapon" that Adidas had prepared for him. He pointed to Bragg, screaming that this man had come all of the way from Germany to deliver the weapon that would make him unbeatable. "It was as if we had written a script for him," said Bragg. The tassled boots, called the Ali Shuffle, made miles of copy.

From then on, Bragg performed many diplomatic sports assignments for Horst Dassler in the United States. Among the contacts cultivated by Bragg was Colonel Don Hull, head of the International Amateur Boxing Association. When the world boxing championship was held in Cuba, which was almost inaccessible to Americans, Horst Dassler confidently picked up his phone. Sure enough, Colonel Hull arranged for John Bragg to travel along as a member of his technical staff.

. . . .

There was not much that Armin Dassler could do to counteract his cousin's friendships. The Puma chairman didn't have the stamina, the personality, or the platform to build up such contacts. Although Armin was sly and crafty, he could not compete with the refinement of his cousin. "Horst had an incredible intellect and he could adapt to any kind of situation. He was completely unflappable," said John Bragg. "He could be quite a charmer, focusing entirely on what he was trying to do. He would have been a great ambassador."

In some of Horst Dassler's dealings, it was hard to draw the line between courtesy and bribery. Without openly encouraging them to act unfairly, Horst made it clear to his executives that he was not against their bending the rules. In the early days, some former Adidas executives felt uneasy about the manipulative aspects of their supposed friendships. "Don't worry, we're controlling them," they often heard Horst say. He rarely discussed manipulation, yet those who worked closely with him could not

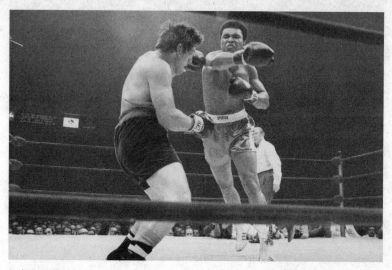

Muhammad Ali in his three-striped boots with red tassels, made for the fight against Oscar Bonavena in New York.

fail to observe that some doors unlocked with unnatural ease. "We never saw it and he never talked about it, but we knew it was going on. They couldn't all be bosom buddies," as one of them put it. Abundant press investigations later uncovered sickening abuses of Olympic funds by high-ranking members of the Olympic movement, as well as odd bank transfers.

Jean-Marie Weber was widely regarded as the man behind the logistics of Horst Dassler's most shady dealings. Hired as an accountant at Adidas France, this unostentatious and refined man soon turned into one of Horst's closest aides. Weber was sometimes described as Dassler's "right-hand man" but often more prosaically as his "bagman." Adidas executives joked that Weber's shoulders were bound to dislocate one day because he was always hauling at least one large sports bag full of personal documents. It was rumored that when the load became too heavy, Weber rented a barn in the small village of Landersheim to make sure the papers would not fall into the clutches of any potential raiders.

By the mid-seventies, Horst Dassler's diplomats relied on a broad network of friends and informants in the international sports world. They had placed their pawns in scores of relatively modest sports organizations. But all the efforts that they deployed in the process would become worthwhile only if they managed to infiltrate the organizations that truly ruled over international sports. The time had come to cash in.

the bountiful game

As much as they annoyed the Dasslers, the increasing demands of the sports people who wore their shoes went hand in hand with the rise of sports as an international business. Unlike his father, Horst Dassler had accepted that this phenomenon was almost unstoppable. And to those around him, it seemed almost inevitable that he would end up ruling it.

The evening meeting that propelled Horst Dassler in the sports marketing business took place at a Frankfurt hotel in June 1974. FIFA, the organization that governs global soccer, had invited scores of delegates to take part in its annual congress and elect their chairman for a four-year term, three weeks ahead of the World Cup.

The annual gathering usually wasn't a very exciting affair, but this ballot was regarded as a potential watershed. Virulent debates had raged among federations over the previous weeks as an unprecedented election campaign confronted two antagonistic views of soccer, business and politics: it pitted former colonial rulers and their supposedly conservative attitudes against a slick, brazen new world.

This was such a weighty issue for Adidas and for the prospects of global soccer that Horst Dassler assigned several of his sports diplomats to try to influence the outcome of the vote. They didn't miss any opportunities to spread their message. As the FIFA delegates settled down in Frankfurt, the Adidas heir himself came to shake a few last hands.

The incumbent, Sir Stanley Rous, was an impeccable Briton who prided himself on his gentlemanly behavior. A former referee and at the helm of FIFA since 1961, Rous had aptly dealt with the rising enthusiasm around soccer, the spread of television, and the organization of World Cups that turned into global events. He coped honorably with political pressure and with the money that began to swirl around soccer. The sixty-one-year-old seemed out of touch, however, with the upcoming soccer nations of the postcolonial world.

While Rous relied on the support of longtime friends, his opponent actively prepared the ground for the election. João Havelange, a tall Brazilian, had observed the workings of sports organizations since 1936, when he took part in the Berlin Olympics as a water polo player. He remained part of the Brazilian team for two decades and acceded to the International Olympic Committee in 1963.

At the same time, Havelange ran a sprawling business in Brazil, generating enough returns to fund his exhausting FIFA campaign. As the official South American candidate for the chairmanship, he visited eighty-six countries—often flanked by Pelé, the greatest crowd-puller the continent had to offer.

Havelange's manifesto unashamedly pandered to the wishes of emerging soccer nations. Among his eight election promises, he vowed to raise the number of non-European participants in the World Cup; he would organize a junior championship, to be held outside Europe; he would fund the construction of soccer pitches in developing economies, as well as training and medical centers. And unlike Rous, Havelange pledged to firmly ban South Africa from FIFA until the end of apartheid rule there.

In contrast with the buttoned-up Rous, Havelange excelled at sports diplomacy. A Brazilian of Belgian extraction, he had grown up as a cosmopolitan young man, a polyglot who gladly and fluently mingled with officials from all continents.

With far more political flair than his opponent, Havelange used all the means at his disposal to swing the vote in his favor. As one observer wrote, "The struggle was between a decent man who has served [soccer] loyally and been rewarded by just being there, and a slippery one who has no illusions about the true nature of the world and coveted glory for himself."

As he headed toward the bar of his Frankfurt hotel on the evening before the vote, Horst Dassler was convinced that Europe would prevail. His English friend Stanley Rous would remain in place, and Rous would surely remember the support offered by Adidas. Just to be sure, Dassler called up his Yugoslav friend Blago Vidinic for a few drinks downstairs.

Since their encounter in Mexico, Vidinic had moved on to Zaire. With the personal backing of President Mobutu, he had scoured the remotest corners of the country to assemble a team of healthy and lean youngsters. Mobutu was just as chuffed as Vidinic and the players when they received their free kit from Adidas, with a leopard's head emblazoned on their shirts. Entirely three-striped, the Leopards went on to win the 1974 African Nations Cup, held in Egypt, which qualified them for the upcoming World Cup in Germany.

The Leopards returned to an ecstatic welcome by the people of Zaire: they would be the first black African team to take part in a World Cup. "I left the celebrations early, saying that I was tired, because there were all these delirious people chanting my name, which is a little awkward when you're standing next to Mobutu," said Vidinic. The qualification still earned him "a sack stuffed with banknotes," delivered by one of Mobutu's goons.

To Horst's shock, the night before the FIFA presidential vote, Blago Vidinic was adamant that Stanley Rous would fail. In Egypt, on the sidelines of the African Nations Cup, he had witnessed a meeting of the African soccer federations. "They all promised to back Havelange," Vidinic told Dassler. The Brazilian had chiefly obtained the support of the African federations through his position on South Africa, as well as through "little presents and that sort of thing."

Deeply unsettled, Horst pondered his next move. Although it was getting late, Blago Vidinic urged him to change his tack right away. "Here's Havelange's room number," Vidinic said. "Tell him you had been backing Stanley Rous but you have been defeated, and from this moment you will be at Havelange's disposal."

This turned out to be an inspired move. As João Havelange had found out over the previous weeks, Horst Dassler could be a mighty opponent. By backing Stanley Rous, the German had nearly undermined Havelange's conquest of FIFA. It seemed much more comfortable to have Horst Dassler on his side. When Dassler returned from his chat with Havelange, he ordered champagne for Vidinic.

The next day, after some tumultuous debates and two rounds of voting, João Havelange was elected chairman of FIFA by a thin margin of 68 to 52 votes, applauded by Horst Dassler. In the aftermath of the congress, the two struck an informal deal that would reshape the soccer business: Havelange would hold the door wide open for Dassler in international soccer, provided that the German helped him garner the funds he needed to fulfil his costly election promises.

There was just one little hitch: Horst Dassler was already stretching his budget to such an extent that he certainly didn't have any extra millions in his pockets for FIFA. To fulfill his part of the deal, he would have to find a new way to raise the money required by Havelange.

. . . .

Ever since modern sports existed, some shrewd agents had made a few bucks by whipping up matches and turning them into entertainment. But in the seventies, Horst Dassler could not fail to observe the rise of professional sports agents, who made their money by seeking lucrative sports endorsements for media-friendly athletes.

The instigator of this business was Mark McCormack, an American lawyer who launched his agency in the sixties on the back of a handshake with golfer Arnold Palmer. McCormack soon turned into the rainmaker of the sports marketing business, and his company, IMG, into a sprawling sports and entertainment group.

In these early days, McCormack was building up his business chiefly in the United States, where sports and business seemed a natural match. The company's European offices were established in the Brussels garage of Eric Drossart, a former Belgian tennis player, who handled the business of erstwhile opponents, from Rod Laver to Ken Rosewall.

Horst Dassler and Mark McCormack regularly met to discuss the increasingly blatant relationship between sports and money. "They were talking as friends," said Eric Drossart, who took part in some of the lunches. "They recognized each other; each of them had made a huge contribution to this business."

Horst became more intimately acquainted with another American in the business, Donald Dell. For the former captain of the U.S. Davis Cup team, it had all started during a cab ride with Arthur Ashe. A lawyer by training, Dell had offered to assist Ashe by introducing him to McCormack. However, the two men weren't on the same wavelength, and Ashe became weary. During their fourth visit to the IMG offices, Ashe turned around to his friend: "Donald, why don't *you* just represent me?"

Over the next years, Donald Dell would deliver Stan Smith and countless other tennis and basketball players for Adidas. He spent many long evenings in Landersheim, and he was one of the few people who could have a laugh at Horst's expense without offending him. The relationship became even tighter when Horst began to rely heavily on Frank Craighill, one of the partners in Dell's law firm, to deal with all his contractual issues in the United States.

Wheeling and dealing in the middle of it all, Horst Dassler saw with interest that, in the early seventies, these agents were exploring new ways to make money from sports, by drawing corporate sponsors into the game. They had come to realize that the large crowds attracted by international sports contests formed an interesting audience for large companies, even if they were selling completely unrelated products.

Although a handful of companies had long paraded their wares at sports events, the spread of television gave an altogether new dimension to this formula. By investing in partnerships with exciting international sports events, companies could reach huge audiences at a stroke and make a mark on millions of consumers by associating themselves with the supposedly clean and energizing values of sport.

Horst Dassler quickly realized that, in this respect, there could not be any more interesting sports product to sell than soccer: it remained by far the most popular sport of all, drawing unmatched audiences and creating excitement that reverberated around the globe. If only he could build a bridge between soccer and international companies, then in no time he would raise the money he'd promised Havelange.

As the Adidas France managers scratched their heads over this new assignment, they discovered an interesting little outfit in London that was making a name for itself in sports marketing. West Nally was built on a partnership between Peter West, a former BBC commentator, and Patrick Nally, a former advertising manager: while West provided the contacts in sports and media, Nally established a reputation as a relentless salesman.

What West Nally proposed was to act as an intermediary between sports events and companies that wanted to be associated with sports. To begin with, they would help organizers package their event in a way that made it more appealing for broadcasters and sponsors. Then they would persuade international companies to cough up the sponsoring money—and reap a hefty commission on the sums they were able to raise.

This was a textbook example of the right concept at the right time. Since the borders of consumer goods markets were becoming increasingly blurred, international companies were exploring new ways of building up a global brand reputation. Sports sponsorship could have a more positive impact than advertising, because it could be regarded as a less obviously commercial investment.

The execution of the idea was just as remarkable. While Peter West brought in many of the contacts with event organizers, it was Patrick Nally who put the deals together. A dashing man in his early twenties, exuding youthful charm and enthusiasm, Nally wooed hard-nosed international executives to unlock stacks of commercial dollars. As they liked to say at the agency on Berkeley Square, Patrick Nally could sell fridges to Eskimos.

A few years into the partnership, West Nally had convinced large companies such as Gillette and Benson and Hedges to invest in cricket and snooker. By the early seventies, the agency employed about forty people and was beginning to open foreign offices. But West and Nally figured that, with the right connections, they could move on to a much larger stage.

When one of the Adidas France managers called, Nally eagerly agreed to meet Horst Dassler in Landersheim. The two young men were to be introduced shortly after Havelange grabbed the leadership of FIFA. And once they had shaken hands, they barely stopped talking for two days.

Patrick Nally was deeply impressed by Horst Dassler's operation and his drive. Seated behind his desk in Landersheim, he seemed constantly busy. "He fired instructions to his four secretaries and picked up the phone to speak to executives and dignitaries around the world, often in their own language," Nally marveled. "He was an unbelievably intense and charismatic man."

Horst Dassler was equally charmed by Nally's boldness and quick wit. Horst soon came to realize that, between the two of them, they could stamp a phenomenal business out of nothing. Due to his handshake with Havelange, Horst Dassler could easily obtain rights for the sale of marketing deals in international soccer. A tireless and highly creative salesman, Patrick Nally could rake in millions.

. . . .

For several months, the two men battled hard to get their business off the ground. All they had to sell was a nondescript partnership with FIFA, and they barely had any factual arguments to support their pitch. Dassler and Nally suffered innumerable rejections, until they landed in Atlanta.

Coca-Cola had long regarded international sports as an interesting means to reach its consumers. Its investments could be traced back to 1928, when the Olympics came to Los Angeles, and it had since appeared on the sidelines of each of the Games. Coke executives were always particularly pleased to see snapshots of Soviet athletes guzzling the imperialistic drink.

But in the seventies, as Coca-Cola sought to crank up its European business, soccer seemed a judicious alternative. Jonathan Parker, the hard-headed executive in charge of Coke's sports investments, was sufficiently intrigued to commit on an experimental scale.

In 1976, after many months of negotiations, the company agreed to pour some of its money into the organization of the soccer youth championships pledged by Havelange, which would take place in Tunisia. In exchange, the fences surrounding the pitches would be plastered with Coke's red posters. In line with Havelange's promises, more dollars were invested in soccer academies set up in developing countries, to grow those countries as soccer nations, supported by European trainers and physicians.

Yet Coca-Cola could hardly expect to get any returns on such remote investments. The real prize was the upcoming soccer World Cup, which was to take place in Argentina. In 1976, two years before the opening game, Dassler and Nally could start testing the waters, after they obtained the rights to sell "Gauchito," the mascot of the championships. Unfortunately, they had just hit the road when murderous generals seized Argentina's leadership. Protesters vehemently argued that the soccer World Cup could not decently be organized by a regime that sanctioned torture and eliminated political opponents by the truckload. Although FIFA rejected the pleas, the rustling rifles and click-clacking army boots made poor sales arguments for Patrick Nally.

As they struggled to sell their rights, Dassler and Nally were constantly short of cash to fund their informal partnership. For several years they would have to invest substantial sums in the business that would begin to yield full revenues only after the World Cup. And since Horst Dassler had made sure not to inform his family about any of these dealings, he could not fund them all too openly with Adidas money.

To get around these headaches, the two men established a partnership in Monte Carlo, called Société Monégasque de Promotion Internationale (SMPI). The local royals had decided to turn their patch of land into a haven for sports business, and Horst Dassler was interested in the opacity Monaco had to offer. Run by Patrick Nally but owned at 55 percent by Horst Dassler, SMPI sent its money through a financial carousel that spun from Switzerland to Monaco, the Netherlands and the Dutch Antilles.

Undeterred by the political upheavals in Argentina, Dassler and Nally bought more sponsorship rights for the 1978 World Cup. They agreed to give FIFA a guarantee of $8 million, in exchange for the right to sell billboards around the Argentine pitches. Although they didn't have the money, they had the backing of Coca-Cola, which blithely put up the guarantee.

They ended up raising $14 million, chiefly flogging boards to American and Japanese companies. Once it had covered abundant costs and paid the rights to FIFA, SMPI could just about afford the rent on its offices on Rue Grimaldi. But Horst Dassler had delivered on his promise to João Havelange, and the Argentine warm-up had convinced him that this soccer marketing business could grow far beyond his initial expectations.

There is no denying that Horst Dassler saw, much more sharply than others, the prospects of the sports-rights business. Nally had already managed to unlock millions of dollars from international companies for Argentina, under the worst of conditions. If this business was run properly, it could disgorge more cash than Adidas. He therefore didn't hesitate to up the ante.

This time, for the 1982 World Cup, FIFA requested $23 million for the marketing rights. The organization could argue that the championships would be held in Spain, an enticing market, and costs had risen sharply because Havelange had promised to draw more non-European teams into the event, raising the number of participants from twenty-four to thirty-two.

The setup behind the "Mundial" marketing deal was more opaque than ever. The rights were formally attributed to a holding company called Rofa, based in Sarnen, Switzerland. Only a handful of insiders knew that the *Ro* stood for Robert Schwan, Franz Beckenbauer's manager, and the *fa* for the player himself. In turn, Rofa assigned SMPI in Monte Carlo to handle and sell the marketing rights.

To raise the required funds, Nally put together a remarkable program, called Intersoccer, which would enable a small group of international companies to buy extensive soccer sponsorship rights for the Mundial. He defined eight separate categories, to make sure that rights would not be attributed to competing companies. Each of them would have four billboards around the Spanish soccer pitches, and large allotments of tickets.

The agreement would be valid not just for the World Cup: as part of a joint arrangement with UEFA, the European soccer federation, the deal would further cover European championships, as well as the forerunner to the Champions League and the UEFA Cup, for four years. The package came at a hefty price, as each of the eight companies would have to fork over 20 million Swiss francs ($11.7 million).

Some of the executives approached for such a deal burst out laughing, telling Nally and his partners that he should begin by removing a zero from the figure. Unfazed, the plucky advertiser put together a flurry of unprecedented soccer marketing deals. His Intersoccer package would form a blueprint for the multimillion-dollar deals that proliferated in international sports over the next years.

As part of their budgets for Intersoccer, Dassler and Nally drew up sheets projecting income and expenses for the next eight years. The sheets featured huge contributions from the likes of Coca-Cola and Canon. When it came to costs, the two men precisely outlined the price they would have to pay to FIFA and UEFA for their rights—discreetly placing all sorts of less official payments under an "additional" line.

Over the next years the strenuous fund-raising launched by the two men in Argentina and Spain would turn into a full-fledged soccer marketing industry, drawing hundreds of millions of dollars to the sport, and Horst Dassler would remain at the forefront of it all.

The money went to FIFA, which spent it on international projects to further popularity for the game and enlarged subsidies to national federations. Another chunk of the money was used to fund the expansion of FIFA itself, including the increasingly lavish payments and expenses of the international federation's board members.

. . . .

The partnership between Horst Dassler and FIFA was further tightened over the next years as the organization hired more of his friends. Among them was a Swiss executive under the name of Sepp Blatter. A well-mannered polyglot in charge of public relations at Longines, Blatter had been recommended to João Havelange and Horst Dassler when the two on the lookout for a suitable general secretary at FIFA.

The position was then filled by a dowdy Swiss, Helmut Käser, but Havelange and Dassler had come to the conclusion that Käser was out of his depth in the modern soccer business. Until Käser could be removed, however, Sepp Blatter would be introduced to FIFA as an unofficial marketing manager.

For several months Blatter worked from an office in Landersheim, where Horst groomed him intensely. "From the beginning, Horst Dassler and myself felt that we were kindred spirits," the Swiss recalled. "He taught me the finer points of sports politics—an excellent education for me." Since their birthdays were just two days apart in March, the two men regularly celebrated together at the Auberge. "That often included smoking a good cigar, another thing that I learned from Horst Dassler," Blatter recalled.

Others felt that Dassler was blatantly using his new protégé. "They had discussions in which Horst plainly issued instructions to Blatter," recalled Christian Jannette. "Horst openly talked of Blatter as a puppet; he introduced Blatter as one of us," another partner agreed. "He was an insignificant character, entirely at Horst's command. When the three of us had lunch together, Blatter looked up at Dassler as if he was God, knowing full well that he wouldn't stand a chance to get the FIFA job without Dassler."

Once Helmut Käser was brutally ousted and Sepp Blatter launched into orbit as general secretary of FIFA, huge marketing contracts were issued to Horst Dassler, behind closed doors. This hegemony gave rise to widespread suspicions that Dassler shared at least some of the spoils with his executive friends at FIFA and other sports organizations.

Over the following years, both the price and the returns of this business would rise at exponential rates. Yet in the second half of the seventies, the financial aspects of the undertaking were still shaky, so Horst remained constantly on the lookout for opportunities to further his personal business. Always at the back of his mind was the hypothesis that the situation with his family would become untenable and that he would have to break away. Just to be on the safe side, he decided to build a vast undercover business.

the clandestine empire

While Horst smelled unprecedented prospects in sports marketing, he suffered from the permanent strain of growing this business far away from his parents' eyes. It was almost by chance that he bumped into the solution: as part of a raggedy package to take over Le Coq Sportif, he found just the right partner to build up his clandestine empire.

Horst had worked closely with Le Coq Sportif since the sixties, before Adidas began to turn out its own clothes. Belonging to the Camuset family, Le Coq Sportif was established as a French maker of sports shirts and shorts, all emblazoned with a rooster. Under the deal with the Camusets, sanctioned by Käthe Dassler, Adidas France and Le Coq Sportif teamed up to offer a complete kit: while Adidas provided the boots, Le Coq Sportif manufactured three-stripe shirts and pants at its expanding plant in Romilly-sur-Seine, a small town in the Champagne region.

Le Coq Sportif was born from an ordinary knitwear factory run by Emile Camuset, who often spent his evenings at the Bar Romillon, a meeting place for locals who enjoyed chatting about sports. Over a round of drinks, they suggested that Emile try to design some sports shirts. Le Coq Sportif was registered as a brand in 1948 and it shot to prominence three years later, when it was asked to make shirts for the Tour de France. Over the next few years, Le Coq Sportif spread rapidly on French tracks and soccer pitches. Fittingly, the French rooster graced the shirts and sweat suits of French athletes at the Olympics, and the chests of the country's soccer players.

Yet the relationship soured when Adidas began to build up its own textile line. One of the problems was that Le Coq Sportif, which was making three-striped pants under the Adidas brand, had been selling clothes with roughly the same design under its own label. Horst Dassler pleaded with Le Coq Sportif to quit selling such products, but the Camusets staunchly refused, insisting that they held the rights to the three stripes in France. In June 1973, Horst Dassler sued.

In spite of the fact that Adidas's French and German operations remained at odds, this move by Horst was fully backed up by the Dasslers in Germany. They couldn't tolerate the fact that Le Coq Sportif caused confusion and unduly benefited from Adidas's investments. But the case took a nightmarish turn in February 1974, when the court of Strasbourg ruled in favor of Le Coq Sportif. The verdict unequivocally identified Le Coq Sportif as the owners of the three stripes, thereby undermining Adidas France's entire textile business.

From then on, Horst Dassler fought Le Coq Sportif relentlessly. Adidas France's lean textile facilities in Troyes worked at full capacity to swamp the market with Adidas shirts. Salespeople were deployed on an all-out offensive to squeeze Le Coq Sportif out of the market. Due to the dispute, Le Coq Sportif was also deprived of its most precious endorsement, by the French soccer federation; the contract had been obtained as part of a deal with Adidas, which supplied boots and left the shirts to Le Coq Sportif. However, the agreement hinged on the personal relationship between Horst Dassler and Jacques George, head of the federation. It took only a few whispers in George's ears to get Le Coq Sportif booted out. A complaint filed by the Camusets in June 1974 was duly rejected by Paris judges, who felt the federation had merely picked the supplier of its choice.

The move that proved most devastating for Le Coq Sportif, however, was orchestrated by the Camusets themselves. Weakened by heightened competition from the early seventies, they still decided to invest massively to expand their production. They acquired one plant and started constructing another one in Romilly. But under attack from Adidas, Le Coq Sportif continued to lose ground in the market. They were up to their necks in debt and stock, as the thousands of products turned out by the new factories remained unsold. By March 1974, Le Coq Sportif was besieged by anxious creditors. One month later the Camusets were expelled from the company, and a court-appointed manager led the search for takeover candidates.

Leaving their squabbles aside, Horst Dassler and his parents agreed that it would be disastrous if the rights to the three stripes, owned by Le Coq Sportif, fell into the wrong hands. Käthe Dassler therefore backed her son's bid to acquire Le Coq Sportif on behalf of Adidas, but the move was met with unexpectedly virulent resistance at Le Coq Sportif.

The bid was rejected most firmly by Mireille Gousserey-Camuset, the founder's daughter, who controlled just over half of the company's shares. Pointing to her activities in the Resistance during the Second World War, she balked at the thought that Le Coq Sportif would fall into German hands. Her brother, Roland Camuset promptly committed his 49 percent package to the Adidas bid. But Mireille stubbornly refused to surrender her shares to "the Krauts."

As Le Coq Sportif edged closer to liquidation, the French government became concerned and came forward with its own buyer for the company. All breathed a sigh of relief when Mireille Gousserey-Camuset gave her blessing to André Guelfi, a swashbuckling investor. His father was Corsican, his mother was Spanish, and he resided in Switzerland—but at least he'd been introduced by the French government. In March 1976, Mireille

Gousserey-Camuset surrendered her 51 percent of Le Coq Sportif to André Guelfi. Adidas France held on to the 49 percent committed by Roland Camuset nearly two years earlier—ending a two-year stalemate that had brought Le Coq Sportif to the edge of collapse.

When the request to buy Le Coq Sportif landed on his desk, André Guelfi had regarded it chiefly as a political favor. He smelled a very interesting opportunity, though, when a manager at Le Coq Sportif helpfully pointed to the ruling on the three stripes. Armed with the court papers, Guelfi arranged a meeting with Horst Dassler. "I went over in a bellicose mood, to tell them that they couldn't just walk away with the three stripes," Guelfi recalled. "But then we hit it off and decided to become partners."

The seduction worked both ways. André Guelfi rightly figured that Le Coq Sportif would do much better if Horst Dassler took it under his wing. As demonstrated by the incident with the French soccer federation, fighting Horst Dassler was a losing battle. As for Dassler, he was instantly charmed by André Guelfi. While Horst shunned the limelight, he relished the company of such gregarious characters. And Guelfi had amassed enough money to discreetly back up Horst Dassler's solo ventures.

The two came to a secret agreement. In the eyes of the Dassler family, Adidas France owned just 49 percent of Le Coq Sportif. But André Guelfi gave 2 percent of his own package to Horst, and granted him an option to acquire the remaining 49 percent at any time. The 2 percent and the option were issued to Horst personally, as opposed to Adidas. In other words, unbeknownst to his family, Horst had taken over control of Le Coq Sportif. The agreement marked the beginning of an intense partnership between the two men.

. . . .

André Guelfi was a dazzling man. In his mid-fifties at the time of the agreement, he had twice lost his fortune and rebuilt it with gusto. Some of the dealings behind his millions remained murky, but he swaggered through his troubles with exuberance and panache.

Growing up in Mazagan, on the Atlantic coast of Morocco, he made his debut as a gofer at a local bank. While he was cleaning up the archive room, Guelfi discovered a stack of files marked "unrecoverable loans." He struck a deal with the bank manager whereby he would get a hefty commission on any of the loans he could recover. After less than one year, the gofer was earning more than the bank manager. He amassed enough money to invest in several fishing vessels, which earned him the unglamorous nickname of "Dédé la Sardine."

Guelfi's nose for dodgy deals was sharpened during his time in Indochina, where he was sent in the mid-fifties as part of France's efforts to reassert its control over the provinces that would later form Vietnam. A reluctant fighter, he spent most of his time scouring the jungle for well-preserved statues. He had to leave the region in a hurry when one of the twenty-seven women to whom he'd gotten engaged took the promise seriously and sent her family around to speed up the proceedings.

Upon his return to Morocco, Guelfi made a fortune with his fishing trade, but this was entirely ruined in the earthquake that devastated Agadir in 1960. He bounced back in Mauritania, however, where he built up another fortune, operating the first fishing vessel with freezer facilities—"They were frozen alive!" he marveled—and several processing plants ashore. He resolved to give up this business, however, when the ship caught fire under dubious circumstances.

This time Guelfi fled to France, persecuted by the Mauritanian government and the Moroccan royal family. The Mauritanians were after him for alleged bribery. It may not have helped that, when the Mauritanian prime minister turned up to visit his frozen-foods plant, Guelfi thought it funny to lock him up in a freezer for a couple of minutes. As for King Hassan II of Morocco, he repudiated Guelfi after an attempted coup by the brutal interior minister, General Mohammed Oufkir, a close friend of Guelfi's.

When he resurfaced in France, André Guelfi went on a spending spree. His dealings in North Africa had left him with enough money to acquire some of the most renowned luxury hotels in Paris. When he applied for a Swiss residence permit in 1975, he reported assets of about 50 million Swiss francs. His mansion in Lausanne was next door to the headquarters of the International Olympic Committee.

His personal life was equally fast. Guelfi took part in six Formula One races as part of Team Gordini. By the time he became tied up with Horst Dassler, he owned a Lear jet, which he flew himself. His yacht was described as "the fastest boat in the Mediterranean." Once he had shaken hands with Horst on the Le Coq Sportif deal, Guelfi regularly popped up at Dassler's side, perpetually suntanned. The jet was almost permanently at Dassler's disposal, with Guelfi in the pilot's seat.

Some in the Alsatian team frowned upon Horst's new partner, who appeared to have come out of nowhere. His flamboyant style was out of sync with the hardworking ethos in Landersheim. Guelfi's extraordinary glibness was most helpful for lobbying purposes, but he admitted that his knowledge of management was restricted to the notion of "right pocket, left pocket."

The French managers laughed at the wild tales circulated about Guelfi—often by the man himself. With waving arms, he recounted the sinking of his vessel: he had managed to save a couple of masterpieces from the wreckage, swimming ashore with a Renoir tucked under his arm (his insurance company apparently bought the story). Other tales were more worrying, involving secret services and illegal funds transfers. A French judge later described Guelfi as "a business parasite," "an old bandit," and "a manufacturer of false bills by the kilometer."

But Horst Dassler ignored all the warnings. He increasingly relied on Guelfi as a jovial sidekick and a deep-pocketed financier. "Between the two of us," said Guelfi, "we became the masters of the world."

. . . .

To finance his undercover business, Horst Dassler teamed up with a dazzling Corsican. As Guelfi saw it, the two became the "masters of the world."

Since Guelfi had thrown Le Coq Sportif into his lap, Horst Dassler pushed the brand with the same drive with which he had contrived to sink it a few years earlier. If the tensions with his family took a dramatic turn, he could always exercise the option offered by Guelfi. Le Coq Sportif wasn't just an investment; it was an alternative brand that Horst could leverage in the stalemate with his family.

Together with Guelfi, Horst plotted far-reaching investments to overhaul Le Coq Sportif. An established player in the French market for sports textiles, the company was to become a serious contender in the international sports business, with a full range of products endorsed by some of the most coveted athletes and soccer teams around the world.

In Landersheim, Horst briefed his most trusted aides. As far as his parents were concerned, Adidas France owned a 49 percent share of Le Coq Sportif. André Guelfi had to invite the Dasslers to official shareholders meetings and politely consult them about expansion projects. But Herzogenaurach was not to find out about all the efforts that the French team was deploying to push Le Coq

Sportif around the world. "When someone came from Herzogenaurach, the Coq Sportif files were safely locked up in the cupboards," one of the Landersheim managers recalled.

The instructions to disguise the French managers' direct involvement in Le Coq Sportif led to some strange arrangements. A French executive recalled that, when he was recruited by Horst Dassler, there was an odd clause in his contract. He was officially hired by Adidas France, but an appendix in the contract indicated that he was to perform the same tasks for Le Coq Sportif. Adidas France was so anxious to keep the arrangement secret that they asked the executive to sign a confidentiality agreement about it.

Johan van den Bossche, head of legal affairs at Adidas France, came to realize the bizarre aspect of the situation a few weeks after his recruitment. He received a phone call from an Asian hotel from a Mr. Gary Heller. The lawyer didn't remember anybody by that name. He was even more startled when Mr. Heller addressed him by his first name and began to issue precise instructions regarding a licensing deal. "I'm sorry, sir. I can't take instructions from somebody I don't know," Van den Bossche calmly replied. It turned out that Mr. Heller was Klaus Hempel, special assistant to Horst Dassler. While traveling in Asia on Le Coq Sportif business, Hempel routinely booked hotel rooms under the name of his brother-in-law.

Horst Dassler and André Guelfi went through elaborate rituals to inform the Dassler family in Herzogenaurach about the progress of Le Coq Sportif in France. "Horst sometimes pretended to side with his mother, rejecting investments which I advocated," Guelfi recalled. At the same time, however, the two established a holding company called Sarragan, located in Freiburg, Switzerland, to regroup all of Horst Dassler's covert activities—including most of the international business for Le Coq Sportif.

The treachery was made possible by the acting talents of all the French executives involved, as well as by the opacity of their accounts. Horst heavily relied on Jean-Marie Weber, his accountant and bagman, to blur the picture for Herzogenaurach. When he dutifully submitted his reports to his parents, he could rest assured that they would not reveal anything awkward. Dassler's unauthorized dealings were aptly disguised in a maze of Swiss holdings and fictitious service agreements. "In such a jumble, even a cat would not be able to trace its kittens," Weber said.

Descente, the Japanese licensee of Adidas, was drawn into the plot. The managers in charge of the Adidas business at Descente seemingly remained loyal to Herzogenaurach, but they agreed to play along with Horst Dassler by also distributing Le Coq Sportif—behind Käthe Dassler's back. The Adidas business was handled by Murakawa-san. But this same man had another set of business cards for Le Coq Sportif, where he was known as Nakamura-san.

Another full-fledged Le Coq Sportif operation was hurriedly opened in the United Kingdom by Robbie Brightwell—the male half of the British runners' couple that had made romantic headlines at the Tokyo Olympics, with gold and silver medalist Ann Packer in the female lead. Since then the two had married, and Brightwell had been hired by Dassler to run an Adidas operation in the United Kingdom (under the formal supervision of Umbro, which distributed Adidas in Britain until the mid-eighties).

Privy to the twisted relationships in the Dassler family, Brightwell understood perfectly that the new operation had to be kept away from Herzogenaurach. Le Coq Sportif UK was therefore established in the Cheshire village of Congleton, a few doors away from the Brightwells' home, and funded with their personal accounts. This caused a bit of a panic at the Congleton branch of the National Westminster Bank, which normally dealt with small local transfers. "Mr. Brightwell, a very large sum has been transferred from Switzerland to your account," a nervous bank manager whispered to him. Sent by Sarragan, the Swiss holding company set up by Dassler and Guelfi, the money enabled Brightwell to build up a fast-growing operation.

All the contacts Horst Dassler cultivated for Adidas were exploited to boost the international standing of Le Coq Sportif. The brand, which a few years before had been thrilled to obtain a deal with the French soccer federation, was suddenly worn by some of the world's most revered sports people, from Arthur Ashe, the American tennis player, to the Argentine soccer team.

The investments were particularly generous in the United States, where Le Coq Sportif was oddly positioned as an upscale tennis brand. At Horst's request, Donald Dell persuaded not only Arthur Ashe but many other players to wear Le Coq Sportif. While the company had American sales of about $1 million, it spent more than twice that amount on athletes. The situation was only reversed in the late seventies when Dassler hired an experienced manager, Pete Mahmet, to run Le Coq Sportif in Cranbury, New Jersey, with a typically succinct assignment: "Make it big and profitable."

Still, Horst Dassler acknowledged that Le Coq Sportif alone could never attain the same scope as Adidas. He therefore entered several other undercover agreements, ranging from a joint venture with Daniel Hechter, the French designer and soccer club executive, to another with Façonnable, all bundled under the Sarragan holding. Due to the clandestine aspects of the setup, the operations remained somewhat haphazard, but they still added up to a sprawling sports and leisure business.

As Horst explained to some close managers, the accumulation of secondary interests was meant to reach a critical mass that would enable him to survive in the sports business by himself. His undertaking was both farsighted and amazingly devious. He would build up another sports conglomerate—behind his family's back.

. . . .

Horst Dassler's least publicized partnership was sealed with Roberto Muller, a flamboyant young man from Uruguay. The dapper executive was the driving force behind Pony, an American sports company established in 1974. A former vice president of Levi Strauss, Muller had extensive contacts in the Far Eastern sourcing industry. His plan with Pony was to concentrate on the all-American sports of baseball and football. Muller quickly grasped the workings of the sports business—and he distinguished himself as a particularly shrewd operator.

A swashbuckling character with a Latin temperament, Muller had all the right credentials to seduce Horst Dassler. His father had originated from a Slovak brewer's family; his mother came from the Austro-Hungarian aristocracy. On a business trip in Brazil when the Second World War erupted, the Jewish family ended up in Uruguay. Roberto was sent to school in Leeds but returned to join Uruguay's junior soccer team. He went on to become one of the country's youngest oil and fashion executives, fluent in eight languages.

There were other aspects to Muller that weren't mentioned in his CV. One of them was his taste for glitz and glamour: his office was decorated with pictures of himself as a dashing young man, on the staircase of a private jet surrounded by stunning women. A fanciful storyteller, he easily captivated his audience. As one former Adidas executive put it, Muller displayed "flashes of genius and flashes of something else."

But Horst Dassler was mostly charmed by Roberto's glibness and his sense of intrigue. The two hit it off when the Pony chief agreed to take part in a prank at the U.S. Olympic trials in 1976, by canceling Armin Dassler's car reservation in Seattle. Shortly afterward, when Muller needed financial backup for Pony, he turned to Horst Dassler.

The deal was set up at Les Pirates, a festive restaurant on a Caravelle ship that was anchored between Monte Carlo and San Remo. On the boat, Horst introduced Muller to André Guelfi. The snapshot that was taken at that dinner would have appalled Horst Dassler's arch-conservative parents: there was their son flanked by two grinning and suntanned men who could have walked straight off the set of *Miami Vice*.

Shortly after this encounter, André Guelfi agreed to acquire a large minority stake in Pony. Just as in the case of Le Coq Sportif, however, Guelfi was merely a front man. In a side letter, Dassler and Guelfi agreed that Dassler was entitled to take over Guelfi's shares in Pony at any time.

Backed up by Horst Dassler, Pony turned into an aggressive contender in the American sports business. Roberto Muller was promptly introduced to the Riu brothers, the Adidas partners in Taiwan. The deal with Dassler considerably reduced production costs for Pony, encouraging Muller to push the brand in the American mass market. Pony made further progress in American sports, endorsed by Wilma Rudolph and O. J. Simpson. It became prominent in the New York boxing scene, and even obtained the endorsement of Pelé when his deal with Puma expired and he ended his career with the New York Cosmos.

But due to the slippery aspects of the New York connection, the deal was kept secret from Herzogenaurach with more care than any of Horst Dassler's other side interests. While Le Coq Sportif and Daniel Hechter belonged to Sarragan, the stake in Pony solely featured in the books of André Guelfi—presuming he kept any.

Only a handful of French executives were thoroughly informed of Dassler's dealings with Roberto Muller. Others who bumped into the clique without warning were somewhat unsettled by what they discovered. André Gorgemans, former financial manager of Le Coq Sportif USA, was thus invited for drinks at a New York apartment owned by one of Roberto Muller's business relations. As he entered the flat, Gorgemans was intrigued by an ornamental bowl filled with white powder on the mantelpiece.

Remarkably, Horst Dassler had managed to hide most of these dealings from his family in Herzogenaurach. But the pressure became untenable for many managers, who were torn between Horst and his inquisitive family. "Sometimes I wondered whether I was in international business or in diplomacy," said Robbie Brightwell.

The same thought occurred to Dieter Passchen, who headed up the Adidas operation in Hong Kong. Passchen once traveled to Herzogenaurach with a delegation from Descente, the company's Japanese licensees, who had a separate deal with Horst for Le Coq Sportif. The talks between Käthe and the Descente managers were meant to extend their deal with Adidas. Just before the meeting, however, Käthe discovered Descente's double role with Le Coq Sportif. "She completely flew off the handle," Passchen recalled. "She branded the Japanese as traitors and refused to sign with them again." It took several days for the dust to settle.

Horst Dassler would never sort out the issue with his father. In his darkest moods, he shared his sadness with close colleagues and showed them long, bitter letters in which Adolf Dassler disowned his son.

Right until the last months of his life, Adolf Dassler was permanently harassed by the conflicts between his son and his German managers. One of the last skirmishes erupted before the 1978 soccer World Cup. For the occasion, Adi Dassler had discreetly developed a soccer boot with all the latest enhancements. Horst Widmann, his personal assistant, was sent to present the boot in Argentina. But when he met up with the Adidas France delegation, at the Sheraton Hotel in Buenos Aires, Widmann was stunned to discover that the model they had brought along was, as far as Widmann was concerned, a crude copy of the German boot. He was fuming, certain that the French had used a mole in the German organization.

Widmann agitatedly called the Dasslers in Herozgenaurach. "Adi Dassler was livid," he recalled. "He gave me the official order to steal a boot from the French delegation to check out how it was made." Then, the two parties still had to work out which of the boots would be launched by Adidas at the World Cup. "Adi and Käthe were breathing down my neck, on the phone all the time to make sure I would stand firm," said Widmann. They ended up reaching a compromise whereby the German team would wear the German boots, while Horst Dassler would hand out French boots to all the other players.

Oblivious to the business aspects of Adidas, Adolf continued to walk around with his notepad and to tinker in his workshop. The obsession that drove him perpetually to seek improvements for his shoes never appeared to fade. Over fives decades he registered nearly seven hundred patents to his name, ranging from the screw-in studs to minute inventions that would stir only the most fanatical shoe buffs.

In his seventies, Adolf Dassler continued to shy away from the honors that were bestowed upon him. When strangers turned up at the gates in Herzogenaurach, hoping to catch a glimpse of Adi Dassler, he turned them away unceremoniously. "One day he was walking his dog in the compound when someone called him to the fence, asking for Adi Dassler," recalled Karl-Heinz Lang, another of his close assistants. "Adi just shrugged. Don't know, he told the visitors. I'm the gardener." Clad in his three-striped sweatpants, he tended to look the part.

Adi once confessed to his friend Erich Deuser, medical adviser to the German soccer team, that he didn't have a clue how many factories Adidas owned—and, frankly, he didn't care. By 1978, the company he had founded in his mother's washroom employed nearly 3,000 people in Germany alone. About 180,000 pairs of three-striped shoes were produced daily in the factories that Adidas owned in 17 countries. They were officially distributed in 144 countries.

By then, Adi had been advised to slow down. He had been gently told after a medical checkup that he should cut back on soccer and tennis, which he still regularly played. Since the warning, Adolf dutifully swallowed handfuls of colored pills. On August 18, 1978, Käthe found him almost motionless in his bed, felled by a stroke. He was rushed to an intensive care unit in Erlangen and lay there for nearly three weeks, surrounded by all of his children. He passed away at the clinic, aged seventy-eight, when his heart finally gave up on September 6, 1978.

The Dassler family strictly followed his instructions to keep pompous speechmakers and other intruders at bay. To make sure the funeral would remain private, Käthe, her five children, and their families assembled one hour before the time that had been scheduled publicly, on a rainy morning two days after Adi's death. He was buried under a plain marble stone in the upper right-hand corner of the Herzogenaurach cemetery—exactly at the opposite end of the spot where his brother Rudolf was laid to rest four years before.

olympic friends

The demise of Adi Dassler marked the end of the days when sports could still be regarded as just a game. As he had watched in frustration in his last years, the enjoyment of sports had been increasingly spoiled by the business that was built around them. It was just as well that he never watched his son turn the Olympics into his most spectacular business deal.

Christian Jannette, the former chief of protocol at the Munich Olympics, intensely prepared the ground. For many years Horst Dassler had been rebuffed by the heads of the International Olympic Committee (IOC), who refused to mingle with lowly merchants and rejected any suggestions to relax the rules around business at the Olympics. He had hired Jannette precisely for the purpose of tearing these barriers down, and the Frenchman was making remarkable progress.

His mission had already started at the Montreal Games in 1976. In line with his brief, Jannette paid particularly close attention to delegates from the Soviet Union. It had been decided two years earlier that the next Olympic Games were to be held in Moscow and that the Soviet capital would host elections for the next chairman of the IOC. The Adidas men knew that nothing could be left to chance.

Jannette's thorniest assignment in Montreal was to organize an odd journey for Sergei Pavlov, the Soviet sports minister at the time. Mikhail Mzareulov, head of protocol for the Soviet delegation, whispered in Jannette's ear that Pavlov would be thrilled to see Niagara Falls. It was left to Jannette to make the arrangements. The excursion would have to go unnoticed, because the Soviet authorities would not have looked too kindly upon an escapade by their team leader to a capitalist attraction.

Pavlov and Mzareulov were therefore smuggled out of Montreal at four o'clock in the morning, then flown on a regular flight to Toronto, to a little private jet, and finally driven in a car with smoked windows to Niagara Falls. "Pavlov was like a kid," recalled Jannette, who accompanied them all the way. The two Russians insisted on having a picture taken behind barrels for a tacky montage, with just their heads sticking out, Niagara Falls in the background.

Sergei Pavlov reciprocated the favor many times over. In the six years before the Moscow Olympics, Christian Jannette made sixty-two trips to the Russian capital. His friends treated him with every consideration, and they made special allowances for him to travel around the country unimpeded. Jannette was likely among the first Westerners in the communist era to travel to the steppes of Yakutia—thousands of miles away from Moscow, to outposts for which Russians themselves needed visas.

. . . .

When Christian Jannette arrived in Moscow on one of his numerous trips, he often headed straight to the Spanish embassy. There, he was certain to be treated to a copious meal by Juan Antonio Samaranch, the ambassador. They became such personal friends that when Jannette was taken to a Moscow hospital with a hernia, the ambassador's charming wife, Bibis, brought him fresh fruit and Spanish dishes every day.

Christian Jannette began to cultivate his contacts with Samaranch shortly after he joined Adidas in 1973. It did not seem to upset anyone that the Catalan had previously shown unrestrained fervor for the Franco regime. In December 1966 Franco's government appointed him to a position in charge of sports. He was later elected as a member of the Cortes, the Spanish parliament, for Barcelona, under the fascist banner—although the ballot didn't have much in common with the basic principles of democracy.

At the same time, Samaranch made his ascent in sports politics, beginning with his election to the IOC in 1966. He gradually reached one of the most coveted positions in the Olympic movement: the chief of protocol. Insiders could not fail to recall that the two previous chairmen of the IOC had held the same position. Jannette was further charmed by Samaranch's smooth manners, astute business sense, and multiple language skills. "He distinguished himself from the brigade of small-time Olympic officials with green blazers," Jannette said.

Jannette pounced at the wedding of Avery Brundage, former IOC chairman, to Mariann Princess Reuss in June 1973. In between two speeches, Jannette asked Samaranch, another wedding guest, if he would be interested in a meeting with Horst Dassler. Samaranch instantly grasped the potential interest of the proposed encounter. The date was set for a few weeks later, in September 1973.

Juan Antonio Samaranch arranged an elaborate welcome. Horst Dassler was taken around Camp Nou, the mythical grounds of the Barcelona FC soccer club. He had lunch at the private residence of the Samaranch couple. He was taken to an impressive nautical show in Barcelona. And he was treated to a black-tie dinner with the Samaranches, in the grandest Catalan style.

The dinner sealed a lifelong understanding between the two men, who would become the most influential executives in the sports world. Both of them were driven by an insatiable thirst for power, and they acknowledged that they could attain it together: if Horst Dassler helped Samaranch to reach the chairmanship of the IOC, Samaranch would hold the door wide open for his German friend.

Horst Dassler at Camp Nou in Barcelona, where he was introduced to Juan Antonio Samaranch (not pictured). They teamed up to take over and sell the Olympics.

Samaranch invested heavily to fulfill his part of the unwritten deal. Shortly after Franco's death, in November 1975, at a time when Spain didn't have an ambassador in the Soviet Union, he persuaded the government to send him to Moscow. He shrewdly figured that, ahead of the Moscow Games, all the people who counted in the Olympics would spend much of their time in the Russian capital. They would be grateful for the support and hospitality of the Spanish embassy. Given the lavishness of the parties thrown by the Samaranches, it was widely suspected that they pumped some personal funds into the diplomatic efforts.

For its closest friends, the Spanish embassy was prepared to sort out more mundane matters. After its deal in Montreal, Adidas had again obtained an exclusive agreement to outfit all of the officials for the Moscow Games. This turned out to be a monstrous task: while the organizers of the Montreal Games had required about ten thousand such outfits, the Russians coolly asked for thirty-two thousand pieces. As the Adidas managers joked back in Landersheim, "for every task there was one chap performing it, another one supervising him, and then the KGB man watching the two others."

Just a few months before the opening of the Games, however, another blazing row erupted between Horst Dassler and his family in Herzogenaurach. The huge equipment deal for the Moscow Olympics had suddenly been transferred to Arena—revealing Horst Dassler's personal clout. Putting his oar in, U.S. president Jimmy Carter decided to protest the Red Army's invasion of Afghanistan by ordering a boycott of the Moscow Games, making it all the more complicated for Dassler to seal partnerships with other suppliers.

Not unlike Havelange a few years earlier, Samaranch campaigned openly for the IOC chairmanship. His unofficial manifesto was based partly on the principle that the amateur ethos of the Olympics should be somewhat relaxed. This position infuriated his opponents when Samaranch dared to express it at a meeting in Olympia, and it continued to irritate some IOC members, who thought it indecent to talk about money at all. However, more down-to-earth members became convinced that the hypocrisy of the existing rules was unsustainable.

Another problem that played in Samaranch's favor was that the Olympic movement was teetering on the brink of collapse. The Montreal Games had punched a massive hole in the city's accounts: its mayor, Jean Drapeau, was quoted as saying that "the Olympics could no more produce a deficit than a man a baby," but the Games left Montreal with debts of about $1 billion (up to $2 billion with interest payments). The reputation of the Olympics was further tarnished by the large-scale boycott of the Moscow Olympics, which badly disappointed some sponsors and looked certain to deprive broadcasters of millions of viewers.

Controversial as they were, Samaranch's plans concretely addressed this urgent situation. He intended to set up a task force that would concentrate entirely on raising funds. It would help to package the Olympics in a way that made them more attractive for broadcasters, and would seek much more comprehensive sponsorship deals. This was where Horst Dassler came in.

On July 16, 1980, the Catalan beat all of his opponents—including Willy Daume, the German candidate favored by executives in Herzogenaurach. That evening, those who had most intensely contributed to Samaranch's triumph convened to celebrate it in a rented meeting room at the Moskva hotel. Among the fifteen guests around the Samaranch couple was Christian Jannette. The caviar was most certainly Russian, but the foie gras for this special party had been flown over from Landersheim.

. . . .

By then, Horst Dassler had become completely fascinated by the mechanics of power. He had turned into a chief manipulator, influential enough to bend weighty decisions in his favor. He enjoyed rubbing shoulders with high-ranking people, thrived on his role as a puppet master. He relished the intrigue, building on the life of deceit he had cultivated since deep disagreements erupted between him and his parents. But since Horst had become involved in international sports politics, his power games acquired a razor-sharp edge.

Although Dassler was permanently on guard, he was particularly suspicious in the Soviet Union. Convinced that he was being bugged all the time, the Adidas chief always traveled beyond the iron curtain with a debugging device, which he used in his hotel room even before he unpacked his bags. He taught several leading executives to use such devices, and encouraged them to plant misleading documents in their briefcases.

Frank Craighill, Horst Dassler's American attorney, watched exactly how the Adidas chief operated in the Soviet Union when he accompanied him on a trip to Moscow, to help deal with the threat of a lawsuit around the television rights for the 1980 Olympic Games. "You have just spoken your last unoverheard word," Horst told Craighill as their plane touched down in the Soviet capital.

During the meeting in the Kremlin, Craighill saw in astonishment that the Soviets didn't even bother to hide the microphones that were stuck on the walls. Later that day, he went along with Horst and Vitaly Smirnov, Soviet member of the IOC, for a more personal discussion. "They went to this large heated pool in Moscow," Craighill recalled. "Then they swam to the middle of the pool and had their conversation there."

The suspected surveillance sometimes became so stressful that Horst Dassler relieved the tension with a playful touch. During a dinner meeting, he would share a piece of fresh information

Christian Jannette, who wove relationships for Horst Dassler in the Soviet Union, sits to his left for an evening at the Lido in Paris. With them is the Soviet sports minister Sergei Pavlov *(front left)*. The young man at the end of the left row is Patrick Nally.

with his Soviet partners but then conclude casually, "Well, you already know this anyway since you've read all the documents." The hosts remained poker-faced.

The obsession was not entirely in jest nor unjustified. After all, Soviet rulers were notoriously inquisitive about capitalist guests, and the stakes of the sports business became so high in those years that the fear of bugs apparently spread to the IOC itself: the Olympic headquarters in Lausanne were rumored to have one meeting room for sensitive discussions that was guaranteed bug-free, constantly checked by technicians.

Conversely, an American salesman was stunned to discover, while staying at the Sportshotel in Herzogenaurach, that its bar appeared to be wired. By then the hotel had been upgraded and it was regularly used by entire delegations of high-ranking dignitaries, who were most likely to share their impressions of the day over a drink at the bar. The salesman was trying to tune his transistor to the radio station of the U.S. Armed Forces in Germany, but distinctly heard conversations at the downstairs bar instead.

The same happened to Jörg Dassler, Armin Dassler's second son, when he was still a teenager in the late seventies. He was sitting in his living room fiddling with his radio, while Armin was talking on the phone. "And all of a sudden, I heard my father on the radio," Jörg Dassler recalled. "That's how we found out that the phone was bugged. We found the device in the receiver."

Such methods caused disbelief and outrage, but many felt that they had become an integral part of the sports business. The boycott at the Moscow Olympics aptly demonstrated that sports had come to be regarded as a sharp political instrument. Horst Dassler and his managers operated in the awkward political climate that characterized the period, fraught with suspicion and intrigue.

As Horst became more deeply involved in the exploding sports business, however, his own behavior acquired an obsessive, paranoid edge. "He was permanently hiding," said Klaus Hempel, his personal assistant. "He would make phone calls from his desk and make people believe that he was at the other end of the world."

At the zenith of his sports political might, from the late seventies, Horst Dassler appeared most concerned about the loyalty of those around him. One of Dassler's managers witnessed how the Adidas chief went berserk at a soccer match when he spotted Franz Beckenbauer, the German soccer player, at the other end of the stadium casually chatting to a competitor. "The next day Dassler called the German police to find out where he could get hold of long-range microphones, so he could eavesdrop on such conversations," the aide remembered. "When I told him he may be overreacting, he rolled his eyes and called me naïve."

He distanced himself from several executives on grounds that turned out to be entirely unfair, or grossly exaggerated. Christian Jannette was gruffly rebuked when he asked Brigitte Baenkler, Horst Dassler's sister, for an innocent dance at the annual German sports ball. Since Frau Baenkler was unaccompanied, Jannette thought it would be polite to ask her, but Horst didn't see it that way. "He quizzed me aggressively, asking what we had been talking about, what she told me," Jannette said. "It was most unpleasant."

The Frenchman was dismissed shortly thereafter, and he would not take part in the outcome of the Olympic project he had initiated by introducing Horst Dassler and Juan Antonio Samaranch.

. . . .

Once the Spaniard had reached the pinnacle of his sports career, it was easier for Dassler to obtain the deals he was after. While his predecessors had scrupulously kept business away from the Olympics, Samaranch urgently set about raising money for the IOC, and there was only one person who could adequately steer this thorny project.

The proposition was roughly the same as with soccer: Dassler would sell the Olympic rings to large corporations as an international marketing tool. It should have been easy, since the Olympics were even more universal than soccer and supposedly inspired by a higher moral order. But the project still seemed to be an aberration, because the rights to the Olympic rings were scattered among scores of National Olympic Committees (NOCs).

The implications were head-spinning. To be able to offer international packages, Dassler would have to persuade nearly all of the NOCs to surrender their rights to the Olympic rings. His leading argument was that the IOC could then draw much larger investments from international companies, which would be partly distributed to the NOCs again. Still, it would take years to meet and convince them all, and the project could still falter if any of the large countries refused to take part.

However, Horst Dassler was not intimidated. The time had come to reap the rewards of the many lonely hours in front of hotel elevators: owing to this relentless lobbying, he knew many of the heads of the national committees himself. The people appointed in his sports politics team had befriended many more.

Samaranch identified broadcasting rights as the most promising source of heightened revenues for the IOC. This business had come a long way since the fifties, when broadcasters boycotted the Olympics because they deemed it unacceptable that they, unlike their newspaper colleagues, should have to pay for the privilege of covering the games. Since then, broadcasters had seen how the Olympics jacked up their ratings and Samaranch rightly figured that, if properly marketed, the broadcasting rights could yield much higher revenues. But unlike FIFA, the Olympic Committee judged that it could handle such negotiations itself, to avoid paying large commissions to Dassler or any sports rights agency.

Next in line were marketing rights. Due to the fragmented control over the rings, the IOC had been unable to draw to the Olympics the million-dollar investments that were spreading in other sports. Samaranch gladly leaned on Horst Dassler, his longtime friend, to deal with the practicalities.

In the interval, Dassler had abruptly broken with Patrick Nally, his young partner in London, based on apparently unsubstantiated allegations that the Englishman was double-crossing him. Unaccountably furious, in April 1982, Horst booked three adjoining suites at the Scribe Hotel in Paris, called a lawyer, and locked himself in for several days to end his partnership with Nally in SMPI, their joint sports marketing company.

"He fired off letters and faxes to the whole world, telling them that he didn't want anything to do with Nally again," one of his executives recalled. Patrick Nally relinquished his shares in SMPI in exchange for a compensation of just 3.6 million Swiss francs ($1.8 million), and West Nally never fully recovered from the split.

Instead Horst Dassler teamed up with Dentsu, the Japanese advertising behemoth. The advantage was that, under the agreement, Dentsu invested 51 million Swiss francs ($25.1 million) in the business and let Dassler keep half of it. The deal was sealed at the Mundial in Spain, where Dassler invited Tetsuro Umegaki, Dentsu's chairman. Based in Lucerne, Switzerland, the joint venture with Dentsu was called ISL (International Sport and Leisure). It was headed up by Klaus Hempel, Dassler's personal assistant, and Jürgen Lenz, former international marketing manager at Adidas.

Their most zealous supporter was Juan Antonio Samaranch. When he persuaded the IOC to set up an international marketing package at a session in New Delhi in 1983, it barely seemed worth mentioning that the deal would go to ISL. Horst Dassler and Jürgen Lenz then set out on an Olympic world tour, to strike a deal with each of the national committees.

To assuage the fears of some reluctant committees, led by the United States and Germany, Juan Antonio Samaranch sent them all a personal letter to explain the benefits of the sale. It took much politicking and several rounds of drawn-out talks to turn around the wealthiest committees. Dassler and Lenz called it quits when the United States had given in and all but thirteen of the NOCs had signed. There was no point in entering further talks with the likes of Afghanistan, Albania, and North Korea, which held on to their rights for political reasons and which were almost meaningless for the sponsors anyway.

This exhausting tour enabled ISL managers to push through an all-encompassing marketing plan for the Olympics. Dubbed The Olympic Programme (TOP), it would raise hundreds of millions of Swiss francs for the organization in Lausanne. Under the same principles as Intersoccer, sponsorship deals were offered to international companies. ISL collected about $94 million for the first edition of TOP, in the run-up to the Seoul Olympics in 1988.

Jean-Marie Weber, Horst Dassler's former "bagman," regularly turned up at ISL in Lucerne to deal with financial issues. He later became known there as the man with the "blacklist," which described the recipients of unusual bank transfers. Other ISL managers professed to turn away from such matters, but they all agreed that the list was long. As one of them put it, "the right question would be who wasn't on it."

Apart from that, the sellout of the Olympics to international marketing powers would cause appalling scandals over the next decades, as reporters exposed widespread abuses of the funds garnered through TOP. While some of them went to aid plans, others were wasted on the egos and expenses of tacky IOC members.

But for Horst Dassler, it was the ultimate reward. With the Olympic program, ISL had established an unshakeable stranglehold on the sports marketing business, which was catching on at breath-taking speed. Horst Dassler protected it fiercely. He had built ISL all by himself, and it would remain his personal patch. He conscientiously preserved it from the nerve-racking squabbles in his family. His undercover dealings came back to haunt him, however, when his cover was blown.

the return

While Horst Dassler hobnobbed with the masters of world sports, Käthe Dassler continued to share plum cake with her guests on the terrace of the Villa. In the early eighties, many weighty decisions at Adidas were made during daily sessions of coffee drinking, when Käthe spent long hours chatting with her sister, Marianne, and her daughters.

In line with Adolf Dassler's will, Käthe Dassler had inherited control of the company, but she insisted on drawing all of her children into the management. Under the family structure, each of the four Dassler daughters supervised her own department. Inge Bente, the eldest daughter, contributed strongly to sports promotion in Germany, but she lost much of her influence after she suffered an unexplained stroke that paralyzed half of her body. Karin Essing, the second eldest, meddled with all things marketing. Brigitte Baenkler seconded her brother, Horst, when it came to relations with East European countries. Sigrid Malms, the youngest daughter, briefly supervised the textile business until her move to Switzerland with her husband.

Other issues facing Adidas were discussed in informal family meetings, involving the four sisters and their husbands. Alf Bente, Inge's husband, wielded the strongest influence. He had been integrated into the company for a long time, supervising the expansion of its production. When Adi began to fade out, Bente informally took up some of his duties. Hans-Günther Essing was less involved in the daily running of the business, but he was seen as reliable and as having solid analytical skills. Hanns-Wolf Baenkler listened much more than he spoke. Christoph Malms, Sigrid's husband, didn't spend much time in Herzogenaurach. Having honed his skills at Wharton Business School in the United States, he became a management consultant with McKinsey.

Some of the family's methods were chiefly designed to keep a tight grip on the management. Among the most outrageous rituals was the opening of the mail. Marianne Hoffmann, Käthe Dassler's sister, spent more than two hours going through every single letter that reached Adidas in Herzogenaurach. It didn't matter if the letters were marked for specific managers; she went through the contents of each package and dispatched them to the recipients of her choice.

Unfortunately, the judgements of the Dassler sisters weren't always in line with the preoccupations of professional managers. One of these managers was in the middle of going through urgent and intricate files when he was called by Frau Essing. "Come up immediately. Our reputation is at stake!" she said. When he arrived in her office he found a sports magazine lying open at the center of her desk. It featured an ad for an odor remover, illustrated with a small drawing of a sports shoe. "And with a magnifying glass, you could just about make out that the shoe in question had a few stripes on its side," as the young manager recalled. He struggled to retain his cool as Frau Essing ordered him to handle the matter instantly—deeming it outrageous that Adidas could be associated with smelly shoes.

Most of the managers accepted such interventions. After all, they had joined a family business. This was made clear to them from the very beginning, during their job interviews—routinely conducted in the Villa and interrupted by unruly children who chased each other in cowboy hats. But the family's habits became damaging when they prevented modernization in the company, which had grown well beyond the scope of a provincial family business.

Jürgen Lenz, the international marketing manager in Herzogen-aurach, was among the most frustrated. Having spent several years at McCann-Erickson, he knew the power of advertising. But when he joined Adidas in the late seventies, it had never run any brand advertising campaign. The only thing that the company had ever done in terms of advertising was to place dull ads in magazines, displaying specific products. As a so-called advertising agency, Adidas continued to use Hans Fick, the small studio in Nuremberg that had been working with Adidas since the fifties. Lenz watched with envy the witty and spectacular brand advertising campaigns run by Nike, with catchy slogans that gave the brand an inspiring identity.

Shortly after his recruitment he was approached by an established German research company that proposed to study the sporting goods market. They offered precisely the instrument Jürgen Lenz had requested since his arrival at Adidas to refine his marketing strategy. He assumed that Käthe Dassler would approve the small investment required for the study. But the reply came in the shape of a short handwritten note: "Herr Lenz. Sold out until 1982!" As Käthe saw it, there was no point in market research if the company was struggling to meet demand anyway.

On her own since the death of her husband in 1978, Käthe Dassler sometimes longed to get away from her complicated family business. She traveled abundantly and attempted to make the best of it, even allowing herself some conspicuous flirtations. She raised many eyebrows at Adidas when she "fell head over heels in love" with the manager of a Brazilian shoe factory. The target of her affections, a married man of Swiss origin, gently rebuffed her advances.

On other occasions, Käthe simply sought to escape the tense atmosphere in Herzogenaurach. When Hansrüdi Ruegger, head of the company's subsidiary in Switzerland, had new offices built

Käthe Dassler was appreciated for her sharpness and warmth. She is pictured here with Helmut Schön, German soccer coach.

there, she asked him to fix up a small apartment for her. She regularly left Herzogenaurach to spend a few days on her own in the plain flat, in a drab industrial neighborhood of Zurich.

But La Mutti, as the French managers called her, was most tormented by the troubles that affected her children. On the terrace of the Villa, she poured her heart out to some of the company's longtime managers, lamenting about the erring ways of her son and the destructive habits of her son-in-law. "One of them is dealing with gangsters and the other should be in rehab," she told one embarrassed visitor.

The jibe on detoxification was targeted at Alf Bente, the husband of Käthe's eldest daughter, who notoriously suffered from alcohol abuse. As some noted, this may well have been caused by excessive loyalty to Adidas. "When Alf traveled to Hungary and Russia, they started on vodka at ten o'clock in the morning," one witness recalled. Alf introduced the habit in Herzogenaurach, where guests were surprised to be offered liquor before lunch.

However, his problem was probably worsened by the collapse of his relationship with his wife, Inge. Apparently, the marriage began to deteriorate after the attack that half-paralyzed her. The disagreements between the two caused awkward problems at Adidas, where some employees had to deal with conflicting instructions.

When it became clear that Alf Bente could no longer function at Adidas, he went missing for several days. Hansrüdi Ruegger, who enjoyed a close relationship with Bente, got a nervous phone call from the owner of the Adidas store at Zurich airport. There was a steaming drunk man in the store who claimed to be the owner of Adidas and was demanding to be picked up. Ruegger rushed to the airport, tucked Bente away at a hotel, and alerted the family. Soon afterward German tabloids revealed that the Bente marriage had come to an end. Alf Bente had moved out of Herzogenaurach to settle down with a young woman in Nuremberg.

The other part of Käthe's tirade, about her son "dealing with gangsters," was targeted at André Guelfi. Her informants soon let her know that Horst and the Corsican were flying around the world together. She began to suspect that André Guelfi was playing a substantial role in all of the murky deals that her son was plotting behind her back. Käthe Dassler was not prepared, however, for all the stories that Guelfi had to tell.

. . . .

Marcel Schmid, the chairman of Sarragan, the Swiss holding company that regrouped the side interests of Horst Dassler, anxiously went through the papers. From his office in Freiburg, he controlled the operations of the sprawling business, covering Le Coq Sportif and stakes in a flurry of other companies. But as he peered at the contracts and invoices handed over by André Guelfi, Schmid became convinced that the figures were wrong.

As Schmid saw it, Guelfi had been cheating Horst Dassler all along. Whenever Guelfi signed a deal, the sum reported to Sarragan was much higher than the figure indicated on the contract. Guelfi routinely argued that the differential had been paid under the table; therefore it could not appear in the papers. But the incidents multiplied at such a rate that Schmid resolved to alert Horst Dassler.

Confronted with the facts, Dassler took furious action. André Guelfi disappeared from the scene just as quickly as he had entered it. Under his agreement with the Corsican, Horst exercised his offer to take full control of Le Coq Sportif, and he stripped Guelfi of his responsibilities at the company.

The dispute ended up in the courts when Marcel Schmid angrily described Guelfi as "an international crook." Guelfi professed to be outraged. He filed a libel suit in a Swiss court. On the day of the hearing, in line with Swiss guidelines at the time, he was led to a small room at the back of the court. He was joined there by Schmid, who had prepared a thick file. When the two emerged from the room, the libel case had been dropped. After careful consideration, Guelfi apparently felt that the tag of "international crook" wasn't all that ill fitting.

Still, there was no way the two parties could be reconciled. They thoroughly disagreed on the sum to be reimbursed to Guelfi for his investments in Sarragan. Guelfi estimated that, since he had struck his confidential deal with Horst Dassler, he had pumped about $30 million into his business—and he wanted that money back. Some of the most explosive rows centered on the exorbitant bill presented by André Guelfi for his travel expenses. The Corsican had meticulously added up all the hours he had flown on Dassler business. "One hour cost about 30,000 [French] francs and I had flown thousands of hours," Guelfi argued.

When Dassler refused to pay up, his managers were confronted with a series of unsettling events. To begin with, shortly after the rowdy breakup, Jean-Marie Weber—the man who oiled the wheels of business with international federations on behalf of Horst Dassler—reported that one of his bags had gone missing at the Geneva airport. He regularly carried at least one large holdall full of sensitive documents.

Shortly afterward, in April 1982, the Adidas building in Landersheim was raided by French customs police. Several managers were curtly instructed to leave their offices as uniformed men went through their files. Other officers loudly knocked on the door of Horst Dassler's home in Eckartswiller. A third unit was dispatched to the Rue Grimaldi in Monte Carlo to search the offices of SMPI. Patrick Nally was questioned at length by the head of the customs department in Marseilles. Yet another unit fetched Marcel Schmid at his office in Freiburg.

The enquiry centered on illegal transfers of currencies. The socialist government that came to power in France after the presidential elections of May 1981 had imposed rules requiring companies and citizens to report any sizeable currency transfers. This badly complicated the operations of all French-based international companies, but given the intricacy and the hidden aspects of Horst Dassler's business, it was simply unthinkable for him to comply.

The case was eventually settled without any disastrous repercussions for the Dasslers. As several executives pointed out, the French budget minister from March 1983 was Henri Emmanuelli, a socialist member of parliament. One of the plants operated by Adidas France was situated in his constituency, in the Landes region. But Dédé la Sardine still had a trick up his sleeve.

Armed with his documents, André Guelfi made a trip to Herzogenaurach and blithely spilled the beans. To her utter dismay, Käthe Dassler discovered that the charming Frenchman had backed her renegade son for several years, spending millions to build a side business of unexpected scope.

Käthe Dassler was enraged. She had long suspected that her son was cheating the entire family, but the coming-out of Sarragan was still a devastating blow. It revealed the scope of the investments that Horst had committed to his concealed business, and all the resources that he had diverted from Adidas for his own purposes. It exposed duplicity of staggering proportions.

The discovery caused such explosive rows that it sometimes became impossible to tackle the ensuing problems through rational discussion. "There were entire periods when Horst Dassler only agreed to talk to other family members in the presence of lawyers," said Günter Sachsenmaier, then export manager in Landersheim. "He was evidently depressed."

From then on, it became much harder for Horst to divert investments from Adidas to Le Coq Sportif and other brands. Tensions rose to boiling point before the 1982 soccer World Cup, as Horst Dassler sought endorsements for Le Coq Sportif from weighty teams that the Dasslers in Herzogenaurach would have liked to draw to the Adidas side.

In the course of the arguments between Horst Dassler and his sisters, the option of a breakup was repeatedly thrown on the table. Several Adidas managers were told of a bid issued by the Dassler sisters to buy out their brother's share and his operations in Landersheim. Horst rejected the offer, however, and Käthe pleaded with her children to reconcile.

As for the André Guelfi situation, after several months of recriminations, it was agreed that Guelfi would walk away with about 15 million Swiss francs ($7.4 million). The brands and shareholdings under Sarragan would fall under the control of the Dassler family. Unwittingly, André Guelfi had helped Horst Dassler enter negotiations about his return to Herzogenaurach.

The mistrust between Horst and his sisters was so deep that it proved hard for the heir apparent to impose his leadership. Once Käthe Dassler had decided to call her son back, he more regularly commuted between Landersheim and Herzogenaurach, but his sisters still refused to relinquish their influence. Fed up with the family's dithering, several managers demanded Horst's full return.

Käthe Dassler then resolved to remove any obstacles to her son's comeback. After a cerebral attack, her health faded fast, and she was desperate to ensure that her children wouldn't tear each other apart after her death. Her relationship with Horst warmed considerably in her last years, as he showed patience and compassion for his mother. She was particularly sensitive to the understanding her son displayed when it came to her private life.

Shortly after the rebuff she suffered in Brazil, Käthe Dassler, in her sixties by then, had entered an intimate relationship with an Austrian shoe producer, who was placed at the head of Adidas Austria. A longtime supplier of Adidas, he was much younger than the widow. The relationship caused consternation among Käthe Dassler's daughters, and many German managers who watched the pair together also felt distinctly uneasy. "It was obvious that this man was exploiting Frau Dassler's loneliness," as one of them put it.

The Dassler daughters stood united, for once, to undermine

the relationship. They were appalled by the Austrian's suspected opportunism and feared that he would manipulate their mother into a second marriage. Convinced that Käthe Dassler had to be dragged away from this relationship for her own sake, several family members asked Klaus-Werner Becker, Adidas's international controller, to broach the subject with her. But she was unimpressed by this genuine concern and furiously barred Becker from the Villa.

Horst Dassler was just as outraged by the Austrian's behavior. But instead of patronizing his mother, he openly encouraged her to enjoy the relationship. This considerate attitude certainly prompted Käthe Dassler to push ahead with planned reforms at Adidas—ignoring the predictable laments of her daughters. The Adidas bylaws were altered to turn the company into a foundation, Stiftung Adi Dassler & Co KG, with an informal family board at its head. But Käthe Dassler clearly told Horst that he would have a free rein in the management.

Horst Dassler long agonized over his decision. He assembled his managers in Landersheim and informed them of his prospective return to Herzogenaurach. "I'm at a crossroads," he told them, visibly distraught. He could sell out his Adidas shares and embark on other projects—in this case, he wanted to make sure that his trusted managers in Landersheim would follow—or he could return to Herzogenaurach. But in this case, he had to warn them, in all honesty, that the influence of Landersheim would have to be sharply curtailed. "Of course we would all have followed him with our eyes closed," said Jean Wendling, then head of Sarragan France. "But of course we all encouraged him to return."

In exchange for their withdrawal, the Dassler sisters obtained an amazingly generous present. Horst Dassler gave each of them a stake in Sporis, a holding company that owned just over half of ISL, his sports rights agency. When ISL was established, it was controlled equally by Horst Dassler and Dentsu. Two years later, Dassler persuaded the Japanese advertising conglomerate to give him a 51 percent majority in the venture, which he placed in Sporis. As part of the deal with his family, he gave each of his sisters a 16 percent share in Sporis. Although he retained a larger share of 36 percent, he could still be overruled if three of his sisters stood in his way. In other words, he relinquished sole control of ISL.

Walter Meier, Horst Dassler's lawyer, was startled by the gesture. In the course of the negotiations that lasted more than one year, the Dassler sisters apparently turned down "countless reasonable proposals." But the ISL shares were a seemingly disproportionate concession, given the fact that Horst Dassler had built ISL entirely by himself. "For me that was hard to understand," Meier was quoted as saying. "He gave his sisters a very valuable present."

The legal arrangements were finalized on December 19, 1984. A few days later, Käthe Dassler left Herzogenaurach to spend the end of the year with her Austrian friend. While the deterioration of her health called for medical care, she was left behind for several days in an apartment in Klagenfurt. When Käthe's daughters realized that she was suffering badly, they sent a private plane to pick her up in Austria. It was too late. On December 31, Die Cheffin, as the company's German managers called her, passed away in a hospital in Erlangen, at the age of sixty-five. The coroner's verdict was heart failure. Others called it a broken heart.

. . . .

Horst Dassler barely waited till the end of his mother's funeral to place his call to Austria. The man who had forged a dubious relationship with Käthe Dassler was summarily dismissed. Gerhard Prochaska, the former marketing manager who replaced the Austrian at the head of the Austrian operations, confirmed that his predecessor had blatantly abused the relationship for the benefit of his shoemaking factory.

With his mother becoming weaker in the last two years before her death, Horst had commuted between Herzogenaurach and Landersheim. But after she passed away, he immediately took the helm. His sisters cleared out their last belongings, and Horst took full control of the management floor, surrounding himself with a handful of trusted managers.

As he settled into his executive chair, Adidas appeared to be thriving. It had just chalked up an unprecedented turnover of nearly 4 billion German marks ($1.4 billion) and it continued to rule almighty over the sports business. But Horst was fully aware that this picture was deceptive. While he bickered with his sisters, Adidas had come under severe attack.

16

collapse

Bill Closs slammed his fist on the table. Sitting in Herzogenaurach for his meeting with German managers in the early
seventies, the Adidas distributor for the American West
Coast was very frustrated. Over the previous years, they had
repeatedly shrugged off his warnings about a small-time operation called Blue Ribbon Sports up in Oregon. Their Nike running
shoes were popping up on more and more Californian shelves.
Unless Adidas reacted swiftly, there was no telling what kind
of damage Nike employees could inflict on the Adidas business.
"You have to kill them right now," Closs hammered.

To illustrate the phenomenon, Bill Closs brought back several
pairs of Nike running shoes and handed them over for inspection
by the Germans. But to his dismay, the sneakers were cast aside
with disdain. "I told them they were selling like crazy, but they
didn't care," Bill Closs recalled. "They just didn't want to build
running shoes. They said their shoes were as good as they could
make, and that was it."

The same happened to international managers who attempted

to draw Adidas's attention to Nike. Günter Sachsenmaier, export manager in Landersheim, spotted the brand on his U.S. travels and figured that the Adidas technicians would be interested, but the response was invariably dismissive. The Waffle, the running shoe designed by former coach Bill Bowerman in his kitchen, provoked outright hilarity. "They inspected the sample as if it was a piece of dirt, pulled at it, and threw it over their shoulder," Sachsenmaier recalled. "They thought it was all a big joke, these lunatics who designed shoes with a waffle-iron."

Seen from Herzogenaurach, the Nike problem didn't seem all that urgent because the Adidas distributors themselves continued to clamor for more product. Yet the dearth of Adidas supplies strongly played into the hands of Nike. In the exploding American market, retailers became so weary of the haphazard Adidas deliveries that they could not afford to turn down an alternative brand.

To push its advantage, Nike introduced a shrewd mechanism known as Futures. The principle was that they would convince retailers to place firm orders and guarantee payments in advance. With these commitments, Nike could increase its orders from Asian manufacturers without gambling too much. In other words, they shifted some of the financial risk to the retailers. In return, the retailers who took part in Futures would obtain a sizeable rebate on their orders and could rest assured that they would actually obtain the goods. In a market driven by wild demand, this was an unbeatable argument.

With the jogging boom in the seventies, Nike's advances turned into a tidal wave. At the forefront of the movement, Bill Bowerman led many thousands of otherwise unathletic Americans on daily jogs—and this newly formed army of leisurely runners turned to Nike en masse. In Herzogenaurach, the German technicians generally dismissed the trend by contending that "jogging is not a sport." When they finally gave in to the pleas of American distributors, they still couldn't bring themselves to turn out what the customers wanted. While Germans tended to run on forest trails, the Americans jogged on roads and pavement; they needed plenty of cushioning. The Adidas distributors clamored for soft shoes, but their pleas were placated with anatomical drawings showing the alleged damage such shoes could inflict on ankles and knees.

When Adidas responded to the jogging boom at last, it was a question of too little, too late. In the late seventies the company came up with a training shoe called SL, which sold about a hundred thousand pairs during its first year in the United States. Looking at the explosion of the market, the distributors pushed their orders up to at least one million pairs for the second year, which would have forced Adidas to increase its capacity. "Adidas refused to make the required adjustments, because that would have entailed considerable investments," said Horst Widmann, Adolf Dassler's personal assistant at the time. "It turned out to be a bad mistake."

Horst Dassler was equally guilty of aloofness when it came to Nike. Absorbed by his sports marketing and broadcasting rights business, he didn't display much concern about the Nike issue. His French managers had come up with a soft running shoe called Country, but the effort was halfhearted.

Larry Hampton, international marketing manager at Adidas France, long struggled to convince Horst Dassler that he should learn more about Nike. He eventually agreed to meet Phil Knight and some other Nike executives at a trade show in Houston, in February 1978. Hampton was disappointed by the meeting, which he deemed utterly uneventful. But the Nike men couldn't believe what they had just heard: Horst Dassler had let it slip that a strong Adidas shoe sold about a hundred thousand pairs each year in the United States. Blue Ribbon Sports was selling roughly the same number of Waffle trainers *a month*.

Until the mid-eighties, Adidas continued to report double-digit sales hikes in the United States each year. The three stripes remained prominent on American fields, with the likes of Joe Montana, the quarterback of the San Francisco 49ers. Herschel Walker, the acclaimed Georgia running back, joined the Adidas gang in 1983, when he was hired by the New Jersey Generals, a franchise

RUIN A WAFFLE IRON.
START A GLOBAL SPORTS REVOLUTION.

JUST DO IT

At Adidas, they couldn't stop laughing when they heard that Nike designed shoes with a waffle iron. The two men behind the operation were Bill Bowerman *(pictured here)*, the inventive coach of the U.S. track and field team, and Phil Knight.

of the short-lived U.S. Football League, and his agent boasted that he had hooked the largest-ever endorsement deal in American sports at the time, worth between $1 and $2 million for ten years.

Adidas even made some inroads in the Oregon running scene by teaming up with Bill Dellinger, former assistant of Bill Bowerman, who had succeeded him as track coach at the University of Oregon in 1973. The two had since fallen out; therefore, Dellinger didn't berate his runners when they turned up wearing three stripes. Some of the Nike people felt violated when they discovered, in the early eighties, that Dellinger had allowed Adidas to place its name on the scoreboard of Hayward Field, which had seen the American brand's beginnings in Eugene, Oregon.

But the Dasslers failed to grasp that, in this ballooning market, Nike was growing much faster still, grabbing market share at a staggering pace. Blinkered by their competition with Puma, the Adidas technicians were not prepared to regard any other company as a serious contender.

. . . .

For the marketing men at Nike, the Los Angeles Olympics in 1984 were the perfect stage to show what they were all about. Eight years earlier, in Montreal, the brand was barely on the international market. Four years earlier, as an American company, Nike was unwanted in Moscow. But for Los Angeles, Nike was all set.

The company's executives had marked the city as their territory. Among their most spectacular displays was a mural that stretched over more than twenty-six feet long, covering two buildings at the heart of Los Angeles. It was a life-size picture of Carl Lewis, the American runner and long jumper, flying over a sandpit. Drivers who cruised along the Marina del Rey Freeway could not fail to spot it.

As usual, Adidas had meticulously prepared for the Games. Horst Dassler had personally taken part in the diplomatic kowtowing that preceded the event. As the Soviet Union had decided to boycott Los Angeles, Horst flew to Havana to meet with Fidel Castro, but could not persuade the Cubans to send their team. On the other hand, Horst was widely credited for the participation of Romania, the only East European country to ignore the Soviet-ordered boycott. The presence of the three stripes was somewhat diminished by the absence of all the other East European teams, but before the competition started it was almost guaranteed that Adidas would still claim the highest number of medals.

Horst Dassler's marketing men had extensively advised Peter Ueberroth, head of the Los Angeles Olympics organizing committee. Unfazed by the financial debacle at the preceding Olympics in Montreal, Ueberroth had decided to run the Games like a commercial enterprise, using mostly private funds. He benefited from the expertise of Horst Dassler, after he gave Adidas a license to make products with the mascot of the Olympics, an American eagle.

Overall, Adidas had set aside a budget of $15 million for the Games. The company had opened an account with a vault at a bank in Los Angeles, where Joe Kirchner, an Adidas textile manager, and other trusted employees deposited several millions of dollars in cash. Old habits die hard, and the Olympic athletes, supposedly amateur as always, still preferred their payments not to appear on their bank statements.

Bill Closs, distributor for the West Coast, spent several months making other arrangements for Adidas. Premises were rented near the university, for athletes and reporters, while Horst Dassler and his closest lieutenants stayed at the Hilton hotel, to schmooze with scores of Olympic officials. Adidas, Horst Dassler, and the Olympics just belonged together.

The Nike men had other plans. They openly despised the elderly European aristocrats who ruled over world sports. They portrayed their athletes and themselves as mavericks, intent on upsetting the sports establishment. While the Adidas people shared cocktails with the notoriously crooked honchos of the athletics world, Phil Knight and his crew raided the beach for an impromptu beer party.

By then, Nike had changed its marketing tack. It had conquered the American market from the track and had long supported hundreds of runners. But in the early eighties, Nike felt that the benefits of such small endorsements were diffuse. They decided to spend more money on advertising and on a restricted number of athletes and players with whom they could build the Nike brand.

For the Olympics, the Nike men made their presence felt in the streets of L.A. through dramatic advertising featuring some of the most inspiring U.S. athletes. While Carl Lewis jumped through the Californian sky, John McEnroe towered over the city in a leather jacket. During the Games the same cast appeared in a striking sixty-second commercial. To the soundtrack of Randy Newman's "I Love L.A.," the ad contained clips of other American star athletes such as Alberto Salazar, the marathon runner, and Mary Decker, who competed in middle-distance running. Such commercials were completely unprecedented in the sports business. Adidas had yet to run ads that were not entirely dedicated to their products.

When the medals were counted at the end of the Olympics, the first ever to yield a profit for the organizers, Adidas claimed a predictable victory. Adidas athletes had reaped 259 medals, against 53 for Nike. Salazar failed to get a medal. Mary Decker fell in the 3,000-meter finals, the only distance in which she competed in Los Angeles, after a collision with Zola Budd, a South African athlete who ran barefoot. Nike had put on a "costly and ephemeral show," Horst Dassler sniggered.

Yet the marketing people at Adidas knew that Nike was on to something. No matter how many more athletes Adidas outfitted, Nike had hijacked the Games in Los Angeles. Although Converse paid $5 million to be the official partner of the organizing committee, consumers were under the impression that Nike had sponsored the Olympics. All but three of the men's gold medals in track and field had been won by Nike athletes. And Nike's beach party was the talk of the town.

For those who witnessed it all that summer in California, it suddenly became clear that Adidas was under serious attack. As one person recalled, "Los Angeles was a massive wake-up call."

. . . .

The Adidas trump card in the United States was an energetic Italian by the name of Angelo Anastasio. He had emigrated with his parents in the sixties and settled in New York. Once he finished college, he played soccer with the New York Cosmos, the same team as Pelé and Franz Beckenbauer. Toward the end of the seventies, he moved to Los Angeles and got a job with Adidas, in charge of entertainment promotion.

The term *celebrity endorsement* had yet to be coined, but Anastasio knew exactly what he was doing: he became chummy with emerging American celebrities and persuaded them to wear the three stripes. If Adidas was getting thrashed on the courts and in the streets, at least it could still get exposure by being seen on the hips and feet of entertainment celebrities.

Anastasio was perfectly cut out for the job. A voluble talker, he was known in Los Angeles for his Ferrari, which had "Adidas I" on its license plate. He happily hung around at pop concerts to meet upcoming stars, shared drinks with Sylvester Stallone, and rode his Harley-Davidson with Mickey Rourke.

His breakthrough came with Rocky Balboa. The mindless boxer played by Stallone seemed to permanently wear the three stripes. Adidas sold about 750,000 units of the black fleece warm-up suit worn by Stallone in *Rocky IV*, with the Italian flag's color on the shoulders. The practice would become known as product placement, keeping squadrons of public relations people busy in Los Angeles. But the concept was still so fresh at the time that Stallone never asked for a cent to appear in Adidas. Anastasio just made sure that his muscular friend would never have to go barefoot.

The Italian had a budget of only up to $8,000 in merchandise to hand out each month, but he promptly became known in Los Angeles as "Mr. Adidas." Under this guise he bumped into Ziggy Marley, the son of the Jamaican reggae singer. From then on, Bob Marley regularly appeared onstage in three-striped clothing that conspicuously clashed with the rest of his attire. In exchange, Adidas agreed to sponsor Marley's soccer team in Jamaica.

But the most talked about celebrity tie-in came in 1985, when Anastasio was attending a concert in New York's Madison Square Garden. On his way out, he spotted three young black men breakdancing on the street, watched by scores of onlookers. He was perplexed to see that they were wearing Adidas pants known as "rainsuits," made of shiny material. Once they had finished dancing and Anastasio had introduced himself, they explained that the rainsuits helped because they were slippery—which happened to be practical since the young men were dancing on cardboard.

The Italian closely followed the three men over the next years and continuously sent them Adidas gear. It paid off when they became known as Run DMC. The rappers eagerly adopted the Superstars, the Adidas basketball shoes, as an original alternative to other sneakers. They liked the shell-toe design and preferably wore their Superstars without laces. When the band agreed to turn up at the 1986 Supershow, the huge sports trade fair in Atlanta, they were stormed by thousands of fans.

"I gave them $1 million but they ended up generating sales of more than $100 million over the next four years," said Anastasio.

"At a time when Nike was growing like crazy, the endorsement gave Adidas exposure and kept the brand alive in the eye of the public." On the back of the endorsement, Anastasio estimated that Adidas sold an extra half million pairs of Superstars. Another fast-selling product was a pair of black pants with three stripes worn by the rappers.

At the time, street fashion was becoming increasingly influenced by music and the media that carried it. It was fabulous advertising for Adidas to have several pairs of Superstars fill MTV screens for close to twenty seconds, as part of a clip shot by Run DMC in 1986 when they covered "Walk This Way," the hit previously written for Aerosmith.

The endorsement was the first of its kind between a band and a sports company. It went so far that Run DMC and Anastasio jointly composed a song called "My Adidas," for their album *Raising Hell*. "Me and my Adidas do the illest things," the song went.

> We like to stomp out pimps with diamond rings.
> We slay all suckers who perpetrate
> And lay down law from state to state.
> We travel on gravel, dirt road or street.
> I wear my Adidas when I rock the beat,
> Onstage front page every show I go,
> It's Adidas on my feet high top or low.

The song became such a hit that, when Run DMC began to sing it onstage, thousands of enthusiastic spectators waved three-striped shoes and shirts.

. . . .

Still, the exposure could not make up for the company's weaknesses when it came to products and marketing. Just as Adidas was waking up to Nike's strength, the Oregon men were mulling over plans to take their brand farther. They had decided to shrink payments to athletes, and they went ahead with yet more radical cutbacks in basketball: they wanted to make a splash with a talented and inspiring player who could overhaul the entire American business.

By the early eighties, Adidas had almost been swept off American basketball courts. Just as it had crushed Converse with the Superstar in the late sixties, it had been hammered by Nike in the late seventies. While Adidas rested on its Superstar laurels, Nike had come up with an invention known as Air, consisting of air cushions that were visibly inserted into the soles of their shoes. Adidas managers had bluntly turned down the Air concept when it was presented to them, but the Nike men could easily picture the marketing line.

By the mid-eighties, nearly half of the players in the NBA had switched to Nike, while most of the others had returned to upgraded Converse shoes. All of these players were paid up to $100,000 per year to wear The Swoosh, which added up to a considerable sum for the company. The Nike marketing men now wanted out of these small basketball contracts to build one all-encompassing endorsement deal.

The project was led by Rob Strasser, one of the most rambunctious characters in Phil Knight's crew of go-getting executives. As a lawyer, Strasser had fought alongside Nike to win a thorny court case after Knight broke up with Onitsuka, in 1973, and he decided to stay. In other companies, Strasser may have been described as a marketing manager, but at Nike he was known as "Rolling Thunder."

Shortly before the Los Angeles Olympics, Strasser heard about Michael Jordan, a player from North Carolina. Sonny Vaccaro, Nike's basketball scout, was enraptured by the boy: the way he described it, Jordan made such spectacular jumps that it looked as if he could fly.

The player was represented by Proserv, the agency of Donald Dell and his assistant, David Falk. They had planned with Dean Smith, the North Carolina basketball coach, that Dell would never show up on the campus or attempt to recruit players. But on the other hand, Smith would alert Dell to particularly promising youngsters.

To begin with, Jordan didn't seem anything out of the ordinary. "As a junior in high school he couldn't even make it into the varsity team," Dell recalled. "And when he was drafted as a junior he was number three!" Therefore, it didn't seem too far off the mark when Adidas offered only $100,000 for Jordan, the same deal they had with Kareem Abdul-Jabbar at the time.

Michael Jordan himself was set on the three stripes, describing himself as an "Adidas nut." He always wore Adidas while training, and when a game was on he reluctantly laced up his Converse, which was part of the team uniform at North Carolina. When Nike approached him, Michael Jordan bluntly made it clear that he would favor the three stripes over any other brand. "I don't want to go anywhere else," he defiantly told Nike executives, after his mother had dragged him out to Oregon. But when he heard what they were offering, he had to think again.

The Nike men saw something in Michael Jordan that their competitors didn't. On the back of Vaccaro's recommendation they felt that the player, in spite of his unimpressive record until then, had an out-of-the-ordinary aura and style. Rob Strasser and Peter Moore, the designer who had forged Nike's brand identity, insistently courted Jordan and his agents. On one particular Saturday morning they were sitting in Proserv's offices with Donald Dell and David Falk, arguing back and forth about potential shoes, when Peter Moore interjected, seemingly out of the blue: "What about Air Jordan?"

The others were awed by the brilliant simplicity of the concept, and they quickly brushed aside concerns that the name sounded like an airline. It didn't take long to convince the player himself: with Nike, Jordan stood to earn about $2.5 million, with royalties on sales of shoes and garments that bore his name.

With Michael Jordan, the Adidas managers had missed the opportunity of a lifetime. They attempted to retaliate with the next big player: Patrick Ewing, who had dazzled the scouts and his coach at Georgetown, John Thompson. Unlike Jordan, Ewing became the first overall draft pick for 1985, to play with the New York Knicks. He was such a coveted player that his agent, Donald Dell again, could drive a hard bargain: his contract with the Knicks would earn Ewing more than $3 million per year, the highest salary in American team sports at the time.

Dell was equally hardheaded when it came to negotiations with Adidas. The marketing manager at Adidas USA, Dave Morgan, had managed to introduce some performance clauses, but they suddenly disappeared from the contract after Dell resorted to his usual trick of getting his friend Horst Dassler on the line. As part of the deal, which included a signature shoe, Ewing reportedly stood to earn $700,000 per year from Adidas.

However, the two basketball deals neatly encapsulated the contrast between Nike and Adidas. Patrick Ewing went on to shine at the Knicks, to be recognized as one of the all-time greats in the NBA. He was a fiercely loyal person, widely lauded for his work ethic. Yet he didn't have the spark that the Nike men had immediately recognized in Jordan, and that made all the difference. While Ewing helped to sell Adidas shoes in New York, and not much beyond, Jordan propelled Nike to new heights.

The Air Jordan was initially banned by the NBA because it was red and black, which departed too much from the mostly white shoes worn by the other players, yet in the first year, it generated sales of more than $100 million for Nike. In the long run, Air Jordan accelerated the spread of basketball shoes in the United States as streetwear. Basketball would come to represent about 60 percent of sales in the American market—and it was Nike territory.

. . . .

As the eighties progressed, the Nike problem was aggravated by Reebok. The brand was derived from Joe Foster, a British company that had been selling track and field shoes since the beginning of the century. As their business dwindled in the fifties, some of Joe Foster's heirs set up another company, which came to be known as Reebok, and teamed up with distributors to spread it beyond England. In 1979, Paul Fireman, a small-time entrepreneur in Boston, acquired the rights for the United States.

Fireman's business made such a slow start that he nearly went bankrupt. To keep the business afloat he sold 55 percent of the venture to Stephen Rubin, a British investor. But Fireman's fortunes picked up dramatically when he introduced a shoe called the Freestyle, designed for aerobics, a form of exercise that was spreading like wildfire in the United States.

The Freestyle actually originated from a mistake by Reebok's manufacturing partners in Asia, who had erroneously used the sort of soft leather intended for gloves. When they sent the samples to Reebok they apologized for the wrinkles, promising to iron them out before line production. Back in Boston, however, the Reebok managers were thrilled. With the ultrasoft shoe, they raided the women's market. The Freestyle drove an eye-popping sales rise for Reebok: from global sales of about $300,000 in 1980, the brand exploded to $12.8 million in 1983.

As could be expected, the Adidas managers shrugged it off. German technicians threw Reebok's Freestyle over their shoulders just as they had done with Nike's Waffle running shoe a few years earlier. But Nike made precisely the same mistake. The Nike men derided aerobics as "a bunch of fat ladies dancing to music" and contended that the Freestyle was not a sports shoe. By 1987, Reebok sales had reached $1.4 billion.

Nike and Reebok had together created the most spectacular upset ever witnessed in the industry. Before they came along, Adidas owned more than half of the American sports shoe market. But by the mid-eighties, the three stripes were reeling from a head-spinning fall. They had not just lost their leadership; they had been relegated to fourth position, behind Nike, Reebok, and Converse. The time had come for drastic action.

. . . .

In the early eighties, the case was studied extensively by Rich Madden. An independent entrepreneur and Harvard graduate, Madden had been hired by Käthe Dassler to tighten Germany's grip on the company's American operations. Madden was recruited as chief executive of Adidas USA, a structure based in Mountainside, New Jersey, that covered joint textile and marketing activities.

The textile business was headed by Don Corn, a former neighbor of Ralph Libonati, Adidas distributor for the East Coast. When he established the Adidas textile unit in 1974, Corn was rebuked by manufacturers who had never heard of Adidas and questioned its creditworthiness. In less than ten years, the business reached sales of about $100 million.

As for the marketing activities, these were entrusted to Bart Stolp, an executive of Dutch origin. At a time when such things barely existed, Stolp got some celebrity events off the ground, getting the likes of Bill Cosby and the cast of the *Love Boat* to take part in an Adidas tennis tournament. But he was permanently frustrated by the lack of commitment by the company to impose America-wide marketing.

This was precisely one of the problems that Rich Madden sought to redress. As he saw it, the American distributors had become complacent. They had amassed considerable fortunes on the back of Adidas and had lost the impetus to fight back against rivals. Madden was taken aback that the distributors refused to raise their marketing expenses or set up a scheme to harmonize and optimize orders, at a time when their warehouses were clogged with millions of dollars' worth of obsolete inventories.

This harsh diagnosis was paired with a radical proposal: Rich Madden suggested buying out the distributors and floating Adidas USA. Instead of disbursing cash, Adidas could pay out the distributors in shares of the floated company. Called Plan X, the proposal was studied in depth by Lehman Brothers and Merrill Lynch, two leading investment banks. They envisaged one of the largest public offerings in the country at the time, to raise at least $200 million. "Adidas would not have to deplete its cash. It would get about $110 million and I would have kept $90 million for comprehensive marketing and retail plans," Madden explained. "And the distributors would have stayed in there with large minority shares."

Yet Plan X was swept under the carpet. The distributors deemed it "preposterous" to be offered shares in a company that barely existed. The plan was far too bold for Hans-Jürgen Martens, the company's haughty and conservative chief financial officer. But perhaps most decisively, Horst Dassler was reluctant to share control of the American market. Rich Madden was summarily dismissed.

Horst Dassler then sent out an envoy, Joe Kirchner, to have his own man in the Mountainside office and to get a grip on the American situation. To get him in, Horst Dassler demanded the resignation of Don Corn, the American textile manager, arguing that Corn had reached retirement age. Crushed by this crude ousting, Corn sued, obtaining a settlement that considerably added to Adidas's bill. Although Horst Dassler had angrily rejected Plan X, he remained convinced that Adidas would have to acquire control of the American market.

. . . .

The American distributors stared at one another in disbelief. Assembled for the Supershow in Atlanta, they had just heard, seemingly out of the blue, that Adidas intended to buy them out. Gary Dietrich, distributor for the Midwest, was stunned. "We had devoted our lives to this thing, and all of a sudden it was taken from us," he lamented. Bill Closs, who had helped Horst Dassler over rough patches, was angry and hurt. As for Ralph Libonati, distributor for the East Coast, he was so furious that he vowed to sue.

Back in Herzogenaurach, the plans had been germinating for several months. Sure, Adidas owed the American distributors a large part of its international reputation. They had been consistently faithful, and their orders had generated an increasing and relatively easy stream of revenue for Adidas. But Horst Dassler, then in his late forties, had slowly become convinced that, given the seriousness of Nike's assault, the setup was no longer adequate. To bite back, he would have to take the American market in his own hands.

One of his arguments was that the split of the market hampered hard-hitting marketing investments. From the beginning, the distributors had been asked to contribute about 4 percent of their turnover to a marketing fund, for promotion and nationwide advertising. Each of them further invested in regional marketing. Yet Horst Dassler felt that the efforts remained scattered. The situation called for a much more vigorous and tightly steered counterattack.

Another problem was that the U.S. trade rules prevented the distributors from offering the same prices for Adidas products in their respective territories. That would have been construed as price fixing. The discrepancies between the distributors were small, but they still encouraged retailers to shop around.

To make matters worse, the Adidas business began to stagnate. Even the company's endorsement by Joe Montana, the quarterback of the San Francisco 49ers, had turned sour. Montana had received $25,000 per year to wear Adidas and make promotional appearances for the brand. But he still ended up filing suit against Adidas in San Francisco Superior Court because they brought out a shoe called Montana after the team's Super Bowl win in 1982, although his contract didn't include such a signature shoe. Adidas cheekily retorted that the shoe had not been named after the player but after the state of Montana.

Frustrations continued to rise on all sides, and Horst became convinced that he would have to quickly seize control of the brand's sales and marketing in the United States. The apron strings were cut at the Supershow in Atlanta.

After the shock of their meeting with Horst, the distributors went into conclave. Doc Hughes, the Texan trader who covered the South, had already thrown in the towel, and his territory had been carved up between Bill Closs and Gary Dietrich, distributors for the West Coast and the Midwest. The two believed that the writing was on the wall, and both accepted an invitation to discuss the sell-out in Herzogenaurach. But Ralph Libonati was still fuming and firmly intent on suing.

Horst Dassler retained Dick Pound, a Canadian lawyer, to advise him on the matter. The fact that Pound was on the IOC's executive board, in charge of television rights, didn't seem to strike anyone as a conflict of interest. A Canadian swimming champion, Pound was one of Juan Antonio Samaranch's most devoted aides when it came to raising revenues for the IOC. He had worked closely with ISL, Horst Dassler's sports marketing and broadcasting rights agency, in Switzerland, when it embarked on its Herculean project to buy out the marketing rights of all national Olympic committees and hand them over to the IOC.

The talks went awry, as Dietrich and Closs both felt that the opening offer from the Germans was insulting. That evening, Dietrich called Closs to his room at the Sports Hotel. He vividly recalled that, in the same hotel, one of his sales people had tuned in his radio to catch the U.S. Armed Forces station and heard conversations at the bar. If the bar was bugged, they could be certain that someone was listening to their discussion, too. Conscientiously articulating each word for the benefit of the eavesdropper, Dietrich told Closs that they should return to the United States and file a lawsuit against Adidas. "The next day [Adidas's] attitude changed completely," Dietrich recalled. "Horst called us into his office and handed us a little paper with seven points on it. That was our deal."

The negotiations lasted for several months, as Adidas and the distributors debated the value of their inventories. Adidas agreed to take them over entirely. Ralph Libonati was persuaded not to sue, but all of his stock was purchased by Adidas at full value. After nearly two years of haggling, Adidas wound up with tons of obsolete goods, four warehouses, and a sales force of mixed quality. For Ralph Libonati alone, Adidas forked out an estimated $35 million for stock that should have been written off. The final bill was astronomical for Adidas, estimated at over $120 million. To make matters worse, the worth of the dollar had reached an all-time high against the German mark. As judicious as the American buyout might have been, its cost precipitated a vertiginous collapse.

the emperor strikes back

H orst Dassler nodded approvingly. The Frankfurt office of Young and Rubicam, the international advertising agency, had come up with an inspiring concept: "The Adidas Factor. It's either for you or against you," ran the tagline. The executives at Y&R, one of the last two agencies in the running for the Adidas account, nervously waited for Horst to deliver his verdict. Adidas was any creative director's dream, and they assumed that Adidas would have an enormous budget.

Shortly after Horst's return to Herzogenaurach, at the beginning of 1985, the fifth floor of the Adidas management building had been entirely reconstructed. He ruled over it from an imposing desk, at the center of the floor. In the adjacent offices he installed some of his trusted managers from Landersheim and a batch of impressive recruits.

By then in his late forties, Horst Dassler envisaged a complete overhaul of Adidas. The company would buy back the operations that had been picked up as it went along, all to be integrated under one roof. It would shed some of the ludicrous habits that had been holding it back over the previous years. Dispersion was to make way for a finely honed, international organization.

Among other things, Horst had become convinced that Adidas needed to invest in international advertising—like all the high-profile brands he dealt with at ISL, his sports rights agency. Until the mid-eighties, Adidas advertising was still mostly provided by Fick, the small design office in Nuremberg that Adi Dassler had retained in the fifties. Fick provided chiefly product advertising, and each of the subsidiaries could decide what they wanted to run. Horst figured that times had changed. He wanted to switch to a harmonized international message.

Young and Rubicam obtained the budget from Adidas, but they were in for some nasty surprises. To begin with, they found out that Adidas invested very little in advertising, as their marketing budget was still spent mostly on deals with athletes and federations. Ingo Kraus, head of Y&R in Germany, could not believe the numbers: the budget he was given for Adidas in the whole world was smaller than Ford's in Germany alone.

Worse still, the agency discovered that Adidas, as a company, was completely out of sync with its international reputation as a brand. Still steeped in their provincial ways and preoccupied by their internal problems, the Dasslers had completely neglected to adjust their company to the increasingly international market-place. The managers at Y&R had their own line to summarize the problem: "Great brand, dumb company."

The brand had traveled without regard for national borders, but the company's international business was a maze of independent distribution and licensing deals. The small-time traders who had once knocked on the Dasslers' door in Herzogenaurach had since turned into local industry chieftains, who prevented Adidas from imposing a harmonized marketing effort. They were not about to let slick advertisers in Frankfurt decide what consumers had to be told in Argentina or Taiwan.

When Young and Rubicam finally came up with the concept for Adidas's first global television commercial, as requested by Horst, it faced yet more opposition. Unlike the hard-hitting Nike commercials, the Y&R production had an arty touch, based on a cloud motif. The principle was that the clouds didn't require translation. They could be used everywhere around the world. But the national managers still demanded so many adjustments that Y&R ended up producing four versions of the commercial—English, French, German, and international, with an English-language text. "It basically defeated the purpose that Horst Dassler wanted, of having a global campaign," said Tom Harrington, then account manager at Y&R.

The commercial was eventually introduced in August 1986 at ISPO, the international sports trade fair, in Munich. The company's assembled distributors and national managers listened expectantly as Horst Dassler outlined the concept. "We now have a global advertising campaign by a global advertising agency," he said. "And this is not negotiable."

The negotiations started as soon as the presentation ended. One of the loudest protests came from France. Bernard Odinet, general manager in Landersheim, flatly refused to run the commercial, saying it reminded him of a Nazi production by Leni Riefenstahl. He was backed by many other national managers, who didn't care for an image campaign: they wanted products to be featured in the commercials, products that would do well in their particular country. "It was the most hostile environment I've ever had for any sort of presentation," said Ingo Kraus, head of Y&R in Germany. As the advertisers lamented, their global concept turned into a product catalog.

This patchy advertising was compounded by a series of costly marketing failures. The most damaging flop was due to Horst Dassler's drive to move away from performance sports. As he remarked, Nike had begun to expand at a staggering pace when running shoes became part of leisure wear in the United States. Nike had redefined the sports business in the United States; Adidas could do the same elsewhere. "I want to be a leisure brand," Horst told startled executives.

To get his point across, he walked around with a drawing of a pyramid. The peak represented the sports market, while the wide bottom part symbolized the mass leisure market. It didn't take an elaborate marketing study to conclude that Adidas would be well advised to target the much larger leisure market.

It worked well on the clothing side, enabling Adidas to sell millions of colorful T-shirts and sweaters. But the company was far less inspired for footwear, allowing the Adidas logo to be affixed to the most improbable concepts. "Our catalogues and flyers looked wonderful, but some of the shoes could only have been launched out of desperation," sighed Peter Rduch, former head of product development. Among the most embarrassing products were shoes with flavored laces.

The misguided moves caused huge confusion. They alienated sports retailers, who watched Adidas diluting its appeal as a sports brand. It baffled fashion retailers, who wondered what Adidas products were doing on their shelves. And it caused frictions in the company, where lifelong sports designers suddenly had to mingle with people from the fashion industry.

. . . .

The brand's American managers were among the most vocal opponents of the global marketing strategy devised by Horst. Although it might have seemed obvious, they went to great lengths to demonstrate that advertising targeted at Germans just didn't work in the United States. They ended up getting their own commercials, made by the American arm of Young and Rubicam.

With a mixture of opportunism and local investments, the brand still managed to grab some American headlines. Many of them were owed to Jim McMahon, who liked to describe himself as the "punky quarterback" of the Chicago Bears. He "loved bars and night life, leaving residue that sometimes led to the field the next day," as one sports writer put it. But what generated the most abundant publicity for Adidas was McMahon's headbands.

In the run-up to Super Bowl XX, in 1985, the Adidas managers took a bet by encouraging McMahon to wear a headband featuring the brand, although this was strictly forbidden. Pete Rozelle, NFL commissioner, predictably fined McMahon $5,000 for wearing such a headband at a play-off game against the New York Giants. Yet the publicity was worth many times the fine, especially when McMahon retorted by appearing at the next game, against the Rams, with a headband that read "Rozelle."

It was one of the rare occasions when the brand's American managers received a message of personal congratulations from Horst Dassler. The company was otherwise deeply weakened by the sudden and somewhat acrimonious buyout of the distributors. Many of the salespeople had departed, and Adidas USA was left to deal with nightmarish logistical headaches.

The buyout was intended to make sure that Adidas could compete more forcefully against Nike and Reebok, but instead the company seemed weaker and more bogged down than ever. The American business was generating abysmal losses, without any prospects of short-term improvement. To make matters worse, Adidas was coming under increasing attack in Europe, where Nike was beginning to make its presence felt. Still unimproved by Horst Dassler's reforms, the company's financial situation was increasingly precarious.

. . . .

When Horst Dassler boarded the little airplane, his companions noticed that he looked strained. Settling in for the short flight from Herzogenaurach to Landersheim, he unfolded his newspaper. His fellow travelers looked at one another in dismay as they distinctly heard, behind the paper, their unshakeable chief sobbing.

"It was such a shocking sight that I felt compelled to ask him what was up," recalled Blago Vidinic. "Horst then explained that he had just taken one of the toughest decisions in his business life. He would have to close down a plant in the Alsace, which he had acquired himself as a young man. He knew full well that several families would lose more than one job, and it was such a desolate village that they would never find another two jobs. This genuinely distressed him."

The French plant closure would be followed by many others. As much as it pained him, Horst Dassler acknowledged that Adidas could not uphold large-scale production in Europe. Cheaper Far Eastern supplies enabled Nike to work with gross margins of more than 40 percent, while Adidas was stuck closer to 25 percent. It was this differential that enabled Nike to pump money into advertising. There was no way that Adidas could counterattack unless it aligned its production costs.

Over the previous years, Adidas had already shifted much of its footwear production to Eastern Europe and the Far East. By the mid-eighties, the Taiwanese Riu brothers were turning out about half of the Adidas footwear production, reaching roughly forty million pairs annually, with several factories in Taïwan and China. To speed up the shift, Horst Dassler hired Uwe Breithaupt, a footwear production specialist.

However, Adidas still wasn't prepared to relinquish control of its production. While Nike dealt with entirely independent Far Eastern manufacturers, Adidas's production took place mostly in plants that were at least partly owned by the company. Breithaupt led a group of German technicians, who were paid at expatriate rates, to run Adidas plants in Korea, then Malaysia, Thailand, and China. Under these conditions Adidas could not take full advantage of the cheaper production, and it caused an infuriating mess. As Adidas failed to deliver, the company was confronted with irate customers and growing losses.

Under Horst Dassler's isolated rule, only a couple of managers were fully aware of the company's troubles. While Horst orchestrated far-reaching cutbacks and other badly needed reforms, he knew it would take several years for the measures to pay off.

The American buyout had punched a gaping hole in the company's balance sheet, and the ensuing problems generated yet more red ink. Not to mention all the side interests that Horst Dassler had accumulated under Sarragan: his rights to Le Coq Sportif, Pony, and Arena were all bought by Adidas for a symbolic sum, but they burdened the company with further losses and operating headaches.

By the end of 1986, Horst's second year at the helm, the Dassler sisters began to question their brother's ability to steer the family company out of its dire straits. Their suspicions were stirred up most persistently by Christoph Malms, husband of Sigrid Dassler, the youngest of the sisters. Since he had joined McKinsey, Malms made his voice heard with increasing firmness at family meetings.

Although Horst Dassler rarely talked about his family, he made it abundantly clear to his aides that he didn't have much time for Christoph Malms's insights. As he told several managers, he could barely stand his brother-in-law's cockiness, and he wasn't about to take advice from a fresh-faced consultant.

Unwilling to confront Horst directly, Malms persuaded the Dassler sisters to let an independent consultant study the company. They picked Michel Perraudin, a partner at McKinsey in Düsseldorf, who specialized in operations management. At the beginning of 1987, Perraudin agreed to a discreet meeting with Christoph Malms at the Hilton hotel in Zurich. "This felt like a conspiracy, because nobody was supposed to know," said Perraudin. He was asked to prepare a brief study of Adidas, to be presented to the board in May. Perraudin could not have guessed that, by then, there would no longer be any need to hide from Horst.

. . . .

Just before the opening of the 1986 soccer championships, held in Mexico, Horst Dassler slipped away. He told some of his closest managers that he was heading for an unscheduled meeting in New York. He didn't tell them that the appointment was with a medical adviser, who advocated surgery to remove cancerous cells behind his left eye.

One of the few people whom Horst Dassler called during his hospital stay in New York was Pat Doran, a former reporter who had joined the U.S. operations of Le Coq Sportif. Over the years, Doran had often been confronted with Horst Dassler's workaholic's habits and his paranoia, but she was still stunned to watch him run Adidas from a New York hospital. "While he was waiting for the magnet therapy that would reduce the tumor, he was

the emperor strikes back   **211**

making calls around the world to people who thought he was at one of his offices," Doran recalled. One of the reasons he cited for the secrecy of his stay was that he didn't want his cousin Armin to find out. "He really believed that Armin had spies following him everywhere," Doran observed.

When he returned to Herzogenaurach with a patch over his eye, Horst Dassler resumed his harrowing schedule. He sometimes left meetings early, apologizing that he felt tired or dizzy. One of his old-time friends was puzzled when he turned down a business dinner, choosing to spend the evening with his wife instead. Others noticed that his eye was weepy. But he brushed aside any concerned queries, and none of the Adidas board members or other high-profile executives realized the seriousness of Dassler's health problems.

With at least one close friend, Horst Dassler shared feelings of personal unhappiness: his relationship with his sisters remained strained, his marriage with Monika had all but dissolved, he said, and he was uncertain about his children's will or ability to build on his achievements. Several managers had been asked to act as mentors for Adi, Jr., taking Horst's son into their department for several weeks. Their observations weren't all too encouraging: Adi, then in his early twenties, was a fine lad, but he showed more interest in partying than in Adidas, often skipping work in the mornings or dozing off at his desk.

In spite of his innumerable relationships, the Adidas heir had very few friends to share his personal anguish. Ilie Nastase, the impetuous Romanian tennis player, winner of the 1972 U.S. Open, was among the handful of people who continued to call when there weren't any deals at stake. He had learned to play the game wearing entirely flat-soled Chinese canvas shoes, which caused him many slides and falls. Once he had become a notorious haggler in the early seventies, Nike offered him a $5,000 contract to wear shoes with "Nasty" embossed on the heel. But the friendship with Horst Dassler began when the player switched to Adidas in 1973, on the back of a four-year contract for about $50,000 to wear the full three-striped tennis line.

Many at Adidas felt that Nastase was ill suited to endorse the German brand. Prone to arguments with umpires and other tactics that bordered on foul play, he was likely to damage the brand's reputation. "My friend Horst just turned around and told them that was precisely why he picked me," recalled Nastase. "That shut them up." From then on, the two used every opportunity to meet up on their respective travels. Horst proudly exhibited a precious watch presented to him by Nastase: "To my friend Horst," read the message engraved on the back.

As his illness progressed, Horst became increasingly short-tempered, suddenly lambasting some of the people with whom he had worked most closely. Among them was Jean-Marie Weber, his bagman. For many years Dassler had relied entirely on Weber to keep track of his financial affairs in a maze of company holdings and undercover payments. But Dassler felt that all these constructions had turned his business into an inextricable mess, and he placed the blame squarely on Weber. Horst called Weber "incompetent" and told several executives that he intended to get rid of his right-hand man.

Another target of his scorn was Sepp Blatter, the FIFA general secretary. Since Horst had installed him in this position, Blatter had not always displayed as much gratitude as Dassler expected. The two continued to celebrate their near-simultaneous birthdays together in Landersheim, but their business relationship quickly deteriorated. Dassler went berserk when he heard that Blatter was spotted playing tennis in Puma gear. More seriously, Dassler was enraged by Blatter's perceived dithering at FIFA. While others criticized Blatter for blatant collusion with Dassler and ISL, the Adidas chief felt that the Swiss wasn't being helpful enough.

By early 1987, it had become clear that the cure had failed and that Dassler's disease had spread. He rapidly lost weight and began to look somewhat emaciated. Managers who had not seen him for a long time were shocked by his sagging cheeks and bilious complexion. However, Horst Dassler continued to run Adidas with unwavering firmness, as if he had many years ahead of him.

At the end of March 1987, in a six-page memo, he issued instructions to the company's board members: "Unfortunately my illness will drag on a little longer than originally expected," he wrote. "To make sure that these intestine and stomach problems don't become chronic, I will have to rest and to stay on a diet for another two months." But in his tone there was a sense of urgency, coupled with a touch of irritation.

As Horst lay dying, he may have acknowledged that he had failed to clean up the company. He had partly managed to mend its fractured family structure, bringing all the brands under the same roof and instilling a truly international approach. Adidas just about remained the market leader in 1987, with international sales that would reach almost precisely 4 billion German marks ($2.2 billion), compared with roughly 900 million German marks ($500.5 million) for Puma. But this amounted to a decline for both of them, as Nike and Reebok were making their way to Europe. The measures advocated by Horst Dassler to reduce costs had certainly not sufficed to make Adidas as sharp and lean as its American foes.

On the other hand, Horst Dassler could rest assured that ISL had turned the corner. In spite of his tussles with Sepp Blatter, the sports rights agency continued to ride high in the soccer business, and it had pulled off an amazing coup with the Olympics. Since they had bought out the marketing rights of nearly all national Olympic committees in the early eighties, ISL executives had been roaming the world to persuade international companies to pump dollars into their marketing plan, The Olympic Programme, for the 1988 Olympics in Seoul, South Korea.

To begin with, and to their dismay, ISL executives found that international companies weren't rushing to buy into the Olympics at all. By late 1985, Dassler had put up guarantees worth millions of dollars in exchange for the assignment to sell the marketing rights for the Olympics, but ISL had persuaded just two companies to buy such rights. They gave themselves another six months to find more partners—otherwise they would have to give up. Fortunately, the situation suddenly became unlocked when another two partners committed. Horst Dassler could proudly tell the IOC that the Olympic marketing plan had raised about $95 million from nine international companies.

Sadly, Horst Dassler would not live to savor ISL's accomplishments. He passed away on April 9, 1987, barely one month after his fifty-first birthday. When they arrived for work the next day, thousands of German employees were stunned to learn about their chairman's death. Those who had not seen him for several months could not have guessed that he had been unwell. An international sales meeting was interrupted, and the board members gathered to discuss the disaster.

The German response was relatively muted, however, compared with the scenes that unfolded in Landersheim. When they heard the news over the loudspeaker that morning, scores of grown men and women erupted in tears. "It was a gripping sight," one of them recalled. "There were people wailing down the corridors, others collapsed in their office, crying desperately for hours on end."

When he heard the news on a fairway, Donald Dell was stunned. He was even more shocked to receive, a few days later, a personal letter that had been dated and handwritten by Horst Dassler just two days before his death. "What in the hell is he doing, lying in bed writing letters to people all over the world?" Dell wondered. It gave a whole new dimension to Dassler's workaholic ways.

The obituaries published by the German press praised Horst Dassler as "an unostentatious, modest man" who steered the international growth of a company with sales of 4.1 billion German marks ($2.3 billion). Others referred to him as "the most powerful man in sports." He was "a tireless, but not selfless genius," one reporter noted, while another portrayed him as "the man in the background, who pulled the strings."

Monika Dassler, the widow, led the small funeral cortege that brought Horst to his final resting place. Juan Antonio Samaranch and Sepp Blatter both walked behind the widow and her children, Adi, Jr., and Suzanne. They had not seen much of their

Sepp Blatter *(with dark glasses)*, João Havelange, and Juan Antonio Samaranch are among the mourners at Horst Dassler's funeral, walking behind his widow and two children.

father, but they knew him well enough to know what touched him most. They had seen to it that, on his last journey, their father would be wearing the watch he had so gleefully received from his friend Ilie Nastase.

puma's demise

Armin Dassler beamed as he shook the bankers' hands. Since he had taken over the helm at Puma just over a decade earlier, then aged forty-five, he had been through many triumphs and setbacks. But this was undeniably his finest hour: that morning, on July 25, 1986, Puma was to be listed on the Frankfurt stock exchange. While Adidas was still a private company, its smaller rival had entered the select group of German companies featured on the financial pages every day.

The Puma shares shot up immediately. In the eyes of the German public, Puma was closely associated with a freckle-faced tennis player who had shot to fame the previous year. In July 1985, the seventeen-year-old Boris Becker stunned the tennis world by winning Wimbledon—the Puma logo clearly visible on his shoes as he dove along the net.

Puma had been tipped off about Boris Becker by a former Romanian player, Ion Tiriac. With protégés like Guillermo Vilas and Henri Leconte, two leading tennis players in the eighties, Tiriac had become an influential manager. On the tennis circuit, he was known mostly for his thick moustache and threatening gaze. As one British reporter wrote, "Tiriac has the air of a man who is about to close a deal in a back room behind a back room."

In this case it was the Puma board room in Herzogenaurach. After a rejection by Adidas, Tiriac persuaded Puma to fork over 300,000 German marks ($105,450) in 1984 for a shoe contract with Boris Becker, then completely unknown. It paid off wildly as Becker went on to become "Boom Boom," a handsomely popular player. The hype reached its peak in July 1986, just days before the Puma stock market introduction, when Becker won his second Wimbledon title in a row, beating the three-striped Ivan Lendl in straight sets. The company claimed that the Becker effect had nearly tripled the sales of its tennis rackets. Puma was so closely associated with the player that the company's public offering was dubbed "the Becker float."

By then, the split of the shares between the Dassler brothers had somewhat changed to the benefit of Armin. He had agreed to take over an extra 10 percent from his brother, Gerd, when the latter suffered some financial troubles. The brothers sold 28 percent of their shares, while retaining the majority of the stock and all of the voting rights. As Armin Dassler explained, the sale of the shares would be useful to raise cash, but it had been motivated partly by his acute health problems. Several years after a Kenyan safari, Armin had been felled by a severe bout of malaria. It nearly cost him his life. He told reporters that the stock market listing might ease inheritance problems. If he died prematurely, his children could easily draw outside capital to keep the company afloat.

The deal crowned a triumphant run for Puma. Since Armin Dassler had taken over from his father in 1974, the company's turnover had shot up to nearly 820 million German marks ($278 million) in 1985. Rudolf Dassler's sons had inherited a brand with an inspiring heritage but that still couldn't compete with the international exposure of its much larger rival and continued to derive most of its sales from German soccer. When he took control, Armin began to issue a throng of licenses and distribution deals that beefed up the brand's international sales, and he strove to cultivate its position as a snappy underdog.

The most thrilling rewards came from Latin America. Armin continued to benefit from the connections of Hans Henningsen, who still worked for Puma in Brazil. Henningsen delivered much of the Argentine team that won the 1978 World Cup. Among the endorsees was Cesar Luis Menotti, the Argentine trainer. When he spotted a chubby attacker at Boca Juniors, he sent the teenager straight to Armin Dassler. Diego Maradona was still so young that the contract had to be signed by his father.

This deal caused Puma many headaches over the years, as Maradona became increasingly capricious. When he once deigned to travel to Munich for an appearance at ISPO, the international trade fair for the sports industry, the Dasslers had to book several adjoining hotel suites for him. He would not move without his entire family, about twenty people. Other demands were attributed to superstition, which was hard to counter. But the deal secured continuous exposure for Puma, as Maradona shone on international pitches.

At the same time, Armin Dassler continued to run Puma as a family business. For many years he entered the company facilities each day through the factory floor and greeted all of the workers. He endeared himself to the employees through his open-door policy and generous behavior. John Akii-Bua, a Ugandan hurdler, experienced this attitude in the seventies, when he fled the political turmoil in his country. Dassler and Akii-Bua had gotten to know each other at the Munich Olympics in 1972, where the Ugandan won a gold medal for the 400-meter hurdles. When Armin heard that Akii-Bua was in trouble, he put up him and his family in one of his properties in Herzogenaurach, and offered the athlete a job in Puma's sports promotion department.

Compared with Horst, Armin Dassler still had the air of a provincial entrepreneur. Yet he had become established in the sports business as chairman of the World Federation of Sporting Goods Industry (WFSGI), lobbying in favor of free trade on behalf of sports companies. The appointment came about in 1986, when the federation's board convened in Tokyo. The chairmanship was then in the hands of Kihachiro Onitsuka, the man behind the Tiger brand in Japan, who set up the Asics running brand after the loss of his dispute with Nike. But under the federation's rules, it had to rotate among executives from different continents, and it was Europe's turn. Since Armin Dassler already headed the European sporting goods federation, Onitsuka figured the German was the obvious choice for chairman.

Still, the shrewd Japanese knew that the appointment was bound to anger Horst Dassler. Therefore, the night before the announcement, Onitsuka went to the Adidas chief's room in Tokyo and politely informed him. "Horst was very upset and issued all sorts of threats. He said it was completely unacceptable to him and he would leave the federation, but I still managed to appease him," Onitsuka recounted. "I taught him the Buddhist proverb which says that the one who leads the attack will get the punch back in his own face."

Horst eventually agreed not to intervene against his cousin at the next day's meeting. Shortly afterward, he could even be persuaded to shake hands with Armin and be pictured sitting at the same table as him. Again, it was Onitsuka's wisdom that did it: "I told him about another Buddhist proverb, which says that it is one's duty to get on with one's family," the Japanese chuckled.

On the other hand, Armin's efforts to outdo his cousin repeatedly landed Puma in deep financial trouble. Jim Woolner, one of the principals at Beconta, still the brand's American distributor, found out when he received an urgent phone call from Armin Dassler while he was on a break in Colorado. "They needed money right away, and a lot of money," Woolner recalled. "Armin said his Dutch distributor had mortgaged his house in order to get money for him."

Beconta itself still held its own in football and athletics, and obtained some enviable endorsement deals. One of them was a tight partnership with baseball player Reggie Jackson, a phenomenal right-fielder. Jackson was contracted by a Puma agent on the West Coast when he was playing in Oakland, but gained yet more

Armin Dassler (left, with checkered jacket) is persuaded to sit down briefly at the same table as his enemy cousin, Horst, at an industry meeting in Japan.

prominence after he was snapped up by the New York Yankees in 1976. He then became such close friends with Jim Woolner that neither of them felt the need to sign more than "a little piece of yellow paper" to seal the endorsement.

However, in the late seventies, Puma's American expansion began to slow down, suffering from the same woes as Adidas. Armin Dassler repeatedly threatened the Beconta managers, reminding them of a clause in their contract that guaranteed a set growth rate. On at least one occasion he dismissed the distributors, only to come back apologetically a few days later. The increasingly strained relationship was finally terminated in June 1979, for reasons the Beconta managers never understood.

This time, Armin's impulsive behavior proved most damaging. Instead of working out a compromise or organizing a smooth transition, he fired Beconta in a huff. "There was no need for the mayhem which my brother caused by breaking up with them from one day to the next," said Gerd Dassler, Armin's younger brother. "I don't know why Armin flew off the handle this time. From then on, the United States was a mess for Puma."

Armin Dassler asked Dick Kazmaier, a former Converse distributor, to hurriedly replace Beconta with four separate distributors. Their orders and marketing activities were to be supervised by a central office, Puma USA, set up by Kazmaier in Boston. Kazmaier himself took up distribution for the East Coast and found three other partners to cover the rest of the country. The changeover was handled as quickly as possible, but Puma deliveries were still heavily disrupted for at least one year, at a time when the market was undergoing drastic changes.

Over the next few years, the chosen partners struggled to convince Puma that their hard shoes were no longer adequate for the American market. Just like their competitors at Adidas, they failed to get the message across and muddled along with "shoes that felt like bricks" compared with the much suppler Nikes. But the Puma brand suffered an even more damaging blow when Armin Dassler encouraged Kazmaier to sign a massive deal with an American discounter.

As Dick Kazmaier recalled, he received an urgent call from Armin Dassler in August 1983. "He told me that he needed more volume and receivables, therefore he wanted to sell two million pairs by the beginning of September," Kazmaier recalled. "Two million pairs were a whole lot of shoes at the time. There was no way to sell them over such a short period without entering the mass merchants." This led to a large-scale deal with Meldisco, a shoe franchise of Kmart. Armin Dassler apparently flew over to Boston just to pick up the hard copy of the order.

Kazmaier felt uneasy about the deal, knowing that "it would wreak havoc with the other distributors." The deal may have been critical to Armin in the short term, but by selling to an offshoot of Kmart, he was undermining his own marketing efforts. The fact that Puma could be found in discount stores would inevitably tarnish the brand, giving it a tacky reputation. By the mid-eighties, Puma began to suffer the consequences: Foot Locker, the most influential sports retailer in the United States, decided to scrap its business with Puma. If the brand was sold at Kmart, they didn't want it on their shelves.

Just like his cousin had done before him with the buyout of the Adidas distributors in the United States, Armin Dassler then decided to buy out Puma's own American distributors. Two of them had already given up on Puma, but Dassler still had to absorb Dick Kazmaier and Richard Voit, the Puma distributor on the West Coast. Puma USA, the office run by Kazmaier for joint buying and marketing, would be expanded into a full-fledged subsidiary. But Puma USA quickly ran into nightmarish problems. Three chief executives struggled to restore the brand's reputation, but none of them lasted more than a few months. They quickly became frustrated by the company's German leadership, which seemed oblivious to U.S. market realities.

Armin Dassler then turned to his eldest son. Aged twenty-nine, Frank Dassler was a law student. A bright and hardworking young man, he regularly turned up at Puma before his lessons in the mornings, to set up a research department called The Running Studio, which looked into the biomechanical aspects of running. However, his knowledge of the business remained limited, and his managerial experience was nonexistent. When, at the beginning of 1985, Armin Dassler told the board that he wanted Frank to fix Puma's abysmal problems in the United States, several managers attempted to convince him that this was a bad idea. He would not be doing the company, or his son, any favors. Frank Dassler himself felt that the request was "kind of crazy." But Armin flatly overruled.

For all his ardor, Frank Dassler was unable to stem the U.S. collapse. At a meeting in February 1985, he warned the Puma board that the brand's American sales were crashing. But the full extent of the troubles became apparent toward October 1986, just months after Puma's launch on the stock exchange. By then, the value of the Puma shares had soared from an issue price of 130 German marks to more than 1,400 German marks. As news of the company's U.S. woes began to seep out, the shares fell back just as steeply. It became clear that Puma would end the year with a substantial loss, caused mostly by the United States.

To make matters worse, Boris Becker became a millstone around Puma's neck. Once hailed as a German role model, he was suddenly perceived as an arrogant brat. On the court, his performance waned fast. He triggered nationwide outrage when he moved to Monte Carlo, in an apparent attempt to escape German taxes and duck out of obligatory military service. "The retailers told us the

Boris Becker products would sell much better if they didn't have the name on them," sighed Uli Heyd, former Puma board member.

But Puma was stuck with the huge contract Tiriac had negotiated in 1986, shortly after Becker's second Wimbledon victory. Apparently blinded by the euphoria and hypnotized by the hirsute Romanian manager, Armin Dassler had signed a delirious deal to outfit Boris Becker from shirt to racket: the athlete would pocket at least $5 million for each of the next five years, as well as a hefty commission on the sales of Puma products in the Boris Becker line. It would have taken staggering sales to make the deal worthwhile for Puma at the best of times. Under the circumstances the deal was a permanent embarrassment and a growing liability.

The problem assumed such proportions that, in January 1987, Armin and Gerd Dassler resolved to inject 62 million German marks ($34.5 million) into the company through a private subordinated loan. Unfortunately that failed to quell the unrest among shareholders. Two months later there were rumors that to reimburse their loan, Armin and Gerd Dassler had put the company up for sale.

Some Puma shareholders became uproarious over the next few months, as auditors went over the company's numbers. Although he was just weeks away from death at the time, Horst Dassler apparently couldn't refrain from making a personal dig. After a press meeting in Budapest in March 1987, he lashed out at his cousin with vicious remarks. Horst had convened the conference to discuss the opening of an Adidas store in Budapest, but he stayed behind to rail at Armin Dassler and Puma's financial woes. "Puma is looking for a buyer that needs high tax-deductible losses," he sniped. Puma's stock market troubles were bringing disrepute to the entire industry, he said, denouncing the situation as "an absolute bank scandal."

The shareholders, mostly private investors, became yet more agitated as several months went by and Puma was unable to hold its shareholders meeting, pending the approval of its accounts. The meeting should have taken place in May, but by the end of the summer the shareholders still hadn't received their invitations. To quell the unrest, Armin Dassler came up with an amazingly generous offer to the shareholders: to replace the expected dividends, he would pay them out of his own pocket.

As its reputation was dragged through the mud, Deutsche Bank seized control of Puma. Alfred Herrhausen, then chairman of the bank, felt personally responsible for the company. After all, he was the one who had signed the agreement to underwrite the Puma public offering, which was turning into a disaster. Deutsche Bank had been badly tarnished by angry shareholders, but Herrhausen knew that the abuse would get much worse if he pulled the plug on Puma.

Jörg Dassler, Armin's second son, distinctly recalled the evening, in September 1987, when his father crashed on the couch in a state of utter despair. He had just returned from a meeting at the Deutsche Bank. The bankers said that they were preparing to remove him from the company. "You have lost your business," he was apparently told.

This was a devastating blow for Armin, who had dedicated his life to Puma. He had weathered the humiliations inflicted by his cousin and worked relentlessly to make sure that Puma could continue to compete. It was hard for him to comprehend how anonymous bankers could take this family heirloom away from him. From then on, as his wife saw it, Armin would never be the same again.

Shortly afterward, his two oldest sons were called in for a meeting with the bankers. Frank and his younger brother, Jörg, who had long been in charge of the department dealing with "entertainment promotion," were both bluntly asked to clear out their desks. "As the bankers put it," Frank said, "they thought it unacceptable that we should be paid just for being Armin's sons."

The Dasslers were deeply distressed by the bankers' methods and allegations, but they were not in a position to protest. Due to the loan that the Puma Dasslers had obtained from the Deutsche Bank earlier that year, their shares were virtually in the hands of the bankers. Another reason behind the sons' resignation was the fast deterioration of Armin's health. Perhaps due to the malaria he suffered two years earlier, his liver was badly damaged and he was becoming increasingly tired and irritable. He reluctantly agreed to a liver transplant.

The company's long-delayed shareholders meeting was finally scheduled for October 19, 1987, at the Sheraton hotel in Munich. The worst criticism was targeted at the bankers in the supervisory board. Due to his illness and his generous gesture, Armin Dassler was largely spared from the ire of the shareholders, but it was agreed that he would leave his company over the next weeks.

His replacement was Hans Woitschätzke, an experienced manager in the sports business. As Woitschätzke discovered over the next months, Puma's former management had not been overly rigorous when it came to accounts. "The books were filled with questionable dealings, from weird expenses to bad receivables that were parked in an offshore company," he said. "The Deutsche Bank evidently hadn't done its homework as an underwriter. Otherwise it would have come to the conclusion that Puma was heading toward disaster."

The wrongdoings partly reflected the informal methods of the former management board. Under Armin Dassler, as with his cousin at Adidas, many contracts had been sealed on the back of personal relationships. Armin's large office was fitted with a liquor bar, which he regularly used when meetings dragged on until late in the evening. Other restraints imposed on the board members appeared to have been relaxed over the years. Each of the six board members had a driver and, judging from their expense sheets, Woitschätzke thought that "they must have known every bar from Flensburg to Garmisch-Partenkirchen."

Yet more disturbingly, it seemed that the company's assets had been grossly inflated. To help him sort out the wreckage, Woitschätzke hired an external auditing firm to write an unofficial report on the company. The document painted such a stark picture of Puma's hidden liabilities that Woitschätzke decided to destroy it. "If the contents of this report had become known, we would have had no choice but to file for bankruptcy," he said.

Woitschätzke held endless meetings with Puma's bankers, who

were rushing for the door. As promised by Alfred Herrhausen, the Deutsche Bank staunchly backed up the managers, and it permanently put pressure on the other banks to uphold their credit lines to Puma.

The disproportionate Becker contract turned into a burning issue. Woitschätzke braced himself for a tough meeting when he invited Ion Tiriac to discuss changes in the deal. "We went through the whole spectrum, from begging to threats," said Woitschätzke. His strongest argument was that "Becker's reputation would take another painful hit if it turned out that Puma had been driven into bankruptcy just because Boris demanded $5 million from us each year." Under the contract, Puma still had at least $20 million to fork out. Tiriac agreed to a cash payment of $4 million, coupled with an "improvement clause." If Puma managed a profit over the next five years, Becker would be entitled to a maximum of 20 percent of that income.

Meanwhile the Deutsche Bank was anxiously trying to find a buyer for Puma. After several prospective deals fell through, Woitschätzke came forward with another suggestion: Cosa Liebermann, a company born from the merger between Liebermann Waelchli, Puma's licensee in Japan, and another trading company. In the meantime, the former had extensively deepened its relationship with Puma, to act as an agent for production in Far Eastern factories. Woitschätzke intimately knew the company since he had been on its board, and Armin Dassler was equally confident: he had forged a strong relationship with Guido Cherubini, Liebermann Waelchli's chief executive, and trusted him to respect the Puma legacy.

Two years into the cleanup, Puma was still losing money and on artificial life support. The bankers had faced so many rejections that they had to turn to smaller partners to pull themselves out of this quagmire. In May 1989, they gladly flogged the Dasslers' 72 percent stake in Puma to Cosa Liebermann, at an estimated cost of $43.5 million, to be split equally between a cash injection in the company and a compensation for those selling their shares.

As the Deutsche Bank saw it, the second part of the payment should have been transferred straight to their account, to pay off the Dasslers' remaining debts from the loan they had contracted in early 1987. However, Hans Woitschätzke convinced the Deutsche Bank that the Dasslers should receive at least some of the money from the sale. Once they had sealed a compromise, the Puma Dassler heirs were apparently left with a little more than 20 million German marks ($10.6 million) between them.

With that, by the end of the decade, the Deutsche Bank had severed the last remaining ties between Puma and the Dasslers. Frank and Jörg, Armin's two eldest sons, would not return to the company. While Frank set up a law firm in Herzogenaurach, specializing in sporting goods, his brother ran a printing business. Their half-brother, Michael, was still studying when Puma was sold off, and none of Gerd's children were given a chance to pursue a career at Puma. It was no longer a family-owned business, and it seemed that the new proprietors could barely wait to erase the family's legacy at the company.

Armin Dassler became increasingly prone to depression. His liver trouble turned out to be cancer, which was quickly spreading to his bones. After a short bout of chemotherapy, he was advised to return home. He passed away in the early afternoon of Sunday, October 14, 1990, at the age of sixty-one. Although it was the cancer that destroyed his body, Armin Dassler's family remains convinced that he was mortally shattered by the loss of his company. "Put it this way," said Irene Dassler, his widow, "he didn't fight."

Once the two Dassler heirs passed away, the battles between Adidas and Puma lost their personal sting. The two companies had spent several decades mostly fighting each other, but they began to falter under intense pressure from other market forces, which brought them to the edge of the precipice.

part three

Multibillion-
Dollar Rescue

shark attack!

Ensconced in the largest office of the management floor in Herzogenaurach, René Jäggi marveled at his fate. There he was, a thirty-eight-year-old manager, at the helm of an emblematic company. True, his ascent had been accelerated by circumstances he could not have predicted, starting with the sudden death of Horst Dassler, but Jäggi had still played his cards right.

As Jäggi himself explained, he won the leadership contest at Adidas in November 1987 by constantly moving. "Think of a shark," he said. "It is the only fish that cannot keep still, otherwise it sinks. This gives the shark an unbelievably elegant swimming movement. The type of person that I am is a shark."

Jäggi had all the charisma that was required to head Adidas—he was equally at ease with soccer players, slick sports officials, and politicians. With his tall frame, square shoulders, and cool charm, he could have breezed off the set of any Hollywood blockbuster. Warm, witty, and outgoing, he was almost everyone's favorite partner for a round of drinks. Only the most old-fashioned German bankers felt uneasy about his lack of titles or wrinkles.

René Jäggi's ordinary Swiss youth took an unexpected turn when he bought a one-way ticket to Tokyo in 1970. Aged twenty-one, he had already studied philosophy and sports, reaching a highly competitive level as a judoka (a competitor in the martial art of judo). Jäggi flew over to Japan so he could sharpen his skills ahead of the 1972 Olympics in Munich. He never made it to Munich, but he did learn to speak Japanese fluently and made contacts that would rescue him from several tight spots over the next years.

Upon his return to Europe, Jäggi rapidly built up his résumé with several international companies. He was general manager at the Daimon-Duracell batteries group when Adidas came along. With a convincing pedigree as an athlete and fluent in five languages, the Swiss had exactly the right profile to seduce the Adidas chief executive, and he was recruited in 1986 as a marketing manager.

When Horst passed away, René Jäggi immediately seized control among the board members—in line with the catchy motto framed in his executive office: "There are three kinds of people: those who make things happen, those who watch things happen, and those who wonder what's happening."

Jäggi was boiling with impatience to steer the company. While Horst had been hemming and hawing about the transfer of production to the Far East, Jäggi used the McKinsey study to push ahead with closures and layoffs. Thousands of redundant workers mortified the Dassler family by demonstrating in front of the company headquarters in Herzogenaurach. "Shirts and shorts in three stripes, employees ripped off," they chanted. From 1987 to 1992, the global workforce would be nearly halved, from about 11,000 to 6,400 people.

Among the chief burdens of the Dassler legacy was the enormous line offered by Adidas. When Jäggi took over, one of the oddities he found in the inventory was a line for *Bosseln*, a sport he had never heard of. It turned out to be a street game practiced in some parts of Friesland, a province in northern Germany. Adi Dassler's quest to make the best possible shoes for each athlete had made Adidas the best in the world, but the breadth of its line was now strangling the company. "The inventories were clogged with left foot size-sixteen curling shoes," said Roddy Campbell, international marketing manager in Herzogenaurach. Over the next four years the line was shrunk by more than 60 percent.

Another costly leftover was the improbable array of athletes and others paid by Adidas. It seemed generous that Franz Beckenbauer, the German soccer player, should still receive 1 million German marks ($590,000) from Adidas each year long after he had stopped playing. But it was altogether ludicrous that Adidas continued to sponsor all but two of the teams in the Bundesliga, Germany's top soccer league, although it drew benefits from only a handful of the teams. Worse still, the sports promotion people were still trying to contract the remaining two.

Roddy Campbell wasn't sure what to make of regular payments from Adidas to the son of Juan Antonio Samaranch, the chairman of the International Olympic Committee. He checked if there was a business partnership with him but could not find one. His investigations uncovered many other puzzling payments to people from sport and broadcasting organizations, which were promptly curtailed.

Yet the thorniest task for René Jäggi's men was to dismantle the organization built up by Horst Dassler in France. The parallel organization in Landersheim was a thorn in their side—a remnant of the old regime and a prime example of the absurdities that were holding back Adidas from competing with Nike and Reebok. Jäggi tackled these absurdities without regret: "When Hannibal trekked through the Alps by forced marches there were also a few falls."

Several men who had worked closely with Horst Dassler left the company, and others felt so alienated by René Jäggi's moves that they attended group therapy. "For several days we all sat there in a circle, unloading our feelings about the loss of Horst and all that he meant to us," said Johan van den Bossche, former legal adviser.

The former soccer players who had learned everything with Horst suddenly had to adjust to the basic principles of business organization. They were stripped of their power, if not their position. "As soon as the boss passed away, it was 'Deutschland über alles,'" sighed Jean Wendling. "The whole French operation was dismembered."

Once he had finished tidying up, Jäggi drew up an all-encompassing plan for the next five years. Nearly all of the reforms engineered by the Swiss were urgently needed, and many others were inspired by smart strategic insights. Yet the Dasslers continued to dither, and they didn't always allow Jäggi to implement the changes as radically as he would have wanted. And in the meantime, Adidas was letting in water from all sides.

. . . .

The Adidas managers gulped hard as they leafed through the document. After all the blurredness of the Dassler years, they were suddenly confronted with a sharply focused picture of Adidas—and it looked scary.

The figures were emerging as Adidas managers, McKinsey, and other consultants disentangled the octopus-like structure Horst Dassler had created. Once they had integrated Arena, Le Coq Sportif, and the rights to Pony, then gone through long months of numbers crunching, McKinsey had come up with relatively straightforward accounts for Adidas.

The worst losses came from the United States: since the buyout in 1986, the American operation had been losing at least $30 million a year. After the acrimonious split with the distributors, the transition was bound to be awkward, but the Adidas managers hadn't anticipated the extent of the difficulties.

The American sales force was badly dispirited as Adidas USA appeared rudderless, having changed its leadership several times already in the first few years of its existence. The Americans still couldn't see any signs that the company's management in Germany had grasped the depth of its troubles in the United States, or that it would be committing any spectacular investments to turn things around.

Adidas's and Nike's contrasting fortunes with basketball endorsements encapsulated the German brand's desperate situation in the United States. While Nike was running away on the back of its endorsement with Michael Jordan, Adidas was scrambling to restructure its deal with Patrick Ewing. He was playing well but still wasn't selling enough shoes to cover the annual $700,000 he was receiving from Adidas.

One of the most immediate problems was the inventory. The distributors had always been encouraged by the Dasslers to order from the entire Adidas line: they could not just buy a few containers of Superstars but had to carry a much wider offering, such as high-jump shoes for left-footed athletes in all sizes. Over the years, these unsold and unsellable shoes had piled up at the back of their warehouses.

Roddy Campbell, international marketing manager, was sent to the United States to clean them out. "We shipped it into Kazakhstan and the Falkland Islands, Mars and Venus," he said. But the margins on these sales were so low that they only added to the losses. They stood to reach about $75 million for the year, on sales of a measly $300 million.

The inventories issue was worsened by a seemingly absurd warehousing problem. Adidas USA had decided to close down all the warehouses belonging to the distributors and to build another large unit in Spartanburg, South Carolina, instead. But the person in charge had come from the music industry and didn't seem to realize that compact discs and shoe boxes weren't exactly the same size. "The boxes just kept falling off the racks!" sneered one of the managers at the time.

Roddy Campbell got so leery of the whole situation that he called up salespeople from all around the country to convene in Spartanburg. They were all hoping for the announcement of some energizing investments, but instead Campbell merely informed them that the warehousing wasn't functional and that they would therefore have to hurry along the aisles and pick out their own orders.

Until the early eighties Adidas barely had any debts and it continuously disgorged profits. But for 1988, debts reached roughly the same level as the company's capital. McKinsey extrapolated that, if Adidas included all their loss-making subsidiaries, as they should have done under accounting rules in other countries, the debt would have reached nearly four times the company's capital.

Under the circumstances, René Jäggi continued to maneuver adroitly. The chief executive attempted to convince the four Dassler sisters that his cleanup measures were beginning to pay off, but at the same time he kept them on edge by pointing to the crumbling financial situation. Armed with the latest McKinsey findings, Jäggi explained that the vital closures and cutbacks could not be completed without a quick cash injection. They would require at least 300 million German marks ($160 million), he insisted, and he rightly guessed that the Dassler sisters were not prepared to cough up the money.

The obvious solution was to raise cash by selling off sizeable chunks of the company, which would require a change in the company's statutes. Adidas would have to be converted from a foundation into an AG, a limited partnership. Somewhat overwhelmed, the Dasslers caved in: in February 1989, they approved the proposed amendments to the Adidas statutes, paving the way for capital changes.

René Jäggi was bursting with suggestions. One of them germinated on a flight transfer in Tokyo, as the chief executive was scanning international newspapers. His gaze landed on the name of Peter Ueberroth, the dapper Californian who had steered the organizing committee for the Los Angeles Olympics in 1984. The Games had yielded unprecedented profits of $225 million for the organizers, turning Ueberroth into a celebrated entrepreneur. *Time* magazine picked him as Man of the Year: "The Achievement was Olympian," ran the introduction on the cover.

If anyone could drag Adidas out of its slump, it was Peter Ueberroth. As Jäggi read in the newspaper, the American had just teamed up with a few other seasoned executives to found the Contrarian group. Unlike some of the raiders who wreaked havoc on Wall Street, Contrarian professed to make friendly investments in undervalued companies. As the newspaper indicated, Peter Ueberroth had just been embroiled in a drawn-out battle with shareholders and trade unions to rescue Eastern Airlines, though this had failed.

René Jäggi rushed to an airport phone and, to his own amazement, quickly persuaded Ueberroth to jump on board. Under the agreement settled in September 1989, the Contrarian group would take over the management of Adidas USA. Owing to the change in statutes, Ueberroth could obtain some of the compensation in share options, and he was promised a seat on the company's supervisory board in Herzogenaurach.

René Jäggi's prize was greeted with excitement. Jäggi was widely praised for hooking such a talented and influential manager. With Ueberroth at the helm, there was a chance that the company's American woes would come to an end at last. But at the same time, the move precipitated a terminal family clash.

. . . .

After the death of Horst Dassler, his children, Suzanne and Adi, Jr., inherited his rights in Adidas. Exactly like each of their four aunts in Herzogenaurach, they would now jointly have 20 percent of the company and a seat on the *Beirat*, the supervisory board. Horst Dassler's children were eager to make their voices heard, to protect their father's legacy at Adidas. But the four Dassler sisters wouldn't have any of that.

As Suzanne Dassler explained much later, she and Adi, Jr., felt persecuted by their aunts. "They didn't spare us anything," she said. "Forty-eight hours after the death of my father they were on our doorstep in Lucerne, to make us sign succession papers." Horst's children refused, deeming the conditions indecent. From then on, the Dassler sisters made it unceremoniously clear that they were not interested in any contribution from their niece and nephew.

The heirs on the German side of the Dassler family apparently longed to get rid of anything that reminded them of Horst—which his children did with devoted persistence. Suzanne and Adi, Jr., heard the complaints of the French managers and watched angrily as their father's citadel in Landersheim became just another

The two most influential Dassler daughters: Inge Bente with her husband, Alf, and Brigitte Baenkler, in charge of relations with East European partners.

subsidiary of Herzogenaurach. In their eyes, the chief evildoer was René Jäggi. "This man imposed himself through the distress of the shareholders," Suzanne Dassler was quoted as saying. "He can't stand my father's shadow. The employees are no longer allowed to speak out his name. The company's brochures no longer refer to his career. But they won't kill him. We will continue to defend his past."

The children's bitterness turned into an ugly battle when the Dassler sisters began to discuss the sale of their shares in ISL, the sports rights agency. As part of their demands before the return of their brother to Herzogenaurach, the sisters had obtained shares in Sporis, the Swiss holding company that held 51 percent of ISL. Each of them owned 16 percent of Sporis, while the remaining 36 percent was in the hands of Horst Dassler's children. Under mounting pressure, the sisters figured that they could sell some of their ISL shares to pay off their inheritance tax and pump some more money into Adidas.

René Jäggi, who happened to be the chairman of Sporis, gladly took up the assignment to look for a buyer. He held talks with

All four daughters held equal shares in Adidas: Karin Essing *(left)* supervised the marketing department, and Sigrid Malms, the youngest of the daughters, was briefly in charge of textiles.

Klaus Hempel and Jürgen Lenz, the two leading executives behind ISL, and asked them to prepare a management buyout offer. At the same time he placed a call to Yoichi Hattori, the man in charge at Dentsu, the Japanese advertising agency. While Sporis held 51 percent of ISL, the remaining 49 percent was still in the hands of Dentsu. As Horst Dassler's children knew all too well, the Japanese would need only one of their aunts' 16 percent package to seize control of the sports rights agency.

If Suzanne and Adi, Jr., were deeply angered by the criticism of their father at Adidas, they were absolutely determined to save his legacy at ISL. Their aunts could shut them up at Adidas, but there was no way they would let some Japanese advertisers grab hold of their father's crowning achievement. They vowed to block the sale of any ISL shares held by their aunts, for which they had preemptive rights.

The sisters attempted to retaliate by removing the representative of the Dassler children from the Sporis board: Walter Meier, the Zurich lawyer who executed Horst Dassler's will, had turned into another nuisance for them. The problem was that under the

ISL statutes, Meier could be removed from the board only for "serious reasons"—and there didn't seem to be any.

Under attack from their aunts, Horst Dassler's children faced another imminent threat: a towering tax bill. Since they were determined to hold on to their ISL shares, the only way Suzanne and Adi, Jr., could settle their inheritance tax was to sell some of their Adidas shares. They turned to Erwin Conradi, general manager at Metro, the German retail behemoth, who had known Horst Dassler. They discreetly held talks until May 1989, when Conradi confirmed that they had come to an agreement: Metro had acquired an option to buy 15 percent of Adidas. Once Metro exercised the option, Adi and Suzanne Dassler would jointly retain a share of only 5 percent.

The Dassler sisters expressed shock at the sale, which they learned of in the newspapers. Their niece and nephew had apparently conducted it behind their backs, something they construed as a form of betrayal, and which aggravated their anger about the stalemate at ISL. The recriminations continued for several months, until the Dassler daughters found another way to hit back at Adi and Suzanne—by using the deal with Peter Ueberroth.

Ueberroth's contract unequivocally stated that he should join the Adidas supervisory board. To make space for Ueberroth, Jäggi and the Dassler sisters agreed that one of the sitting board members would have to give up his seat. And predictably, they picked their niece and nephew's sole representative.

Adi, Jr., and Suzanne were aghast to hear that, at the general meeting of October 1989, their aunts had unanimously voted to evict Walter Meier from the Adidas board. Since the four sisters jointly controlled 80 percent of the company, there didn't seem to be much that Horst Dassler's children could do, but they fought tooth and nail to get the vote annulled. The battle took a grotesque turn: the supervisory board had to convene three times to vote on the same issue; the outcome was always the same, 80 percent in favor. But Walter Meier still argued that his eviction was unlawful due to a legal flaw.

Yet again the family dispute ended up before the judges. Suzanne and Adi, Jr., lodged a complaint at the administrative court of Nuremberg, arguing that they had been fleeced by their aunts. They had voted in favor of the change of the Adidas statutes on the condition that they would continue to be represented on the supervisory board, they said, but less than one year later they had been booted out.

Amid all these skirmishes, the Dassler sisters anxiously watched the upheavals in the international sports market. They had barely digested the reports for 1988, which placed Adidas just ahead of Reebok, but they could already tell that their company's results for 1989 would be the worst ever: the restructuring measures would contribute to unprecedented losses, and the three stripes were continuing to retreat in the market.

The turn of the decade officially sealed the demise of Adidas. By the end of 1989, Reebok could rightly claim that it had become the largest sporting goods business in the world, with sales of just over $1.8 billion. This was hurtful enough for Nike, which was recovering from a sharp dip, with sales of just over $1.7 billion. But it was altogether humiliating for Adidas, which was relegated to third place, a few thousand dollars behind Nike.

The Dassler sisters became all the more nervous about their financial woes. Under normal business circumstances the bankers, shareholders, and managers could have come to some arrangement. Carl-Hainer Thomas, one of the independent members of the board, certainly didn't regard the company's predicament as insurmountable. The chief executive of a multibillion-dollar division at Siemens, he advised the Dassler sisters against any rash moves. "The speed of the collapse was scary, but there was no rational need to sell," he said.

Yet the Dassler sisters became convinced that they should exit while Adidas was relatively untarnished. They anxiously watched the drama unfolding on the other side of the Aurach, where their Puma cousins were thrown out of their company with a pittance. The panic-stricken Dassler sisters made up their minds. They wanted out.

· · · ·

The assignment to sell Adidas was thrown into the lap of Gerhard Ziener, the new chairman of the Adidas supervisory board. A former chairman of Röhm, a chemicals company in Darmstadt, not far from Frankfurt, Ziener protested that he was ill suited to orchestrate such a deal and recommended a merchant banker. However, the sisters balked at the commission fee required by bankers and insisted that Ziener conduct the talks.

Reluctantly, the chairman prepared a study about the worth and prospects of Adidas. A well-connected businessman, Ziener easily spread word that the company was up for sale. He still felt awkward about the assignment, though, and was greatly relieved when René Jäggi stepped in—always at the ready. Through the Swiss chief executive, Ziener was introduced to a flurry of would-be buyers. The Benetton family and Timothy Fok, the Hong Kong entrepreneur, among others, politely declined. The most serious talks were held with two German investors.

Gerhard Ziener was set on Metro, the German retail group that had bought the 15 percent option from Adi and Suzanne. However, the sale had provoked much unrest among small German store owners, who feared unfair competition from Metro discount stores. After some talks with Ziener, Metro decided to hold on to their 15 percent as "an investment opportunity" but turned down the rest of the shares.

Then there was Klaus Jacobs, the owner of Jacobs Suchard, the Swiss coffee and confectionery group. Ziener didn't think much of the investor, who made a "very arrogant impression." The chairman was further unsettled by the relationship between Jacobs and Jäggi, who "became all starry-eyed whenever the name Jacobs came up." He suspected that Jäggi would not be impartial toward a bid from Jacobs.

Since Ziener was dragging his feet, Jäggi decided to further the talks himself. He knew full well that the Dassler sisters still didn't have any offers lined up, and they didn't seem to have any hang-ups about Klaus Jacobs. They appreciated the fact that he was German and owned a family company. If Jäggi presented them with a commitment from Jacobs, they would certainly bite.

On a Saturday in June 1989, four Adidas managers discreetly made their way to the Jacobs mansion in Zurich. They were so wary of leaks that they asked Hansrüdi Ruegger, longtime head of the Adidas subsidiary in Switzerland, to pick them up at the airport.

Warmly greeted by Jacobs, René Jäggi made the introductions. Axel Markus, the chief financial officer, outlined the figures. Michel Perraudin, the former McKinsey man on the Adidas board, provided another bite-size audit. And Herman Homann tagged along as Jäggi's personal assistant.

The four Adidas men were jubilant as they drove back to Zurich airport. They excitedly told Ruegger that they had saved the company. They had struck a detailed agreement that fulfilled all the Dassler sisters' requirements. Jacobs would fork out the asking price to acquire Adidas, and he promised the managers that they would get a chunk of the cake.

On the plane back to Nuremberg, René Jäggi and Axel Markus celebrated with champagne. The two managers, who had become very close over the previous months, both knew that the price required by the Dassler sisters was a bargain. And with their own options in the company, Jäggi and Markus stood to make a killing. Michel Perraudin, who took another flight to Hong Kong, felt just as confident. "It was a done deal," he recalled.

The following Monday, René Jäggi called Christoph Malms, husband of Sigrid Dassler, to obtain the family's go-ahead. Excitedly, Jäggi began to recount the meeting held in Zurich two days earlier. But Malms swiftly cut him off. The Dassler sisters mistrusted Jacobs since he had just sold his family company, Jacobs Suchard, to Philip Morris. If Jacobs flogged his business to American tobacco merchants, they felt, there was not much of a chance that he would care to preserve the heritage of Adidas.

They had found another suitor, Malms said. The man turned up from nowhere and his pretensions seemed incongruous, but he had swept the sisters off their feet. For once, Jäggi was utterly speechless.

the sellout

The man spoke English with a subtle French accent. He introduced himself as Laurent Adamowicz, a consultant with Paribas, the investment bank. He said he was calling on behalf of a French investor who may be interested in acquiring Adidas, but he was reluctant to provide the person's name. Adamowicz wisely judged that it would be safer not to mention him during the first phone call.

Ulrich Nehm, who picked up the phone that day, was somewhat bewildered. The Munich lawyer had been hired just a few months earlier and he found himself dealing with calls from mystery investors on his private number. Still, this Adamowicz sounded serious enough and Adidas could not really afford to snub potential cash providers.

During their meeting at Nehm's offices in Munich, the man from Paribas confirmed the lawyer's intuition. A young man with round glasses and little hair, Adamowicz already had an impressive pedigree as an investment banker. Having just returned from a stint with Paribas in New York, he had been asked by the bank to come up with large-scale buyout suggestions in Europe. The Wharton graduate came across as a no-nonsense, efficient guy. But when he walked out of Nehm's office, Adamowicz still hadn't revealed the identity of his client.

The bizarre approach was partly justified by the nature of the proposed deal. After all, Adidas was still an institution: whoever ended up buying it, the sell-off of the three stripes was bound to trigger some emotional reactions. And given the explosive reputation of his client, Adamowicz had reason to fear an outcry that would torpedo the deal before it was properly tabled.

Over the previous years, Bernard Tapie had hardly ceased to dominate French business headlines. Starting off as a small-time electronics dealer, he had risen to prominence by taking over near-defunct companies and turning them around. He shook up the French establishment with his charisma, loud mouth, and go-getting attitude, which earned him a slot as the host of a prime-time television show. But Tapie's name became truly ubiquitous in 1989, when he won a seat affiliated to the socialist group in the French parliament, in a hard-fought district of Marseilles.

In business, the tallest feather in his hat was Wonder, a batteries company, which Tapie acquired in 1984 and sold again five years later at a huge profit. Then came Terraillon and Testut, two companies best known for their weighing scales. Another of his investments was a small stake in TF1, France's leading private television channel. His shares in these companies were regrouped under a company called Bernard Tapie Finances (BTF), which was floated on the Paris stock market in November 1989.

Tapie liked to remind his audience that he had built this all by himself—a tough lad who grew up in a drab Paris suburb, his modest family crammed into a flat with a plain basin as their sole washing facility. By the late eighties his lifestyle had undergone a radical change. Tapie convinced his bankers to acquire one of the most beautiful estates in Paris, the Hôtel de Cavoye, a private hotel with a lush garden on the Rue des Saints-Pères, at the heart of the Latin Quarter.

But when Tapie really wanted to impress his guests he took

them on the *Phocéa*, a seventy-four-meter boat whose refurbishment had lasted four years and cost Tapie more than 60 million French francs ($7.6 million). Tapie transformed the former Club Méditerrannée racing boat with four masts and ten luxury cabins, and proudly moored her in the port of Marseilles.

Some regarded Bernard Tapie as France's answer to the swashbuckling self-made men who ripped through corporate America with their leveraged buyouts in the eighties. He was applauded wildly by business students who yearned to get rid of the country's staid business establishment. On the other hand, he was reviled by many of the ruling caste—the men who ran state-controlled companies, rarely made a speech without quoting obscure poets, and abhorred insolent outsiders. To them, Bernard Tapie was just a vulgar charlatan, an impudent dare-it-all: a former TV salesman who had twice filed for personal bankruptcy.

The irritation turned to bewilderment when Bernard Tapie began to appear in the company of François Mitterrand. The wily socialist president had been seduced by Tapie's exuberance—or at least he figured that it might come in handy. This turned out to be a smart judgement when Mitterrand needed a daring ally to face Jean-Marie Le Pen, the leader of the openly racist National Front. While many others were reluctant to battle with the astute and notoriously combative Le Pen, Bernard Tapie took up the fight and verbally crushed the populist leader.

Marseilles became Bernard Tapie's launching pad in politics, and in the sports business, when he acquired L'Olympique de Marseille. Back in 1986 the soccer club was whiling away in the second division—a depressing state of affairs for its supporters in Marseilles, where l'OM is an institution. The squad's dismal performance was certain to have unpleasant political consequences for the city's mayor, Gaston Deferre, so Bernard Tapie was invited to acquire the ailing OM. Within months he had assembled a team with international players, and Olympique de Marseille soon reached the semi-finals of the European Champions League.

Tapie relished the limelight and the heroics of sport. In the eighties he was deeply involved in the cycling world when La

Vie Claire, a dietary products chain he owned, became sponsor of a cycling team on the Tour de France. The team won the Tour twice in a row, with Bernard Hinault and Greg LeMond, the French and American cycling champions. Tapie took over Look, a French manufacturer of ski bindings, and he still owned Donnay, a Belgian company making tennis rackets that were endorsed by André Agassi.

But when Adamowicz cold-called Bernard Tapie with buyout suggestions, Tapie's business was dwindling. Adidas was precisely what he needed: an international company with a high-profile brand would propel him on the international sports scene and dramatically alter the contours of his business. After all, Adidas reported sales equivalent to more than 10 billion French francs ($1.57 billion), while BTF's sales were only around 1 billion French francs ($157 million). A takeover of Adidas, a German institution that dwarfed any of Tapie's previous acquisitions, would be a coup spectacular enough to silence his most ardent critics. Could he possibly pull this off?

As part of the project, code-named "Lendl," Adamowicz began cautiously to investigate the company. However, Tapie was boiling over with impatience. He didn't need lengthy audits and wordy analysis—he had it all sussed out. "All the people who fight for the right to claim they have saved Adidas are just clowns," said Tapie. "A first-year business student would have grasped the company's problems." And no matter how empty the coffers, he could always find a solution. After all, this was Adidas.

Still, Adamowicz had to convince the Dassler heirs that Tapie was the right investor to steer the turnaround. After some phone calls it became clear that the children of Horst Dassler were at loggerheads with their four aunts in Herzogenaurach. Since the women together held 80 percent of the shares, it seemed wiser to concentrate on them. Then it still took Adamowicz several weeks to discreetly locate their lawyer in Munich.

Adamowicz insisted on withholding the potential buyer's identity for several months. In the two months after his opening meeting with Ulrich Nehm, in February 1990, Adamowicz returned to Munich several times, but none of the encounters enlightened the Germans about the identity of the French investor behind Adamowicz. It was only at the beginning of May that the banker agreed to lift the veil.

The news didn't seem to upset Ulrich Nehm as badly as Adamowicz had feared. In fact, Nehm headed straight for the Dassler villa, and the sisters instructed him to enter negotiations, together with Gerhard Ziener, head of the supervisory board. At the end of May 1990, the two of them met up with Laurent Adamowicz and Bernard Tapie in Darmstadt, in a meeting room at Röhm, the chemicals company Ziener headed.

The get-together was somewhat awkward because Bernard Tapie didn't speak a word of English and Adamowicz had to translate everything. Still, the spiel worked perfectly, as Tapie deployed his remarkable acting talents. The two Germans had never seen anything like this. Deeply impressed by Tapie's charm and his impassioned speech, they walked away with "the impression that Tapie would throw his heart into the company," Nehm recalled.

Back in Herzogenaurach, Nehm and Ziener ordered some checks on Tapie's financial situation, which were not very encouraging. "It appeared that his slate wasn't entirely clean," they concluded—and that was a very mild assessment. To anybody who knew the staunchly conservative Dassler sisters and their emotional desire to leave their parents' heritage in safe hands, Bernard Tapie would have seemed an absurd proposal. Unlike their father, the flamboyant Frenchman constantly bragged and sought the limelight—more like one of the characters their brother used to deal with. He reveled in controversy and had been caught repeatedly breaching his promises and reneging on deals.

Still, the lawyers and decision-makers at Adidas ably defended Tapie's case. As they explained to the Dassler sisters, Adidas needed a strong personality to whip up the company. Tapie's sheer charisma would be invaluable for the brand. He didn't haggle over the asking price and pledged to invest fresh money into the company. The parliamentarian had the support of the

French government—which could not possibly drop an emblematic German company. And on a more practical note, they didn't have any other offers on the table.

After a personal meeting with Bernard Tapie at a Basel restaurant, René Jäggi had further motives to believe that the takeover by Tapie would turn out well—for himself. Since Klaus Jacobs was out of the picture, Jäggi was keen to make a good impression on the potential new owner. He convincingly explained to Tapie that the turnaround was under way. In turn, Tapie assured Jäggi that the management would stay, and it was his habit to reward management with options in the capital of his companies.

For the second meeting with the Germans, on June 27, 1990, Bernard Tapie put on another dazzling show. This time Ulrich Nehm was accompanied by Hans-Jürgen Martens, Adidas financial manager. The two of them stayed in Paris, where Tapie came to pick them up in the morning in a black BMW. As soon as the two Germans were ensconced at the back of the vehicle, Tapie took his seat behind the wheel, pulled out a little brass badge reading "Membre de l'Assemblée Nationale," and placed it behind the windshield. The BMW then screeched off into the morning traffic, escorted by a blue police car with flashing lights. The convoy's destination was Le Bourget, a small airport near Paris, where the group was joined by René Jäggi for further talks. The two Germans were paralyzed with fear.

. . . .

The Dassler sisters handed over their father's heritage on the morning of July 4, 1990, at the Röhm chemicals company in Darmstadt. They were represented by Brigitte Baenkler, the third Dassler daughter, who had always been particularly attached to the company. The other Dassler envoy was Christoph Malms, the husband of the youngest Dassler daughter, Sigrid.

Brigitte Baenkler knew all too well that the contract with Bernard Tapie would put an end to more than half a century of family dedication to the Adidas brand, which had shaped her parents' lives and her own. Yet the sisters had not deemed it useful to get to know Bernard Tapie. They had apparently given their blessing to the sale without ever meeting the buyer.

As they walked into the Röhm meeting room, Gerhard Ziener, the supervisory board chairman, pulled Adamowicz aside. "The shareholders have one last request," he whispered. With a mixture of exasperation and concern, the Paribas consultant protested that the contract had been discussed and agreed down to the smallest details. But as Ziener explained, the request was not about the terms of the sale. "The shareholders would like to make sure that they will still be allowed to buy Adidas products at the company stores with a corporate discount," Ziener pleaded. Adamowicz couldn't believe his ears: the Dasslers were about to sell their company and all they worried about was a 20 percent rebate on their Adidas shirts!

This time Gerhard Ziener had obtained a relatively prestigious meeting room, but this failed to lift the mood as the two parties ran through the contract one last time. Brigitte Baenkler was unable to contain her emotions. A gloomy and unpalatable lunch, fetched at the Röhm canteen, ended with a sullen handshake between Bernard Tapie and the Dassler representatives. The latter would come to regret it immensely.

. . . .

Scores of reporters filled the red velvet chairs at the theater of the Forum Olimpico in Rome, on July 7, 1990. João Havelange, president of FIFA, had assembled them to discuss the final of the soccer World Cup, which would take place the next day between Germany and Argentina. After an hour he was preparing to leave, but he softly asked the reporters to remain seated, because Adidas had "an important message" to convey.

As the reporters obediently remained in their seats, the FIFA logos on the screen were replaced with the Adidas Trefoil, and a beaming Bernard Tapie strode onto the stage. Some of the sports reporters gasped as they recognized the maverick owner of the Olympique Marseille, but there probably wasn't anyone in the theater who knew the two other men, Gerhard Ziener and René Jäggi.

Sporting a beige suit with a Trefoil pinned to his lapel, the Frenchman easily hijacked the stage. "Save for the birth of my children, this is the most beautiful day of my life!" he crowed. As Bernard Tapie explained, Adidas combined the three things that fascinated him most: sports, business, and politics. "The purchase of a majority stake in Adidas by a French company symbolizes the privileged and friendly relationship between Germany and France," he stated grandly, adding that it should rid the French of their complexes toward the economic might of the freshly united Germany.

The news shook the German and French establishments to their roots. For the Germans, it signified the loss of an emblematic company to a controversial French "juggler." Some newspapers described the sell-off as a national tragedy. But to the French it seemed an extraordinary catch. François Mitterrand, the French president, was quoted as saying that he was impressed. There was no denying that Bernard Tapie had struck a masterful deal.

The day after the press conference, Tapie was invited to take part in the lunch hosted for the sponsors of the World Cup. There he was, swapping stories with leading executives of Mars, JVC, and Coca-Cola. The triumph was complete when the Adidas-clad German squad won their third soccer World Cup the next day, beating Argentina, and Diego Maradona's tears fell onto his Puma boots.

Back in Herzogenaurach, Adidas employees were glued to their television screens. While some of them had heard about takeover talks, Bernard Tapie's name had never come up before. The encouraging part was that he promised to inject capital into the company. He pledged to keep the management, and Adidas was likely to be better off without the bickering Dassler sisters. On the other hand, Tapie was known for chopping up and selling his companies. This time he said he would "not sell Adidas in ten years, not in a hundred years, never."

Suzanne and Adi Dassler were equally startled by the news. Adi, Jr., was in Rome when he heard that his aunts had flogged the company to Bernard Tapie. Horst Dassler's children had granted

Described alternatively as a savior and a buffoon, Bernard Tapie proudly unveils his acquisition of Adidas at a press conference in Rome, in July 1990.

options to Metro behind their aunts' backs to pay their inheritance tax; now it was their turn to protest that they had "not been consulted in any way during the negotiations" with Bernard Tapie. "We don't know him, but we are disappointed that he chose the side of the managers, who have always been our father's enemy, particularly Mr. Jäggi," Adi angrily told *Le Figaro*.

The aftermath of the Rome conference was just as devastating for the four Dassler sisters. Since Bernard Tapie remained elusive on the price he had paid for his 80 percent of Adidas, reporters had to come up with their own estimates. The consensus was that the company and its indestructible brand should be worth at least 800 million to 1 billion German marks ($500 to $620 million). On that sad morning in Darmstadt, the Dassler sisters had obtained about half of that: they had handed over their shares for the laughable sum of about 440 million German marks ($273 million), valuing the three stripes at roughly 550 million German marks ($342 million). When they confirmed the price to the German press, the sisters stressed that Tapie had pledged to pump another 300 million German marks ($186 million) into the company, but Tapie himself boasted that the price he paid for Adidas was "ludicrously low."

Yet there was still one question that remained unanswered. As *Le Parisien* bluntly put it: "Where will the money come from?"

The honest answer was that Tapie wasn't quite sure himself. Several of his shareholders swiftly made it known that they would not contribute to the financing—it probably didn't help that they had to learn of the deal on television. The only bank that had been informed was the Crédit Lyonnais, and even they had not been given the full story. "Bernard just told them that they would have to open their check book again," Adamowicz recalled.

As the French bankers dragged their feet, Adamowicz probed his foreign contacts and obtained decisive commitments from two Japanese banks. With their faxes neatly laid out in front of him, Bernard Tapie called his French bankers. "How would you like the newspapers to report that, since you didn't have the guts to support the buy of Adidas by a Frenchman, I had to turn to Japanese banks?" he asked.

Bernard Tapie finally unveiled the terms of the financing on July 16. The press gasped again when he revealed the price of 440 million German marks ($273 million), which was to be paid entirely through bank loans. French banks were to contribute the equivalent of roughly 1 billion French francs ($184 million), while several Japanese and German firms would make up the remaining 500 million French francs ($92 million)—all to be reimbursed in a matter of just two years, with the first slice of 500 million French francs due as early as July 1991.

The agreement would soon prove deadly for Bernard Tapie, but in August 1990 he was elated. He had not only bought himself a permanent, prime seat in the most prestigious sports arenas—he had also silenced the critics who had sniped that he would be unable to get the money together.

This called for a rest on the *Phocéa*, where he invited René Jäggi. As they sailed around the Mediterranean, the two men pursued their talks about the Adidas management's stake in the company. René Jäggi walked off the boat with "a piece of paper" stating that he would obtain a 10 percent share option in BTF GmbH, the vehicle that was set up to hold Tapie's 80 percent stake in Adidas. He could not have guessed that this was just the beginning of a nerve-racking battle.

. . . .

Bernard Tapie figured that he would rule over Adidas from his office on the Avenue de Friedland, a stone's throw from the Champs-Elysées. Given his parliamentary seat and the comfort of his Hôtel de Cavoye, the Frenchman hardly thought of settling down in sleepy Herzogenaurach, but he still intended to make his presence felt there. While the managers in Germany took care of the nitty-gritty, he would hold the reins from Paris and regularly amaze the managers with his brainwaves.

To begin with, he would reinvigorate Adidas by adding some marketing chutzpah. Tapie rightly regarded this as his strongest suit. He quickly identified the marketing problems at Adidas, and summed them up with characteristic bluntness: "Adidas was tied with the world's leading javelin thrower as well as the German soccer team—you could hardly think of anything that's more naff," he scoffed. Adidas wasn't going to go anywhere as long as it continued to be seen with such athletes, which he regarded as utterly unglamorous. Bernard Tapie was even more specific when it came to Ivan Lendl, the stony-faced Czech who had won one tennis tournament after another in Adidas attire. "I mean, who on earth would want to look like this guy?" he asked.

Some of the owner's interventions caused more embarrassment. Just hours after Bernard Tapie acquired Adidas, managers were startled to read that one third of the company's (potential) profits were to be spent on charitable causes. Several weeks later he came up with another scurrilous plan that was chiefly intended to hit the headlines. "He called us very excitedly and said he wanted to drop a planeload of sports gear in Iraq during the Gulf war," one executive recalled. "He reckoned it would be great for public relations while also helping us to get rid of stock. He would have done anything to make the opening of the eight o'clock news."

As it happened, Bernard Tapie's privileged relationships with many Paris reporters caused painful headaches for the public relations managers in Herzogenaurach. The people in charge of Adidas textiles thus read in French newspapers that their owner wanted to launch an Adidas haute couture line, to be designed by Azzedine Alaïa, one of the rising Paris designers at the time. Although Adidas would team up with such fashion designers in later years, it seemed grossly inappropriate in the early nineties. While Adidas was struggling to recover its credibility in the sports business, here was Bernard Tapie blabbering on about three-striped tuxedos.

Tapie's compulsive habit of calling reporters was perfectly in line with one of his credos: "A day when I'm not in the media is a wasted day," he told Klaus Müller, the public relations manager at Adidas, who had to clean up the mess after each of Tapie's impromptu press conferences.

Most of the Adidas managers were distinctly unimpressed by the new owner. He had flown to Herzogenaurach to shake some hands after the takeover, but the visit turned into a bit of an embarrassment since only a few of the managers could speak decent French and Tapie still hadn't made any progress in English, never mind German. He talked a lot and kept some managers busy with his incessant requests, but he failed to grasp the workings of a large German company with decades of family tradition.

For all his side dealings with Bernard Tapie at the time of the takeover, René Jäggi stood by his managers. The Swiss chief executive began to irritate Tapie when the Frenchman sent over some of his friends from RSCG, a Paris-based advertising agency. Addressing the assembled Adidas board, an agency manager coolly explained that RSCG would be taking over from Y&R as international advertising agency. "René Jäggi was sitting there and told them firmly that Adidas would not be changing its agency," recalled Tom Harrington, who switched from Young and Rubicam to Adidas as a communications manager. "The one thing that Mr Tapie has to learn in Germany, he said, is that decisions are made by the executive board, not the owners."

Bernard Tapie's irritation turned to anger when Axel Markus, chief financial officer, turned down yet more disturbing demands. To begin with, Bernard Tapie requested an annual consultant's fee of nearly 5 million French francs ($920,000). Later he suggested that the Adidas board meetings could be held on board the *Phocéa*—the company would then carry 20 percent of the boat's maintenance costs. Markus, who became known as "Mr. No," infuriated Tapie by rejecting one request after the other. "I feel like I've bought a Ferrari but the driver won't drive me," the Frenchman sulked.

To exert some influence, Bernard Tapie recruited a hard-nosed board member to closely guard his interests at Adidas. Gilberte Beaux had become known in France as the right-hand woman of Jimmy Goldsmith, the English tycoon, watching over the banking arm of his conglomerate. A silver-haired lady with a penchant for gutsy entrepreneurs, she was widely respected in Paris as a tough and thorough manager. But even Beaux was unable to get a grip on the situation. "For nearly two years the managers just refused to let us take an inside look at the company," she said. "All we got from them was a cleaned-up report which didn't give us any of the details we needed to influence decisions."

Furthermore, Tapie was not making any progress in fixing the company's American problems. The deal with Peter Ueberroth was adding to the costs but it wasn't yielding any significant improvements. One of the angry rumors doing the rounds in Herzogenaurach was that one of the Contrarian managers demanded a seat for his briefcase as he flew around the country. In yet another American management change, Steve Tannen was placed at the helm of Adidas USA. While many felt that the company ought to cut costs, Tannen quickly decided to move into a disproportionately large building in Warren, New Jersey.

Bernard Tapie tried everything to convince the German establishment. To raise Tapie's profile in Frankfurt, the Adidas public relations managers arranged for the new owner to be invited as a guest speaker at a prestigious business get-together, where the Frenchman did surprisingly well. To cajole German football enthusiasts, he hired Franz Beckenbauer, the retired German football player, as a trainer for Olympique de Marseille. Still, all of this failed to alter the sarcastic mood in Germany. Tapie was constantly denigrated in the German press, which laughed at his clashes with Adidas managers. This turned out to be a much more tedious affair than Bernard Tapie had expected.

But while he had been juggling with bankers and reporters, Bernard Tapie had been far too busy to notice that Adidas was undergoing a radical internal shake-up. A gang of young mavericks had virtually taken charge.

stir it up

On a chilly morning in February 1990, a small group of dedicated Adidas executives was called to the Grand Hotel in Nuremberg. René Jäggi made it clear that they should convene discreetly, and he remained vague about the purpose of the meeting: he just wanted to introduce two Americans who had been working on an interesting concept for Adidas.

The first surprise came when the executives entered the meeting room. It seemed to be filled by a huge, bearlike American with a reddish beard and a hearty handshake. Next to him the other guest seemed effaced, with fidgety hands and a somewhat evasive look. The two men were briefly introduced as Rob Strasser and Peter Moore, general manager and creative director of Sports Inc., a small brand management company based in Portland, Oregon.

It was no coincidence that their business was located in the same place as Nike. As insiders knew, Strasser and Moore were among the hardworking and hard-playing men who had forged Nike's soul. Rob Strasser was known there as "Rolling Thunder"—a larger-than-life epitome of the "Just do it" attitude. Peter Moore was the man behind the clean creative work that had given Nike its distinctive identity.

At Nike, the two functioned as an inseparable duo. Strasser's forte was strategic thinking. He hatched business concepts and then encapsulated them in a striking formula. Moore learned to translate Strasser's lines into products that looked equally simple and efficient. Together, they made it all tie up.

Their greatest triumph was Air Jordan. They had both pushed the deal with Michael Jordan because they had immediately grasped the marketing fit, between the player who could fly and the shoes that would propel him into the air. The execution was just as remarkable: while Strasser was still talking to Jordan's agent, Moore had finished drawing the logo of the Jordan line—a basketball with a pair of wings.

However, the two had left Nike on a sour note in 1987. Rob Strasser felt slighted by Phil Knight, bitter that the Nike chief had failed to properly acknowledge the achievements of his ebullient marketing man. When he resigned, he was quickly followed by Peter Moore and several others, who regarded the upcoming Nike managers as uninspiring technocrats.

Cindy Hale was among the departures. When she joined Nike in her early twenties, she was an assistant in the marketing department, but Strasser enjoyed throwing weighty assignments at her. Upon his resignation she wrote him a letter that summed up the feelings of many colleagues. "It is the end of an era, whether you'll admit it or not," it read. "A collection of great people have learned about business, and about a brand, and about themselves, by being at your side. Wherever we go we're your real legacy. Watch us now."

Strasser and Moore then set up Sports Inc., working on several small brands. Most of their time was taken up by Van Grack, a clothing label named after an edgy Washington retailer. Strasser and Moore attempted to establish this as a sporty urban brand. But Van Grack had reached annual sales of just $7 million, and Sports Inc. was barely surviving, when in September 1989, at a Chicago trade fair, René Jäggi introduced himself to Strasser. Adidas had lost its way, the chief executive conceded. As an inspired strategist and a sports business supremo, Rob Strasser could give new impetus to the brand.

Strasser hesitated. He consulted John Horan, editor of *Sporting Goods Intelligence*, the industry's newsletter, who was unequivocal: Sports Inc. and Van Grack were far too small for Rob Strasser's boots. "You can't run on the deck of a canoe," Horan said. Adidas was an extraordinary opportunity to "get back in the game." It was also an unhoped-for opportunity to get back at Nike.

For the Nike men in the early days, Adidas was The Enemy. An advertising executive who entered the Nike building wearing a pair of Adidas shoes was made to sit through the meeting in his socks. Among Nike's gadgets was a bag with the slogan "One swoosh is better than three stripes." At a sales meeting in the late seventies, Phil Knight was even blunter about the rivalry: "This industry is like Snow White and the Seven Dwarfs," he once told assembled sales managers. "Adidas is Snow White. This year, we became the biggest dwarf. And next year, we're going to get in her pants."

To beat Adidas, Nike didn't shy away from dubious references to the brand's German origins. Adidas people were routinely described as "The Huns," loathed for their arrogant supremacy in the sports business. In a pitch to the management of Wimbledon, Peter Moore appealed to the war memories of Buzzer Hadingham, Wimbledon chairman and World War II veteran. A poster for the winning pitch featured an aerial shot of Wimbledon after a German bomb attack—"Courtesy of our three-striped friends," read the tagline.

But by the end of the eighties, Adidas was no longer an issue. Reebok had been recast as The Enemy, while Adidas seemed to have disappeared, at least from the American market. "They seemed to be kind of lost in space, and nobody cared," said Peter Moore. "It wasn't like they were bad, they just didn't exist."

The same applied to Puma. While the brand had long held its ground in the United States, the Kmart fiasco had relegated Puma to discount status. It seemed almost unreal that the brand had once been coveted by world-class athletes, and been sported by such cool icons as Joe Namath and Walt Frazier.

For Adidas, Strasser and Moore quickly figured out that the brand should get back to its roots. They knew Adidas as the brand that equipped athletes, providing them with the tools they needed to compete. Therefore, they suggested a line of clean-cut, no-frills sports shoes and apparel. To distinguish this line from the flowery and fashion-oriented products turned out by Adidas, they called it Equipment.

The intuition of the two consultants was reinforced after their first visit to Herzogenaurach, in November 1989. They briefly outlined the Equipment concept, backing up their presentation with four simple boards. René Jäggi then led them to the second floor of the head office. There, Adidas displayed many of the samples crafted by Adi Dassler, as well as shoes worn by Olympic athletes and soccer heroes.

The two former Nike managers were flabbergasted. It suddenly dawned on Moore that Adi Dassler had invented the whole sports industry. It seemed to him that half of the shoes launched by Nike in the seventies had been unwittingly knocked off from Adi Dassler inventions. "I was truly blown away by it," said Moore. As he saw it, that made the Equipment concept all the more compelling.

Upon their return to Portland, Strasser and Moore built on their idea. Within a couple of weeks they had produced a thick black folder explaining Equipment. Fearing that the project might alienate his German staff, coming from two former Nike managers, René Jäggi called some of his closest advisers to the Grand Hotel. Present were Bernd Wahler, the marketing man; Tom Harrington, in charge of international communications; and Peter Rduch, the steady export and development manager.

Aided by some archive material, Strasser referred to Adi Dassler as "the equipment manager of the world," an unostentatious craftsman who had built his business on inventions that genuinely benefited athletes. That was what Adidas stood for. Strasser rightly predicted that, after the excesses of the eighties, consumers would yearn for a return to basics. The answer was Equipment, the best of Adidas—a line with only simple but high-quality products that would have obtained Adi Dassler's stamp of approval.

As they sat through the presentation, the managers looked at each other in disbelief. Over the previous years they had been struggling to define the identity of Adidas. Under attack, the brand had been going in all directions. And here were these two Americans, flown in from the other side of the world, who hadn't spent a day at Adidas and yet had grasped the legacy of Adi Dassler with more clarity than the men who walked under his framed portrait every day. "We all had goose bumps," said Bernd Wahler. "They caught it all with such simplicity that it was almost humiliating."

As for Peter Rduch, an early export manager, he could not believe what he was seeing. At Adidas since the sixties, he had earned the trust of Adi and Käthe Dassler, and had helped to cover the world in three stripes. Later, Horst Dassler and René Jäggi had come to appreciate Rduch as a reliable manager and a dedicated guardian of the Adidas heritage. They called him "the conscience of the brand." That morning at the Grand Hotel, Rduch was stunned. "They got everything precisely right," he said. "It was just unreal."

. . . .

René Jäggi wanted to keep it all under wraps until an international sales meeting three months later. By then, the Portland crew would have to come up with samples of Equipment products and a spectacular presentation.

The problems started as soon as the Americans began to hold talks with the relevant Adidas managers. The timelines imposed by the former Nike managers were far too short: the Adidas tanker could not be turned around in such a short time. Rob Strasser and Peter Moore heard the same line over and over again: "It can't be done."

The Americans were met with particular resistance in the apparel division. Established in the renovated stables of a castle in Fontainebleau, south of Paris, the division was headed up by Karl-Otto Lang, a hardheaded German manager. His apparel sales had been mushrooming in Europe over the previous years, owing largely to the takeoff of tennis apparel, with lines named after the German tennis star Steffi Graf and her male counterpart, Swede Stefan Edberg. The shirts were all sorts of colors, featuring anything from orchids to pheasants.

Predictably, Karl-Otto Lang was not impressed with the Equipment designs, all plain garments in green, black, and white. "Nobody wants a sweatshirt just like that," he said. But Peter Moore regarded the tennis line as a glaring symptom of Adidas's problems. "Well, there are people in the world who don't want to look like a piece of wallpaper," he shot back. Karl-Otto Lang reluctantly agreed to give Equipment a try—but he still insisted "it can't be done."

Exasperated, Rob Strasser turned to Mary McGoldrick. He had met her several years earlier covered in grease and fuzz while she was cleaning up her grandmother's apparel plant. She was then married to a Nike development manager in New Hampshire, and Strasser had wanted to convince her that the couple needed to move to Oregon. By the end of the meeting, Strasser didn't care much what McGoldrick's husband would do at the company, but he had a firm offer for her. A remarkably talented and tenacious woman, Mary McGoldrick was instrumental in the buildup of Nike's fledgling apparel business. When Strasser and Moore left Nike, she followed suit, becoming the third founding partner of Sports Inc.

McGoldrick was told she had six weeks to develop the fabrics and to produce the samples that were required for the Equipment launch. She spent all of that time in Asia, leaning on trusted partners. When she returned, she was hauling thirteen huge sacks stuffed with Equipment samples. It could be done after all.

. . . .

Hatched under a code name, the Equipment concept was revealed to Adidas employees and distributors in April 1990 at the Vereinshaus, a large hall in Herzogenaurach. Cindy Hale, brands development manager at Sports Inc., had prepared a dazzling presentation. To underline the weight attached to it, René Jäggi invited several members of the Dassler family, who then still owned the company. Nearly all of them turned up.

They listened intently as René Jäggi, Rob Strasser, and Tom Harrington went through the Equipment project. As the managers explained, there was no point in trying to out-Nike Nike. Adidas had something else that was entirely unique: the story and genius of Adi Dassler. Nike could always come up with another Air, but only Adidas could do Equipment.

A ripple of excitement went through the audience when a new logo was blown up on the screen. Strasser and Moore suggested that, to distinguish Equipment from other Adidas products, they were to be fitted with their own logo: instead of the Trefoil, the Equipment clothes and the heels of the shoes would feature three slanted stripes in growing order, forming a sort of triangle.

When the lights went on again, Jäggi stood up to hug the two Americans, and applause erupted in the hall. Some managers felt uneasy about the newcomers, wondering why a bunch of outsiders had been asked to tinker with the soul of Adidas. But the response was overwhelmingly positive, and scores of excited managers rushed to congratulate Rob Strasser. "We should have done this a long time ago," they said. "You are exactly what we need."

Never shy of commitment, Rob Strasser took them at their word. To help implement Equipment, he was prepared to settle down in Herzogenaurach. And while he was at it, he thought he might as well overhaul the company.

. . . .

Rob Strasser always drew inspiration from music. He picked his words with deadly accuracy, and his choice of soundtracks was equally precise. During his stay in Herzogenaurach, the record he played most abundantly was "Stir It Up," by Patti LaBelle.

When he returned to Herzogenaurach in August 1990, the

company didn't exactly roll out the red carpet. Strasser was not properly introduced, and René Jäggi hadn't even thought of an office for him. He just squatted in the staff coffee meeting room and declared it his office.

It was left to Owen Clemens to gather some furnishings. A former driver at Nike, Clemens had turned into Rob Strasser's personal assistant, friend, driver, valet, and shadow. He was the only person who could decipher Strasser's scribbles and turn them into coherent text. When Strasser decided to move to Germany, Clemens didn't hesitate to follow. For several weeks, he spent much of his time befriending the ladies who brought coffee around the offices, and the security guards; they would give him access to the Adidas building after five o'clock, when the halls were deserted. He would then roam around the offices, collecting one stapler here and a couple of pens there.

Once Strasser was all set, the company's managers were in for a vigorous shake-up. Most of them had grown accustomed to the cumbersome Adidas structure. Employees grudgingly respected the formalities that prevailed in other German companies at the time, turning up at the sports company in impeccable suits and addressing each other with "Herr Doktor." They wrote lengthy memos and strictly respected hierarchy.

To Rob Strasser, forty-three, all of this was unbearable. A lawyer by training, he had learned at Nike to ignore bureaucratic obstacles and to bulldoze ahead with concrete projects. He regularly turned up at the office in Hawaiian shirts, and when he didn't, his sleeves would often be covered in scribbles. There was even a rumor that, when asked to sum up his thoughts in a memo, he had handed over a photocopy of his hands.

From his coffee room, Rob Strasser observed German corporate life with disbelief. While Germans were supposed to cultivate a strict work ethic, the company's corridors were deserted long before dark. When they traveled, Adidas executives deemed it normal to spend a few days recuperating. And while he knew that the company was suffering, the parking lot was full of expensive company cars.

When his turn came to pick a company car, Rob Strasser decided to set the example by asking for a Trabant, a boxy East German car. The request was turned down, but Strasser obtained another vehicle that was just slightly less grotty. "In the summer heat, poor Owen had to drive in this smelly old car without air conditioning," Tom Harrington recalled. "That was Rob's way of protesting the corporate culture."

To some Adidas executives, Strasser's unorthodox personality could be overwhelming. He regularly threw fits, which deeply embarrassed the composed German managers. They were perplexed by his occasionally foul language and gruff appearance, as he permanently gestured, shook with laughter, jumped up, waved his arms, and tugged at his clothes. When he braced himself for a rough meeting, he tied a red football sock around his arm, like a warrior.

Yet Strasser's persuasive charm still took Adidas by storm. An intense talker, he filled a room with his presence, as well as with his huge frame. He quickly took over any space he entered, from a coffee shop to an airplane. With sheer charisma and the right choice of words, he could enthuse a roomful of seasoned executives. "He could give someone a fountain pen and tell them to go to war, and they would go," said Cindy Hale, "because he could get them that revved up."

In this respect, Rob Strasser often drew inspiration from war tales. Winston Churchill was his all-time hero. The shelves of his Oregon beach house were filled with war books. After a few months in Europe, Owen Clemens refused to accompany Strasser on any more London weekends because he knew that he would be taken along for yet another tour of the Imperial War Museum.

One of the war scenes that fascinated Strasser most was a sequence from the film *The Battle of the Bulge*. It featured the commander of a Third Reich Panzer unit meeting up with a team of adolescent recruits. Fired up by the commander, the youngsters started belting out, one by one, a fraternal army hymn. "Rob, the Germans are a little sensitive about this Nazi thing," Peter Moore objected. But Strasser invited German executives into his hotel room and played the clip at full blast, excitedly asking them to translate.

His methods ruffled some feathers, yet fresh Adidas executives watched excitedly as Strasser whirled through the company. They had long regarded Adidas as a "sleeping giant" that urgently needed to be shaken out its lethargy. Their efforts had constantly been hampered by the tedious aspects of the organization, which had prevented them from getting things done. "It was like running through a swamp," said Tom Harrington.

While he was meant to watch over Equipment, Rob Strasser quickly became the epicenter of the company. He was mobbed by a group of young executives who yearned to be part of his entourage, because they knew that he made things happen. "He was like Elvis," said Cindy Hale. "All the guys wanted to be around him." From among them, he picked a crew of go-getting Adidas managers who were prepared to stir it up with him.

. . . .

As it became clear that the Adidas battleship could not handle Equipment, Rob Strasser took it into his own hands. To run the concept he recruited Bernd Wahler, the most enthusiastic marketing man he could find, and placed him at the head of a special business unit for Equipment.

For the launch in 1991, Strasser and Moore had prepared advertising material with catchy lines that neatly encapsulated Equipment as a return to functional products. "Enough is enough," they wrote, "All you need and nothing more," and "Only the essentials." Just a few months earlier, the Germans had turned a dark page in their history and changed the face of world politics by tearing down the Berlin wall. With Equipment, "the Germans are about to knock down another wall," read a folder printed for leading retailers. It was then left to each of the distributors and subsidiaries to push the concept as they saw fit.

The two Americans embarked on a long round of presentations to each of the countries, to convince them that they needed Equipment. Time and time again, they were stupefied by the behavior of Adidas salesmen, who seemed to find fault with everything. They had never come across any such hemming and hawing at Nike, where salespeople just took the products and ran out to sell them.

They attempted to whip up the American sales force at a meeting in Arizona, but the response remained lukewarm. The sales force did not seem to believe that Equipment would enable them to take back any shelf space from Nike and Reebok. Their halfhearted efforts were symptomatic of the Adidas setup in the United States at that time: the company's American subsidiary was headed by executives from Peter Ueberroth's Contrarian group, who charged huge consultants' fees but never fully meshed with the company.

Strasser and Moore themselves profited handsomely from Equipment. Under their deal with René Jäggi, Sports Inc. was to pocket 10 percent of the sales generated by the line. Equipment sales ended up making about 10 percent of the company's turnover after two years. Most important, the project and its instigators triggered vital changes. On a small scale, the Equipment business unit worked precisely the way Rob Strasser thought Adidas should operate: with a small team in charge of a specific line, from development to sale.

With René Jäggi's blessing, Rob Strasser strove to expand the concept to the whole company. He traveled all around Europe looking for managers to be placed at the head of other business units. Along with Equipment, five of them were set up to cover running, football, basketball, tennis, and hiking. From then on, Strasser and his gang of impetuous "bums" (business unit managers) virtually ran the company. While Bernard Tapie battled with his bankers and René Jäggi struggled to keep the company out of trouble, they could rightly claim that their drive and focused projects gave the impetus for the brand's revival.

The bums became so self-confident that when Rob Strasser decided it was time for him to return to Portland, they staged a rebellion. It was announced to them in January 1992 that the business units would be led by Karl-Otto Lang, head of the fast-growing apparel business. Alarmed by the news, Bernd Wahler called a meeting with all the other managers and asked for their opinions. The response was unanimous: there was no way they would accept Karl-Otto Lang as their superior. Bernd Wahler then walked over to René Jäggi's office and presented him with an ultimatum. If Karl-Otto Lang were appointed as head of the business units, they would all quit.

Furious, Jäggi called a meeting at his house in Nuremberg that evening. The business unit managers and Rob Strasser were led down to the wine-tasting cellar, where each of them was asked to choose a bottle from the plentiful racks. Then Jäggi resorted to an odd management trick: he asked the young mavericks to pick their own boss.

. . . .

Engrossed in their tasks, the bums ignored the troubles that were gripping the company at large. Only a few of them ever met Bernard Tapie, and they weren't interested in his dealings. To the young executives, the disaster reports about Adidas seemed completely out of sync with what was happening around them. But due to the very long time required for products to reach the market, it would take nearly two years before the repercussions of Rob Strasser's shake-up hit the bottom line.

To make sure that Adidas could still report a profit for 1990, Bernard Tapie ordered an asset sale. The companies Horst Dassler had accumulated on the side were to be sold before the end of the year. Much to the chagrin of Horst Dassler's children, the Auberge du Kochersberg, Arena, and Pony would all be part of the sell-off, along with some rights to Le Coq Sportif.

For Le Coq Sportif, one of the largest chunks, René Jäggi entered talks with Descente, the Adidas licensee in Japan, who was willing to acquire the Far East and Southeast Asian rights. To balance the books and save Bernard Tapie's face, René Jäggi went to Alaska in the middle of his Christmas break.

The meeting in Anchorage turned into a bit of a farce, when Jäggi and the Descente executives got caught in a massive bar brawl between Alaskan bushmen. Anxious to close the deal, they remained seated while beer bottles flew around them. The Japanese-speaking chief executive returned with a generous present for Tapie: a check of 56 million German marks that would enable the company to close its books with a net profit of nearly 52 million German marks. Bernard Tapie had obtained a short reprieve.

Yet there was a much larger problem looming for Tapie, as the French bankers who had lent him the money to buy Adidas would soon be sitting in his anteroom. The unpleasant conversations the Frenchman anticipated turned into a nerve-racking poker game, with Adidas at stake.

triple bluff

With his shock of white hair and his penchant for bow ties, Stephen Rubin cut an original figure among England's business elite. He was known as a philanthropist, donating funds to an array of social causes and giving impassioned speeches about the need for education in the poorest Far Eastern countries.

Rubin had been toying with footwear since his boyhood in Liverpool, where his Polish-born parents, Minnie and Berko, set up the Liverpool Shoe Company, which made ordinary footwear. Stephen, their only child, took over the reins in 1969 and renamed the company Pentland. While the British shoe industry collapsed, he shrewdly explored production in Far Eastern countries and effectively transformed Pentland into an investment and trading company.

But the deal that made Rubin came in 1981. He was then approached by Paul Fireman, the small-time businessman who had obtained an American production and sales license for Reebok. Rubin acquired a 55 percent stake in Paul Fireman's company, at a price of $77,500. Once he had finished selling off his shares in 1991, Rubin had netted $777 million. "I made a few bob," as he put it.

Rubin's track record and his little war chest had inevitably drawn the attention of Bernard Tapie. Already when he had bought Adidas, Tapie had sought the support of Stephen Rubin and offered him an option to buy up to 33 percent in the company anytime over the next three years. When Rubin then attempted to exercise the option, Bernard Tapie cried that there had been a misunderstanding. The two were preparing to face the judges in Paris in June 1991 when the Frenchman suddenly changed his mind.

The problem was that, in just a few weeks, his bankers would call in 500 million French francs ($86.6 million), and his coffers were still desperately empty. Tapie had agreed to repay the entire loan for the acquisition of Adidas in just two years on the premise that his French bankers would manage to sell off some of his other assets. But the economic situation was most unfavourable for any such deals, and many investors wouldn't have touched Tapie's assets with a ten-foot pole anyway. Under the circumstances, Bernard Tapie figured that Rubin's millions could turn out to be providential.

By August 7, 1991, the two men signed a pact that would reduce Tapie's stake in BTF GmbH from 100 percent to 55 percent. As part of the reshuffle, Stephen Rubin would get a 20.05 percent share of BTF GmbH, at a price of 134.5 million German marks ($81 million). An assortment of French banks and insurance companies agreed to swap part of their Tapie debts for Adidas shares. They held a combined stake of 20 percent in BTF GmbH, while another 5 percent went to Gilberte Beaux.

However, Rubin shrewdly exploited Tapie's desperate situation to obtain some extras. Among other concessions, he got voting rights that amounted to a blocking minority, a seat on the supervisory board, and a preemption clause: in other words, if Bernard Tapie wanted to sell his remaining shares in Adidas, he would have to offer them to Pentland first.

The Englishman unambiguously stated that, in his eyes, his investment in Adidas was the opening move for a full-fledged acquisition. "Reebok was just an appetizer; the main course will be Adidas," he boasted.

. . . .

One year further down the road, as the bankers were preparing to call in the second installment of their loan, neither Adidas nor Tapie's financial situation had improved much. But the Frenchman's outlook entirely changed on April 2, 1992, just before eleven o'clock at night, when the secretary-general of the Elysée stood on the palace steps and read out the names of new ministers in the latest government under socialist president François Mitterrand. Monsieur Bernard Tapie would be in charge of urban affairs.

Tapie reportedly wept as he settled into his plush ministerial seat, and he invited all of his friends to inspect the chandeliers. To become part of the government, he had agreed to give up any other activities that could be regarded as conflicting with his new obligations—a list led by Adidas. Less than two years earlier Adidas had been "the deal of [his] life," but the comfort of a VIP lounge in a soccer stadium wasn't quite as seductive as the trappings of his ministry.

The euphoria was short-lived, however. Bernard Tapie had barely learned to find his way in the ministry when he was assailed by a series of embarrassing problems. To begin with, employees of an Adidas plant in the Alsace that was to be closed down threatened to stage a demonstration in front of his office. Then Olympique de Marseille, the soccer club he owned, became embroiled in a financial scandal.

But the toughest blow came from a French judge, who indicted Tapie as part of a dispute with a former business partner, Georges Tranchant, unrelated to Adidas. Under the political mores that prevailed in France, this forced Tapie to leave the government, to make sure that he would not seek to influence the investigations. He resigned on May 23, 1992, after just forty-eight days in office.

He would be allowed to return only if he sold his business and his legal matters were cleared up.

Stephen Rubin was the obvious candidate to help Tapie get rid of Adidas, but the Englishman was in no hurry. "In all the deals we did with Tapie, one of the techniques was to sit back and wait, because it seemed likely that he would dig a hole and fall in it," Rubin explained.

Except that Bernard Tapie had his own plan to secure a quick exit: over the Easter weekend he called René Jäggi for urgent talks at the BTF offices in Paris and persuaded the chief executive to put together a management buyout offer by the end of June. If René Jäggi truly managed to garner the funds for a buyout, that was fine. Just as interestingly for Tapie, a management bid would force Stephen Rubin to give up the waiting game and promptly issue a counter bid.

With Tapie in a hurry and Jäggi somewhat dazzled, the two quickly shook hands and phoned Stephen Rubin. At the other end of the line, the Englishman was aghast. "I wouldn't like to sit in a nuclear submarine with you, René," he said. "With such a jittery fellow at the wheel we would soon have a World War Three." But Jäggi ignored him and spent the next day preparing his bid with John Botts, a London investment banker.

Over the next weeks, the two of them hit the road to meet investors with a thick prospectus called Juno, after the code name of the proposed management buyout. Many of the managers who struggled to redress Adidas were appalled by the new imbroglio. Yet again their company was being thrown into play, and their chief executive was right in the middle of it.

René Jäggi threw his cards on the table when he excitedly declared that he had submitted his bid to Bernard Tapie on June 25, 1992. The offer was worth 1 billion German marks ($640 million) for the whole of Adidas, and Jäggi stressed that it came with a deadline: five days hence, on June 30, when Adidas shareholders were due to convene for their annual meeting.

However, Stephen Rubin didn't rush to his phone. When the Tuesday deadline passed without any response from Pentland, the deadline was discreetly postponed for the following Friday. Adidas employees anxiously waited until the end of the week. They began to believe that the management may well have won when they opened their Saturday newspapers and still didn't find news of any counter offer by Stephen Rubin.

But by then, the Juno prospectus had long been buried in Bernard Tapie's wastebasket. While Adidas employees were left guessing about Rubin's intentions, he had taken his seat at the negotiating table. It was unfortunate that Jäggi's bid had forced him to act immediately, but there was no way that he was going to let Adidas slip.

The talks lasted for two days and two nights. Gilberte Beaux showed remarkable stamina, but Stephen Rubin was equally meticulous. The outcome was revealed by bleary-eyed lawyers at seven o'clock in the morning of July 7, 1992: Stephen Rubin would be the new owner of Adidas. The Englishman, who had acquired just over 20 percent of BTF GmbH one year earlier, would fork over 621 million German marks ($398 million) for the remaining 80 percent.

The news was greeted with huge relief in Herzogenaurach. After all the agitation of the previous years, when Adidas was constantly starved for cash and hitting the headlines for the wrong reasons, their fate would be in the hands of a trustworthy, experienced entrepreneur.

Since he held a seat on the Adidas supervisory board, Rubin was well aware of the company's troubles. However, he felt certain that he could tackle them. After all, the weakness that continued to strangle Adidas was the high cost of its production, which was precisely Pentland's forte. And the Englishman had demonstrated his marketing savvy through his dealings with several others sports brands.

The late-night deal with Gilberte Beaux was subject to a three-month-long audit, which would be concluded toward the middle of October 1992. A lawyer by training, Stephen Rubin was known to be very rigorous with his acquisitions, but all were convinced that the audit would proceed smoothly.

Although the Englishman hadn't yet signed the check for the company, some managers began to report to him. Bob McCulloch and Tom Harrington, in charge of marketing and communications respectively, regularly flew over to London to discuss their plans. For several weeks, Bob McCulloch shared his office with Andy Rubin, Stephen's son, who specialized in marketing. Axel Markus, chief financial officer, had to clear part of his office for Frank Farrant, his counterpart at Pentland.

As it dragged on, however, the audit stirred deep ill feelings in Herzogenaurach. Adidas executives had gladly opened their doors to Pentland colleagues in July, but they hadn't expected their offices to be squatted in for months. Entire armies of lawyers and accountants had descended on Herzogenaurach to go through the books. Some managers felt that they were "crawling all over the place," about sixty of them milling around production plants, talking to distributors and other partners. And still Stephen Rubin hadn't signed that check for ownership of the company.

Bernard Tapie and the other shareholders swallowed their pride in September, when Rubin asked for a cut of about 50 million German marks ($32 million) and the continuation of the audit. For the second time, Bernard Tapie was prepared to give in, but the other shareholders decided to stand firm. At a meeting at Hotel Napoleon in Paris, they agreed that Bernard Tapie should not be allowed to further downgrade Adidas.

Gilberte Beaux, his personal adviser, fully agreed. She was incensed by the methods used for the audit, which was sapping morale at Adidas. Stephen Rubin argued that Pentland was a listed company, therefore he could not afford to leave any stones unturned at Adidas. He was annoyed by the tough behavior of the Frenchwoman, whom he regarded as "an awful amount of trouble." But Gilberte Beaux felt that the Pentland crew "purposely destabilized the company to buy it more cheaply" and "their behaviour was odious."

The matter came to a head on October 5, 1992, just one week before the supposed end of the audit. An emissary for Stephen Rubin then called at the private office of Gilberte Beaux on the

Rond-Point des Champs-Elysées to say that the lawyers had uncovered another problem. There had been some technical irregularities in the acquisition of Adidas shares by Bernard Tapie. Stephen Rubin needed another two months to obtain clearance by the German courts.

But by then, Gilberte Beaux had become completely exasperated with the Englishman and decided that he would not ride roughshod over her. She urgently needed an answer because the banks and shareholders were to convene within days to decide on the company's fate. So Beaux had the full backing of the banks when she issued an ultimatum to Stephen Rubin, demanding that he provide his final verdict on Adidas by midnight on Wednesday, October 14, 1992.

That evening, a group of French and German bankers sat huddled with Gilberte Beaux in her office in Paris, waiting for the phone to ring. To everyone's amazement, it never did. On Thursday, October 15, Pentland issued a statement confirming that it would not proceed with the acquisition of Adidas. "The investigations have revealed a number of matters of which Pentland was not previously aware," it ominously added, without any further explanation.

Beaux was fuming. The withdrawal of Stephen Rubin's offer was a disaster for Tapie and the company, but it was made far worse by Pentland's statement. As things stood, Rubin had blocked the sale of Adidas for three months and then dumped it with an innuendo that was certain to scare off any other potential buyers. Gilberte Beaux vehemently denied that there was anything nasty hidden in Adidas and angrily depicted Stephen Rubin as a carpetbagger who was merely playing around with companies to grab them for a song.

Since Rubin refused to elaborate on the troubles allegedly uncovered by his due diligence, speculation was rife. Some referred to huge inventories that were supposedly found in a warehouse in Antwerp. Others believed that Rubin had decided to walk away due to the massive devaluation of the pound against the deutschemark in the summer of 1992. To finance the Adidas deal in July,

Stephen Rubin had acquired millions of deutschemarks. Due to the rise in the exchange rate, he made a considerable profit on this move alone. Another argument was that Germany had just been rocked by a series of attacks by neo-Nazis. Minnie Rubin feared that her son, a Jewish entrepreneur who would have had to slash jobs in Germany, might have come under attack.

Many years later, Stephen Rubin argued that the failure of the deal was caused partly by the intransigence of Gilberte Beaux. "It was bluff and double-bluff, and she was too clever by half," he said. On the other hand, the Pentland chairman admitted that the due diligence didn't uncover any shattering problem. "It was nothing to do with the inner workings of Adidas," he said. "If it had been just me, I would have gone ahead and bought it."

From there on, Gilberte Beaux had three days to prepare for a grueling meeting with the bankers, who had just seen their last hope turn his back on Adidas.

. . . .

In a drab hotel meeting room in Munich, the silver-haired Frenchwoman was surrounded by about fifteen stern-looking German bankers, leading executives from the country's most powerful financial institutions, who had invested millions in Adidas. They had been extremely patient with the hapless Dassler sisters. They had held their collective breath with Bernard Tapie. But after the Pentland fiasco, many figured that the time had come to cut their losses.

The problems that were stacking up on the other side of the Aurach River in Herzogenaurach weren't very encouraging for the bankers, either. Since Armin Dassler had been forced to sell Puma, the company had been tossed around between several Swiss and Swedish owners. Chief executives had come and gone in quick succession, but none had managed to return any significant profits. Puma made its largest volume of sales with a cheap tennis shoe. Plagued by many of the same problems, it seemed that Adidas didn't have much more of a chance to survive the onslaught of its two American rivals.

Far from being intimidated, Gilberte Beaux went through her opening statement with poise and conviction. Based on her discussions with executives and the figures she had amassed, she pleaded with the bankers to give the company another few months. True, Adidas was heading toward abyssal losses, and sales looked set to decline by at least another 10 percent for the year, but she was absolutely certain that they would pick up imminently.

Most of the bankers around the table did not realize just how urgently Adidas needed their cash. In the corridors at Adidas there were rumors that the company would struggle to pay staff wages for October. Axel Markus, chief financial officer, had warned Beaux that the company had "no liquidity at all," and if they failed to reach an agreement with the banks in Munich, the company's credit lines would cover less than two weeks.

Preparing for the worst, just before the meeting with the bankers, Axel Markus had walked down to the office of Herbert Hainer, then sales manager of Adidas Germany. "How do you think our German customers would feel if we failed to make salaries on time for October?" Markus asked. Hainer was so startled that it took him several seconds to reply that "it probably wouldn't go down too well."

However, Gilberte Beaux easily obtained the backing of the French banks, Crédit Lyonnais and Banque du Phénix. Since the French bankers had agreed that Adidas could not be sold to Stephen Rubin at a reduced price, they would have to lead its rescue. At the meeting in Munich, Gilberte Beaux urged them to make a last-ditch commitment. After all that it had already invested, Crédit Lyonnais promised to secure a decent exit for the German bankers, whatever happened.

The wary German bankers gave their approval. They would close ranks behind their French colleagues and contribute to another cash injection. Gilberte Beaux would be appointed as chief executive until a more lasting solution was found for the company.

In Herzogenaurach, the relief about the rescue was mixed with some incredulity as René Jäggi left the company with the millions he had been promised by Bernard Tapie in case the management bid failed, and Madame Beaux, a demurely dressed Frenchwoman with silver hair tied up in a bun, settled in the chief executive's chair. The sniggers rapidly died down, though. As she bulldozed ahead with cutbacks and restructuring measures, Beaux earned the respect of the most hardheaded managers in Herzogenaurach.

Back in Paris, Bernard Tapie was fidgeting. Bernard Tapie Finance and its majority stake in Adidas were the only things standing in the way of his return to his ministerial office. Gutted by the withdrawal of Stephen Rubin, Tapie harassed his bankers and the finance ministry to find another solution. He closely followed the talks instigated by Beaux and sank into increasing despair as the list of potential investors continued to shrink.

The French banks became so desperate that they attempted to reopen talks with Stephen Rubin. But the Pentland chairman decided to exit entirely, selling off his remaining 20.05 percent stake at the end of November 1992. Not only had the banks failed to get rid of Adidas, they had also exposed themselves a little further by adding 147.5 million German marks ($94.5 million) on Tapie's tab. They began to concoct another improbable plan—one that would draw all the protagonists into an extravagant imbroglio.

. . . .

On November 7, 1992, Jean-Paul Tchang, the general manager of Banque du Phénix, one of the French banks that rescued Adidas, had given up his Saturday morning to meet yet another Canadian investor at the apartment of Gilberte Beaux. But it soon became clear that the talks were going nowhere, and Tchang's thoughts began to drift. He then tore a little piece of paper from his notebook. He scribbled the words "Robert Louis-Dreyfus" and passed on the message to his neighbor, Henri Filho.

As chairman of Clinvest, investment banking arm of Crédit Lyonnais, Henri Filho was leading the search for Adidas investors. He was up to his neck in the Adidas file. The bank was owed at least 1.1 billion French francs ($208 million) by Bernard Tapie, who was technically bankrupt, and it was saddled with 10 percent in Adidas. Trying to sell Adidas, he had suffered one rejection after the next.

When they wrapped up their talks that Saturday morning, Jean-Paul Tchang explained what he knew about Robert Louis-Dreyfus. Heir to one of France's wealthiest banking and trading dynasties, peddling ships, cereals, and weapons, Louis-Dreyfus had long been regarded as its black sheep. After his studies at Harvard Business School and a spell at SG Warburg, the American investment bank, he had spent a few years at the Louis-Dreyfus Group. Yet he quickly acknowledged that he wouldn't have the patience to climb the ladder in the family conglomerate and instead joined IMS, a small American company specialized in research for the health market. Among the tight-knit group of IMS was Christian Tourres, another Frenchman. When Louis-Dreyfus joined the company in 1983, its value was estimated at $400 million. Five years later it was sold for $1.7 billion, and the two Frenchmen both made enough to retire.

That's precisely what Louis-Dreyfus did, until Charles and Maurice Saatchi called, toward the end of 1989. Their advertising agency was in the doldrums after several gluttonous acquisitions, and they needed a new chief executive to clean up the mess. As it happened, Louis-Dreyfus was just beginning to get bored. "My friends weren't available because they were all still working," he explained. With his droopy face, unruly curls, and thick cigars, Louis-Dreyfus came across as the millionaire version of a dilettante. Impeccable British bankers frowned when the relaxed chairman welcomed them in a pair of socks. Introduced by the Saatchis to serious poker circles in London, he soon became known as one of the sharpest players in town. Profiles never failed to mention his Peugeot 205, the sandwiches he wolfed down for lunch, his American cousin Julia, of *Seinfeld* fame, and the date he once allegedly wrangled with actress Kim Basinger.

When Louis-Dreyfus heard of Jean-Paul Tchang's offer to have him and Tourres appointed to the helm of Adidas, he responded coolly. Surely he could not be expected to throw himself into Adidas, which so many others had turned down, for a simple salary. He and Tourres didn't exactly need jobs. They would con-

Robert Louis-Dreyfus anxiously watches the performance of his team, Olympique de Marseille. He had more joy with Adidas.

sider rolling up their sleeves only if the banks offered prospects of sizeable share ownership.

Undeterred, Jean-Paul Tchang invited Louis-Dreyfus and Tourres for dinner in London. He then introduced the two men to Henri Filho, general manager of Clinvest. Before the main course was served, Filho became convinced that Tchang was right: Louis-Dreyfus and Tourres were exactly the right men. Filho didn't hesitate to offer them a substantial stake in the company.

Egged on by the bankers, Louis-Dreyfus delved into the sports market. To check the extent of the brand's problems, he spent three days reading through the thick study commissioned by Stephen Rubin as part of his due diligence, but he could not find any indication of the "number of matters" Rubin had cited to call off his acquisition of Adidas back in October 1992.

In the interval, on December 16, 1992, Bernard Tapie revealed, in full-page ads in financial papers, that he had reached a settlement with Crédit Lyonnais, his lead banker. Paving the way for Tapie's return to politics, the agreement called for the dissolution of Bernard Tapie Finances (BTF) and indicated that Tapie should sell his 78 percent stake in BTF GmbH by February 15, 1993. This self-imposed deadline wouldn't make talks for the sale of Adidas any easier for Crédit Lyonnais. Further reducing any room for negotiations, the public settlement between the bank and Bernard Tapie set a price of 2.08 billion French francs ($367 million) for his stake in Adidas, in line with the Rubin offer. Exactly one week later, Tapie was reinstated as minister of urban affairs.

An avid poker player, Louis-Dreyfus seized on the commitments contained in this settlement to heighten the pressure on the bankers. Less than one month before the deadline set by Tapie, Jean-Paul Tchang's fax machine sputtered out a letter from Louis-Dreyfus: to the banker's consternation, Louis-Dreyfus explained that the whole Adidas deal was off because he had accepted an offer by his cousin Gérard to take a leading position at the Dreyfus Group. "By then I had quit looking for any alternatives," sighed Jean-Paul Tchang. "If the agreement with Louis-Dreyfus fell through, we would have to start all over again, with less than six weeks to go before the deadline imposed by Tapie and a long list of rejections in our pocket."

After a panicked phone call, Jean-Paul Tchang and Henri Filho hopped on the next plane to Zurich, where Louis-Dreyfus spent all of his weekends. The two were even more determined to get Louis-Dreyfus on board when they discovered all the sports memorabilia in his home. "The walls were covered with snapshots of legendary games and players," Tchang recalled. They begged and pleaded until Louis-Dreyfus agreed to reconsider. The condition was that the prospective deal should allow him and his friends to control all of Adidas.

The fax was part of a finely honed routine that Louis-Dreyfus and Christian Tourres further refined over the following weeks. "I was the nit-picker who found fault with everything," said Tourres, "and Robert the somewhat aloof but fundamentally benevolent investor who was always prepared to patch things up." Nearly fifteen years into the deal, the concessions the two obtained along the way would continue to stir controversy.

The sale of Adidas was finally settled at seven o'clock on Thursday, February 11, 1993, after two full days and nights of talks. Completely exhausted, Henri Filho was driving home when he fell asleep at the wheel. The crash caused only minor leg injuries, but when the deal was unveiled the next day, Filho and the other bankers suffered a barrage of criticism.

Based on a leak, a report in *Les Echos*, the leading French financial daily, indicated that state-owned banks had heavily assisted Bernard Tapie in the sale of his 78 percent stake, in a transaction valuing Adidas at exactly 2.085 billion French francs ($368 million). The figurehead of the takeover was Robert Louis-Dreyfus, who would assume the leadership. Together with a group of friends, he had acquired 15 percent of BTF GmbH (the holding company that controlled 95 percent of Adidas).

Meanwhile, the state-owned shareholders, Clinvest, Banque du Phénix, and Worms had all increased their stakes, amounting to a total of 42 percent for state-owned financial institutions. Gilberte Beaux had followed suit, raising her share from 5 percent to 8 percent. The rest was in the hands of two offshore funds: Omega Ventures, described as an offshoot of Citibank, had acquired 19.9 percent, while the remaining 15 percent went to Coatbridge Holdings, a fund that indirectly belonged to SG Warburg.

The press, however, smelled an outrageous intervention by the state-owned banks. As they saw it, the two offshore funds were mere puppets acting on behalf of Crédit Lyonnais. Adding their stakes to those of the French financial institutions, it looked as if Crédit Lyonnais directly or indirectly controlled about 77 percent of BTF GmbH. In other words, the state-owned banks had jumped to the rescue of a government minister ahead of tense parliamentary elections. The banks had justified their actions on the basis that by helping Tapie they were simply easing the transition from Tapie to Louis-Dreyfus, which was a desirable outcome for all. Before the weekend was over, right-wing politicians had called for an urgent parliamentary enquiry. As one of them saw it, the Adidas deal epitomized "the rot, the cancer, the gangrene" that was eating away at the French state. And that was before they learned of the details.

When the deal unraveled several years later, it turned out that Louis-Dreyfus and his friends had barely put down any money for their combined stake of 15 percent in Adidas. They said they had pitched in just 10 million French francs ($1.8 million), while the bulk of their stake was acquired through an almost interest-free loan by Crédit Lyonnais. In return for these generous conditions, Louis-Dreyfus would have to hand over to Crédit Lyonnais a large part of the profits he might make on the sale of the shares he had just bought. In other words, Crédit Lyonnais was taking nearly all of the risk but it would pocket the largest part of the benefits.

The two offshore funds bought their Adidas shares through roughly the same "limited recourse loan" from Crédit Lyonnais. Again, the bank was taking much of the risk in exchange for a large part of the potential profits. The bankers and the offshore funds themselves denied that their participation was a sham. However, the arrangements added fuel to the critics' arguments that the offshore funds had been lured into the Adidas deal at unreal conditions to cover up a state rescue.

To make matters worse, it emerged that Crédit Lyonnais had held separate talks with Louis-Dreyfus, behind the back of their actual client. Unbeknownst to Tapie, Louis-Dreyfus was given an option to buy the Adidas shares owned by the banks and the offshore funds by the end of 1994, at a fixed price: while the bank advised Tapie to sell Adidas based on a valuation of about 2.1 billion French francs ($370 million), their side agreement with Louis-Dreyfus placed the company's (potential) worth at 4.4 billion French francs ($777 million).

Again, this secret, second stage of the deal was most judicious for Louis-Dreyfus. If he managed to turn Adidas around he could exercise his option and take control of the company. Otherwise he could walk away scot-free: he would not even have to reimburse his original loan for the acquisition of his 15 percent. "Not a bad deal," he mused.

In fact, several other investors who had been approached for the same transaction turned it down on the grounds that it seemed fishy. They were particularly tweaked by the multiple parts Crédit Lyonnais played in the deal: it acted as an adviser for Bernard Tapie, the seller; it was offering side deals to Robert Louis-Dreyfus and the other buyers; and on top of that, the bank was itself a shareholder. "In the eyes of many investors, that constituted an outrageous conflict of interest," said Laurent Adamowicz, who held talks with several parties in New York on behalf of the French bank. They all refused to take part in the transaction because it seemed "too good to be true."

The revelation of the secondary dealings between the bank and Louis-Dreyfus would trigger a spectacular court case, but for the time being Bernard Tapie was chuffed—hugely relieved that the agreement had brought him one step closer to the unraveling of his business interests. As Henri Filho and Jean-Paul Tchang recalled, the reinstated minister was so grateful that he called them up excitedly to offer them an official state decoration.

As for the buyers, they kept a low profile. Louis-Dreyfus had been offered the three stripes on a silver plate and his deal would enable him to make a fortune. Assuming, of course, that he could salvage Adidas.

the comeback

Robert Louis-Dreyfus opened his first Adidas board meeting in April 1993 after an early lunch. Utterly relaxed, clad in his habitual jeans and polo shirt, he introduced himself with the promise that Adidas would regain the lead in its industry. "I can't tell you when, but I promise you that we'll be back in the lead," he told them. "It should be a great ride, the opportunity of a lifetime for all of you."

To the Frenchman's dismay, the speech didn't appear to stir as much enthusiasm as he had hoped. He quietly moved on to the next part, asking each of the board members to outline the three problems that worried them most. But again, there were few reactions. Louis-Dreyfus felt that the managers didn't dare speak up, and they certainly didn't have a clear view of what had gone wrong. "They reacted like boxers who have been knocked down too many times," he said.

For several years the Adidas managers had suffered continuous humiliation at the hands of their American rivals. Just as Louis-Dreyfus arrived in Herzogenaurach, it was confirmed that Adidas had made losses of about 149 million German marks ($95.5 million) for 1992, and sales had dwindled to 2.7 billion German marks ($1.73 billion), down by 18 percent. They were trailing far behind Nike and at a widening distance from Reebok.

Their fresh lines had not yet hit the market, and the measures that had been taken to improve marketing would not be felt until later that year. In the meantime, Adidas continued to be constantly mocked as the decaying German brand that just could not compete with the witty, fast-moving market leaders. As Louis-Dreyfus saw it, the board members had spent so much time scratching their heads on the causes of this discomfiture that they had forgotten to fix the problems. By the time they wrapped up the meeting, at nine o'clock that evening, the Frenchman almost wished he'd never set foot in Herzogenaurach.

Unlike Bernard Tapie before them, Louis-Dreyfus and Christian Tourres immediately seized control. Louis-Dreyfus made it clear that he was not about to tolerate executives who constantly made weak excuses for unacceptable problems. There was no way he would compromise with company traditions, and he had no intention of wasting his time on endless discussions: he and Tourres would firmly take charge.

All but one of the sitting board members swiftly left the company. But as Louis-Dreyfus settled in Herzogenaurach, he was much relieved to find that the inertia he had felt among the leading executives had not spread to the entire company. Adidas retained a cast of hard-nosed executives who displayed unwavering loyalty to the three stripes and burning impatience to hit back at Nike. Their plan didn't differ all that much from the measures advocated by several predecessors—except that Louis-Dreyfus and Tourres actually saw it through.

To begin with, Louis-Dreyfus dealt with the problem that had threatened the company's existence and prevented it from competing with the Americans: the high cost of production. The last two French factories were closed down without too much hullabaloo. Steve Liggett, a former Reebok executive, was hired to sweep through production arrangements in the Far East, hacking through the organization. Louis-Dreyfus ignored the predictable complaints: after two years, margins were back on track and, for the first time in many years, retailers were receiving their Adidas products on time. "At least we were in the game," he said.

As Christian Tourres reviewed international distribution deals, he quickly came to the conclusion that Adidas was being cheated by many of its partners. At least one of them turned out to be a genuine crook, but many others were just taking liberties. They had obtained their deals with Adidas many years ago, and no one had ever bothered to check if they were selling the right shoes or paying the right amount of royalties. "They were conning us right, left and center," said Tourres.

There were some deals that, as Tourres saw it, "could only have been signed by our predecessors in a state of advanced drunkenness." It took several years for the Frenchman to disentangle the more than two hundred licenses and other agreements signed by the Dasslers, which had long scattered the company's marketing efforts. With that, the Frenchmen finished dismantling the company haphazardly constructed by the Dasslers, and then rebuilt it along the lines of a marketing-driven and profit-oriented company.

The most encouraging document that Robert Louis-Dreyfus found in his drawers was a marketing study in which consumers were asked to name, out of the blue, the product brands that came to mind. Just as the chief executive had suspected, Adidas was among the most cited brands, along with the likes of Coca-Cola and Marlboro. It backed up his belief that the Adidas brand still enjoyed huge international recognition: all it needed was a little refreshing. While marketing budgets had constantly shrunk over the last years, the new owners ordered a long-delayed advertising blast. Yet Louis-Dreyfus acknowledged that the full recovery of the brand would hinge on the United States, where Adidas had suffered its worst battering.

. . . .

The former Jantzen swimwear building in Portland, Oregon, suddenly came to life again. As the managers arrived they were given a trolley, then asked to pick up a desk at the back and drop it where they saw fit. A half basketball court was set up in the middle, as well as a jukebox and a Ping-Pong table.

The unconventional setup was right in line with the personalities who headed the new Adidas America, Rob Strasser and Peter Moore, the two former Nike executives. They planned to shake up Adidas in the United States with their own team and in their own ways.

Robert Louis-Dreyfus fully supported such a forceful overhaul in the United States. This was by far the largest and the most influential sports market, yet Adidas USA was still not turning a profit, and its market share failed to rise above the humiliating level of about 2.5 percent. Coming from a market leadership of more than 60 percent just two decades earlier, when sneakers were still meant for sports, the implosion of Adidas in the United States must have ranked as one of the most spectacular upsets in any industry.

Even before he settled in Herzogenaurach, Louis-Dreyfus had decided that the halfhearted agreement with Peter Ueberroth could not drag Adidas out of its American quagmire. He therefore encouraged Gilberte Beaux to settle an agreement with Rob Strasser and Peter Moore that would place them firmly in charge of the American situation.

The deal was that Adidas would acquire their small company in Oregon, Sports Inc., and transform it into Adidas America. The former subsidiary Adidas USA in New Jersey would be dismantled. Rob Strasser, Peter Moore, Mary McGoldrick, Cindy Hale, and Owen Clemens, the shareholders of Sports Inc., would all obtain shares and options in the new subsidiary, adding up to a stake of 35 percent. Peter Ueberroth would be elbowed out and would have to surrender his share options.

The agreement was finalized in February 1993, just hours before the opening of the Super Show, the trade fair in Atlanta, at an estimated price of $16.5 million for Adidas. That morning, the four leading Sports Inc. managers walked to the Adidas booth and told Peter Ueberroth's executives that they would be taking over.

They invited about half of the existing staff to join the new Adidas America in Oregon. In an odd remake of the Herzogenaurach split, Portland was to be divided between Nike and Adidas, established on either side of the Willamette River, and the Strasser crew didn't waste any opportunity to make its presence felt.

. . . .

If anyone in the American sports business had missed the news of the Strasser deal, the rambunctious manager made sure that they would quickly find out. Just as he had done back in Herzogenaurach, Strasser shook up Adidas in the United States with his sometimes scrappy and always hardhitting tack. "The only way we can win is with an underdog mentality," he said.

One of the leading executives of Finish Line got a taste of Strasser's attitude at a trade gathering in Atlanta. "Listen David," Strasser told him, "you don't like the way I do business, and I don't like the way you do business, so let's just take a break." With that, he walked out of the meeting with one of the largest American sports retailers.

Some of Strasser's investments in sports marketing were guided by gut feelings as well. The first American basketball player to be signed under the new American leadership was John Starks, a guard for the New York Knicks. Although Starks was a decent player, what really motivated the deal was that the athlete had once blocked a shot by Michael Jordan. "Let's sign him and have posters of that block!" Strasser gleefully ordered.

In the same vein, the Adidas America managers enjoyed hitting at their larger rival in their hometown. When their colleagues returned from trade fairs, they were welcomed at the Portland airport with huge banners greeting them back into Adidas territory. The three-striped welcoming committee cheerfully waved at the Nike executives who inevitably sat on the same plane.

The Adidas managers relished the jolly fighting spirit that Rob Strasser instilled in the small team in the Jantzen building. While they were making phone calls, retailers could hear balls bouncing on the basketball court just a few yards away. The managers often sat around the television in the evening watching the second-rate teams that played in three stripes. Any victory in itself was cause for extensive celebrations at the Club 21 bar across the road.

They were given a little reprieve with the surge of the Originals line. Strasser had predicted American enthusiasm for the retro Adidas products a few years earlier, and Moore pleaded with Robert Louis-Dreyfus to unearth some old catalogues. They then revamped and relaunched a few models, which quickly appeared on the very important feet of Madonna and Claudia Schiffer.

But at the same time, the Strasser crew went about the more fundamental business of making sports products that would be relevant for Americans again, and to let it be known. It seemed as if the brand had just taken the 1980s off, and in most American sports, it had to start from scratch again.

Although they still didn't have two cents to rub together, they made it clear to all around them that a new wind was blowing at the company. Sales would jump from $215 million to nearly $300 million by the end of the year, but Strasser sent out a far more forceful signal. As John Horan saw it, "it was the first time that Nike looked over its shoulder in a long time."

. . . .

As they fought to revive the Adidas business in the United States, Rob Strasser and his crew became increasingly demanding. They permanently railed at the shortcomings of the European organization and attempted to pull more of the Adidas blanket over to their side of the Atlantic.

Some of the claims appeared justified. One of the conditions imposed by Rob Strasser for the setting up of Adidas America was that his friend Bernd Wahler and the business unit for Equipment should be allowed to join the Portland team. The Americans then obtained the global business unit for basketball, arguing that "Europeans wouldn't know a basketball from a hockey puck." Peter Moore was appointed as worldwide creative director for the Adidas brand.

Yet the two sides constantly bickered about other arrangements. The crux of the argument was that, as the Americans saw it, they should be granted full control over their operation. European marketers could not possibly grasp the American market. The Americans should be allowed to source their own products, and to run their own advertising.

One of their most virulent disputes centered around the Adidas logo. The Americans argued that the company should adopt the Equipment logo, the triangle with slanted stripes, as a fresh Adidas logo. But the Europeans thoroughly disagreed, insisting that they should stick with the Trefoil and leave the triangle to Equipment.

The fight brought ridicule on the company at the Supershow in Atlanta. "Some European managers were handing out Trefoil pins to everybody, while we had completely decorated the booth with the Equipment logo," recalled Bernd Wahler. Robert Louis-Dreyfus ended up ruling in favor of the triangle designed by the Americans, while the Trefoil would be used for Originals.

In the heat of their battles, the Oregonians could become nasty. They deprecated their European counterparts and arbitrarily dismissed European-inspired products. Sometimes they became so leery of the Europeans that they pledged to revolt. "We figured that we would just turn off the phones, stop answering calls from Germany," said Peter Moore.

When Rob Strasser didn't get his way, he sometimes displayed the least inviting aspect of his personality, openly rubbishing the Europeans and their products. "Strasser was a phenomenal character, but he was nuts," said Christian Tourres. "They were losing their minds on both sides."

The clashes came to a head in July 1993, when German managers found an unsettling memo. "It was announced briefly and dryly in Herzogenaurach that the responsibility for the entire footwear business, including staff, as well as the stewardship for the Adidas brand image worldwide, would fall in the hands of our American colleagues in Portland, Oregon," read the report in *Intern*, Adidas's internal magazine. "This caused a shock wave, unleashing wild rumours and speculation."

The reshuffle amounted to a virtual takeover by Adidas America. As the German managers saw it, footwear remained the heart and soul of the company. They had already suffered over the previous months, as Steve Liggett hacked through their production ranks. But if footwear development were handed over to the Americans, as well as international marketing, Herzogenaurach would all but dissolve.

The decision was swiftly reversed, but the battles continued to rage. They were among the most controversial issues to be handled at the company's international sales meeting in the alpine resort of Sonthofen, in October 1993. The leading managers from Adidas America all arrived early to go through a list of complaints with Robert Louis-Dreyfus.

At this preliminary meeting, Rob Strasser was getting all worked up again when he felt a searing pain in his chest. The other managers persuaded him to remain still. Although he was just forty-six years old, his weight and unhealthy eating habits had made him a heart attack waiting to happen. He was picked up by an ambulance that took him to the local hospital, but Louis-Dreyfus arranged for Strasser to be airlifted by helicopter to a better-equipped hospital in Munich.

On their way back from the sales meeting, Peter Moore and Mary McGoldrick dropped by to greet Rob Strasser in Munich. He was feeling much better and preparing to fly back to Portland. He promised that, upon his return, he would take up a fitness course to lose weight. But the next morning, when Owen Clemens arrived at the hospital, he found Rob Strasser lying on the floor. His heart had exploded.

Strasser's shattered crew, together with some other former Nike managers, bid their last farewell to Rob Strasser on November 7, 1993. He was buried at the graveyard of Manzanita, Oregon, where he liked to relax during the weekends. His team gathered on the beach and sang along as Bernd Wahler struggled to play Jimmy Buffett's "Pirate Looks at Forty" on his guitar.

"Be Real" and "Don't settle" were the catchphrases that dominated Rob Strasser's memorial service at the University of Portland's Chiles Center the next day, attended by Adidas and Nike managers alike. Former Nike friends depicted Strasser as "center-stage, personified" and compared him with Gen. George Patton. Peter Rduch made the trip on behalf of Adidas in Germany, remembering the day back in 1989 when Strasser had stunned the Adidas managers with the accuracy of his vision. Peter Moore and Mary McGoldrick both spoke of the challenges that lay ahead for Adidas.

But emotions flared shortly afterward when several managers began to lay claim to the control of Adidas America. Steve Liggett, the sourcing manager, in charge of organizing Far East production, was apparently stirring the unrest. When Robert Louis-Dreyfus turned up in Portland to deal with the aftermath of Rob Strasser's death, he felt that Liggett and his supporters "tried to make a coup." As the Frenchman recalled, about twenty U.S. managers ganged up on him in Strasser's former office and demanded control of the Adidas brand. Louis-Dreyfus stood firm.

Steve Liggett then left for lunch and never returned. Although Louis-Dreyfus acknowledged that Peter Moore "couldn't manage his pocketbook," he decided that the designer would be the right person to calm things down for a while.

. . . .

Less than two years after Louis-Dreyfus and Tourres stepped in, Adidas had returned to profits. Nike and Reebok were still sailing far ahead, but the two men became convinced that Adidas was poised for a spectacular return. Everything about it seemed upbeat, from the advertising on the reception's screens to the three-striped sweater on the chief executive's back.

Watching the swift recovery, the two Frenchmen did not hesitate to go ahead with the purchase of the company. Under their deal with Crédit Lyonnais in February 1993, Louis-Dreyfus and his friends held just 15 percent of Adidas International (the holding that itself detained 95 percent of Adidas, while the remaining 5 percent were in the hands of Horst Dassler's children). But he was entitled to buy the rest by the end of 1994, at a price equivalent to 4.4 billion French francs ($800 million) for the whole of Adidas.

As the deadline neared, Louis-Dreyfus and Tourres put their package together. The loan was again provided by Crédit Lyonnais and Banque du Phénix. This time it was granted at normal interest rates, but the banks required a 25 percent share of the profits to be generated by the sale of these shares. In other words, if Adidas were floated successfully, the gains would soon wipe off the bankers' memories of their disastrous dealings with Bernard Tapie.

This was precisely what happened: the two Frenchmen barely waited for the settlement of their acquisition to round up some investment bankers and to prepare the company's launch on the Frankfurt stock market, scheduled for November 1995.

Gilberte Beaux would not share in the spoils. The woman who held the company afloat in its worst days was unceremoniously pushed aside. Horst Dassler's children would not see many of the benefits, either. Of the 20 percent stake they had inherited from their father in 1987, they had already sold off 15 percent, to the Metro retail group in 1990. They held their breath for another few years, while Adidas was poised on the precipice. But shortly after the takeover by Louis-Dreyfus, they flogged their remaining 5 percent to an offshoot of Crédit Lyonnais.

Apart from the two leading executives, the most generously rewarded managers were the Americans. To prepare for the float, Robert Louis-Dreyfus had to buy out the minority shareholders in Adidas America. They all made substantial profits, as more than $50 million were shared among the original shareholders of Sports Inc. and another dozen managers. Some of them let out incredulous expletives as they read through their deals. It did little to reconcile the Americans with their European counterparts, none of whom earned any life-changing sums from the float.

Louis-Dreyfus and Tourres cashed in on November 17, 1995, when Adidas made its debut on the Frankfurt stock exchange. While they acquired the company for the equivalent of 4.4 billion French francs ($800 million), the float valued Adidas at roughly

11 billion French francs ($2.2 billion). They owed at least 25 percent of their profits to Crédit Lyonnais, but they still made enough to retire—again. The largest chunk went to David Bromilow, owner of a publishing company in Hong Kong, who owned most of the package jointly held by Louis-Dreyfus and his friends.

The two French executives both regarded the float as the ultimate reward for the exhausting years they spent in Herzogenaurach. Just over two years after the company's managers scraped to pay salaries and scores of investors declared the brand worthless, Adidas was back. Yet it still wasn't immune to disaster in the United States.

soccer punch II

The young managers at Adidas America couldn't stop staring. They had never seen Tommy Kain, their soccer marketing manager, in such a state before. The Jantzen building resonated with uncouth language, and it appeared that Kain had smashed his telephone against the wall.

Over the previous months, Kain, himself a former player on the U.S. national soccer team, had spent much of his time dealing with American soccer executives. This wouldn't otherwise feature among the priorities for Adidas America, but the mixed interests of business and sports politics had contrived to attribute the 1994 soccer World Cup to the United States. This was the only sport where Adidas still ruled almighty, providing an unparalleled opportunity for the three stripes to shine in the United States at little cost.

FIFA began to think of the United States as a World Cup organizer after the unexpected success of the soccer tournament at the Los Angeles Olympics, in 1984. If they managed to repeat the trick with a World Cup, the Americans could achieve a breakthrough for soccer in the United States at last. The decision was confirmed by FIFA in 1988.

But two years later, FIFA executives were deeply worried about the lack of progress of the American organizers. The U.S. soccer federation was then led by Werner Fricker and run chiefly by volunteers. After a few warnings, the federation was told in no uncertain terms that it would lose the World Cup unless it changed its leadership.

FIFA had already found the person it wanted in charge: Alan Rothenberg, the California lawyer who had organized the soccer tournament at the 1984 Olympics. Werner Fricker's supporters bitterly opposed FIFA's move to impose Rothenberg, regarded as a slippery outsider with little interest in soccer, but after much politicking and maneuvering, he was still elected by a small margin.

Since the federation was in dire straits, Rothenberg immediately revised its endorsement deals. Among them was an agreement with Adidas, which had been outfitting the national team at no cost for many years. As the company saw it, this was a generous deal that was merely intended to support the spread of soccer in the United States.

Still, such agreements did not fit in with Rothenberg's game plan. "It was next to no money!" he objected. Just months after his rise to the chairmanship, in 1990, Rothenberg obtained a four-year deal with Adidas with a somewhat larger cash component. It didn't take too much arm-twisting, since Peter Ueberroth was still in charge of Adidas in the United States at the time, and the two Californians knew each other intimately from the Los Angeles Games.

Three years later, in 1993, Rothenberg was reviewing sponsorship deals again with Sunil Gulati, an economics teacher at Columbia University who spent his spare time working as a marketing manager for the soccer federation. By then, Peter Ueberroth had exited Adidas, so Rothenberg and Gulati didn't have any qualms about turning to Nike.

It might have seemed a problem that Nike still had almost no experience in soccer. A few years earlier it had dipped its toe in the water, when Rob Strasser was heading up Nike in Europe. He had been entranced by the fervor he felt among Liverpool supporters, watching a game at Anfield, and became convinced that Nike could not make it in Europe without soccer. He then set up an English factory for soccer boots, but this turned into an awful embarrassment as the boots fell apart.

So when he flew out to meet with Nike managers in Oregon in 1993, Rothenberg returned empty-handed. "Phil Knight rejected out of hand, with the almost flip comment that he just didn't see the future of soccer in the United States," the lawyer recalled. Only a few months later, however, the outlook had dramatically improved, and Knight radically changed his mind.

To begin with, all agreed that U.S. soccer had patched together a credible squad. Judging from ticket sales, it looked as if the federation had beaten the skeptics and the 1994 World Cup was going to generate excitement. And after many previous trials and failures, it appeared that Rothenberg and Gulati, the marketing manager, were stamping a credible league off the ground at last, Major League Soccer (MLS), which had been one of the prerequisites for the United States to organize the World Cup.

Some questioned if Nike could be trusted to supply equipment at such a juncture, yet Gulati was unconcerned. "When you visit the Nike headquarters, in thirty seconds you know what they can do," he said. "They had been a success in any space they had gotten into. They were hot." It certainly helped that, in April 1994, just months before the World Cup, Nike came up with an offer of about $50 million for the national soccer team and MLS.

When it came to the team, the U.S. soccer federation had the obligation to give Adidas a right of first refusal. However, it didn't occur to the Adidas managers that the U.S. soccer federation could earnestly walk away from them. "In our view there was an implied goodwill, because we had supported American soccer for so long, when things frankly weren't worth it," said Robert Erb, then in charge of sports marketing at Adidas America.

Alan Rothenberg didn't see it that way. He became increasingly frustrated as Adidas declined to exercise its right of first refusal, attempting to stall and negotiate instead. Adidas "just couldn't get their act together," he said. "They did not believe that we were serious, so they didn't respond as they were legally required to."

Sunil Gulati was equally frustrated. "This is it," he repeatedly warned. "Give us your best shot." But the Adidas managers still didn't realize they were in real danger, and failed to respond decisively. Gulati could then table the phenomenal Nike offer: at about ten times the previous Adidas deal, for eight years starting in 1995, it was unanimously accepted.

The Adidas managers were shell-shocked. "There was a lot of anger, frustration, arguments and finger-pointing," said Robert Erb. "We felt like a jilted lover. Finally there was going to be some return on investment with American soccer, and they shopped the deal to Nike." Robert Louis-Dreyfus himself placed a furious call to the head of the federation, but it was too late. There were more hard feelings a few months later, when Tommy Kain switched to Nike.

Phil Knight had changed his mind a little too late for the 1994 World Cup itself. The U.S. men's soccer team would still wear Adidas jerseys during the competition, and Nike couldn't secure the endorsement of any other teams in time.

Still, Nike's newfound interest in soccer opened another front in the battle between the American leader and its two German rivals. Seen from Oregon, the chock-a-block Rose Bowl on the night of the final, pitting Italy against Brazil, made investments in soccer all the more compelling. Ten of the players on the field that day donned American boots, including such headline acts as Romario and Paolo Maldini. And anybody who watched Nike at the time could be certain that the Americans wouldn't leave it at that.

In terms of sports marketing, Adidas America could hardly have started on a more discordant note. If even soccer was no longer their exclusive property, Adidas could expect to fight for every inch of exposure.

Fortunately, the hard-pressed American managers appeared to have international sports organizations on their side, since the United States prepared to host yet another planetary event: just twelve years after Los Angeles, the Olympics would be back to celebrate the centenary of their revival in Atlanta.

In the interval, the International Olympic Committee (IOC) had given up all pretense that business should be kept at a safe distance from the Games. ISL, the rights company set up by Horst Dassler, had sold $95 million worth of marketing rights for the Seoul Olympics in 1988, and even the event schedules were rearranged to fit broadcasters and their advertisers. The interference continued four years later in Barcelona, where ISL raised $175 million from twelve international sponsors, but it reached unprecedented heights in Atlanta.

Viewers were treated to a shower of brown lemonade as Coca-Cola was rewarded for its unstinting investments in international sports. The sports marketing business had changed beyond recognition since Jonathan Parker, in charge of sports marketing at Coca-Cola, inked his deals with Horst Dassler and Patrick Nally, his English partner in the early days. The Atlanta behemoth now had a dedicated sports department with multimillion-dollar budgets and enough executives to fill an entire floor.

The brand's presence at the Atlanta Olympics was so pervasive that they were dubbed the Coca-Cola Games. The jaws of many reporters dropped as they landed in Atlanta to find themselves surrounded with entire walls of red posters, towers in the shape of Coke bottles, and even a full-fledged Coca-Cola Olympic City in downtown Atlanta. The company invested an estimated $200 million in the Games, and it still had to compete with a multitude of other sponsors.

"Sporting event? Or merely a branch of the advertising and entertainment industry?" an editorial asked. "In the centenary of their reinvention by Baron Pierre de Coubertin, the Olympic Games look more like a celebration of the marketing muscle of Coca-Cola, Kodak and BMW than a display of human prowess and courage. The gold, silver and bronze that clinks loudest in Atlanta is that handed over for the rights to televise, sponsor and advertise through the games."

The time of the amateur rules imposed on Olympic athletes seemed light-years away. Professional tennis players had been allowed to take part in 1988, and the amateur rules were officially abolished in 1990, when the IOC adopted a new Olympic code of admission that no longer barred professionals. By then there weren't many athletes who still believed that taking part should be their ultimate reward.

After the change in the rules, some of the athletes didn't hesitate to broadcast their commercial interests, which led to embarrassing scenes at the 1992 Olympics in Barcelona. A "Dream Team" of American basketball players, from Michael Jordan to Magic Johnson and Scott Pippen, supposedly performed a patriotic duty by competing at the Olympics, but it became clear that they chiefly served Nike's business plan when they refused to wear Reebok uniforms at the medal ceremony. In a crass publicity gesture, several of the players draped the American flag around their shoulders to cover up the Reebok logo on their team jackets.

The battles between the brands had become an integral part of the excitement. Since the cold war had ended, the confrontations no longer pitted the United States against the Soviet Union. The media were more likely to concentrate on the stories of a handful of poster boys, and their respective sponsors.

In the meantime, Peter Moore had been relieved to hand over the leadership of Adidas America to Steve Wynne, the Portland lawyer who dealt with the buyout of Sports Inc. Wynne later arranged the buyout of minority shareholders of Adidas America, and caught the eye of Robert Louis-Dreyfus. As Wynne saw it, Rob Strasser had sparked Adidas America but it still returned marginal profits. While Strasser had cut back on sports marketing investment to get the products right, Wynne intended to fully deploy the brand in the United States again.

In Atlanta, Adidas could still rely on the celebration of its past, and on its ties with innumerable sports federations. The company had just produced a commercial featuring Muhammad Ali, who provided one of the most gripping moments of the Games by appearing in the stadium with the Olympic torch. Another commercial featured Adi Dassler himself, tying the destinies of Adidas with the august tradition of the Olympics.

For the occasion, Adidas bought a row of seven brick-and-timber warehouses directly across from Altanta's new Olympic Park. They were converted into a hospitality suite that enabled guests to mingle with some of the seventy athletes who won medals in Adidas shoes and clothes. The three stripes had their own fine moment on the feet of the Canadian sprinter Donovan Bailey, the world's fastest man at the Atlanta Games.

But Nike and Reebok threw so much marketing weight behind the Olympics that Adidas struggled to grab any attention. Nike was up to its usual provocation, producing a flag of the United States with swooshes instead of stars. Then it plastered the city with huge billboards, and unapologetically used its track and field champions to act out marketing stunts, like the gold sneakers that Michael Johnson tossed into the crowd after his stupendous 400-meter dash.

The more laborious line adopted by Adidas caused deep frustration back in Portland. Steve Wynne and his managers could not help feeling that, next to the headline-grabbing antics of their competitors, the investments made by Adidas's international team in Atlanta had failed to make an impression in the United States. The Americans had no choice but to take the matter into their own hands, and hit Nike where it might hurt most.

sneaker wars II

Many of the wealthiest American basketball players owed their breakthrough to Sonny Vaccaro, a failed gambler who had turned into the most assiduously courted scout in the trade. He was the man who had spotted Michael Jordan and delivered him straight to Nike. Since then, a spot on Sonny's short list was the safest way to reach the el dorado of American basketball.

Vaccaro enjoyed a controversial reputation. Some argued that he had enabled young men from underprivileged families to earn their rightful due as ultratalented showmen. Others countered that he had corrupted basketball by introducing summer camps for promising young players, luring them away from their schools and homes at a young age with promises of unheard-of riches.

This entire business was built on the back of Michael Jordan. The deal with Jordan had reshaped the American endorsement business: by generating hundreds of millions for Nike, it appeared to prove that players with exceptional talent and that extra spark could justify even the most exorbitant deals.

Sonny Vaccaro walked over to Adidas in 1993. He wasn't directly employed by Adidas but operated as a sort of extraordinary consultant: in exchange for funding his ABCD training camp, it was understood that the three stripes would have privileged access to players who emerged from it. The camp had turned into a preying ground for team scouts and shoe company executives, all avidly looking out for the next Michael Jordan.

Paul Fireman's executives at Reebok had just taken a bet on Allen Iverson, a prolific young guard from Virginia. As a quarterback, Iverson led his high school football team to a state championship, but his mother persuaded him to try basketball as well. Although Iverson was in jail at eighteen, on a conviction that was later overturned, his mother begged Georgetown's basketball coach to give him a chance. After two years there, Iverson made himself available to the draft and a shoe endorsement in 1996, to be snapped up by the Philadelphia 76ers and Reebok.

But another remarkably talented and attractive young player had caught Sonny Vaccaro's eye: he convinced the Adidas executives that the next basketball hero would be Kobe Bryant, a seventeen-year-old player who had just graduated from Lower Merion High School in suburban Philadelphia.

Kobe Bryant distinguished himself from other young players in many ways. He was bright and articulate, was from a middle-class family, and had spent part of his childhood in Italy. His father, Joe "Jellybean" Bryant, was a former NBA player. Kobe could have gone to almost any university, and he wasn't motivated by money, yet he was still determined to join a professional team as early as possible. He therefore announced that he would skip college and make himself available for the 1996 NBA draft.

By waiving his ability to go to college, Bryant invited the shoe companies to place their bets. The risk seemed enormous, since the young man had never played an NBA game. He demanded a seven-figure contract just to wear three-striped shoes. But the Adidas executives became convinced that they could not afford to let Bryant slip through their fingers. "Sonny was absolutely sure that Kobe was going to be the guy," explained Robert Erb, then in charge of sports marketing at Adidas America.

Kobe Bryant obediently listened to a pitch by Nike managers, but the relationship he had built up with Sonny Vaccaro over the two previous years still proved decisive. Vaccaro had enabled him to shine by inviting him to the ABCD basketball training camp two summers in a row, and the scout made sure that Bryant would take part in other tournaments where he would be noticed. Vaccaro had been around long enough to have known Bryant's father and his uncle, Chubbie Box, when they were aspiring NBA players. It helped that Sonny's friends at Adidas offered a deal of $5 million for five years even before the player had been drafted.

Much of Bryant's value would depend on his destination. The team that had its sights most firmly set on him was the Los Angeles Lakers, which suited Adidas down to the ground, but unfortunately the team didn't have a pick that year. Bryant was eventually picked as the thirteenth draft by the Charlotte Hornets, but Jerry West, the Lakers coach, who had spotted Bryant at the ABCD camp, swiftly traded the starting center Vlade Divac for him.

Down the road in Beaverton, the Nike men raised their eyebrows. They weren't too sorry to hear that Bryant was going into the season with a broken arm that would keep him on the bench for several weeks. But the Bryant deal indicated that Adidas was back in the game, and they had to make sure that the next upcoming player would be on their list.

As things turned out, the prospect who whetted all appetites in 1997 was even more directly indebted to Adidas. Tracy McGrady had been spotted on a basketball court in Auburndale, Florida, by Adidas scout Alvis Smith. McGrady didn't hesitate to pack his belongings and head for the Mount Zion Christian Academy, in Durham, North Carolina, which served as a prep school for basketball players. From there he was sent to the ABCD camp.

The circumstances that led Bryant and McGrady to Sonny Vaccaro could hardly have been more different. McGrady had little hope of academic achievement and he had enjoyed a modest up-bringing, in which dinner often featured his grandmother's catch from the local pond. However, the two athletes still drew many comparisons, and they headed in the same direction: just like Bryant, McGrady hired Arn Tellem as an agent and declared his intention to join the draft without attending college.

Due to McGrady's relationships with Smith and Vaccaro, Adidas seemed to be at an advantage. But Arn Tellem was not about to let such details spoil a megadeal. He eagerly responded to the advances of Nike, which aggressively pursued McGrady. Just as Adidas was quietly preparing to wrap up its proposal for the player, Tellem called to let them know that McGrady would be signing with Nike.

The Adidas managers could barely afford to up the ante. McGrady was a promising player, but rumors had it that he would begin his career at the NBA with the Toronto Raptors, which would not open up the juiciest commercial opportunities. Still, the company's American executives figured that they couldn't afford to let Nike run away with Tracy McGrady. Partly as a defensive move, and partly as a bet, they urged Robert Louis-Dreyfus to personally woo the young player.

The cagey seventeen-year-old thus found himself sitting at a restaurant table in New Jersey surrounded by his agent, Arn Tellem, Sonny Vaccaro, assorted Adidas executives, and Louis-Dreyfus. Unlike Kobe Bryant, who had asked pointed questions and closely studied Adidas's marketing plan, McGrady relied on his agent to do the talking. He just nodded his assent here and there as the Adidas managers guided him through their offer.

Arn Tellem had played his card rights: the lunch in New Jersey cost Adidas about $2.4 million, with the deal rising to about $12 million for six years—a far cry from the $25,000 paid for Kareem Abdul-Jabbar back in the seventies. McGrady insisted that his finders, Adidas scout Alvis Smith and Joel Hopkins of the Mount Zion Academy, each get a six-figure chunk of the sum agreed for the contract.

Over the next months, many executives at Adidas questioned

the deals, which seemed exorbitant compared with the budget at the company's disposal and the money they could expect to make. But it reflected a heightened appetite for sports assets in the United States, which had the sneaker companies feverishly outbidding each other for individual stars as well as teams.

. . . .

When it came to football, Adidas appeared stuck. It had failed to impress on the fields since it had fallen out with Joe Montana, and Herschel Walker was nearing retirement. The three stripes were almost barred from the sport anyway, since Nike and Reebok had a joint deal with the National Football League (NFL) that prevented any other brands from making an appearance on the field.

To rule out any repeat of the McMahon incident, there were always a few heavies around to make sure that the agreement was strictly respected. "The NFL guys would stand at the players' entrance of the field and make them take off things that had logos not related to the NFL," moaned Steve Wynne. And when the players still managed to smuggle the three stripes on the field, they were in for some trouble. Troy Aikman, quarterback of the Dallas Cowboys, faced a fine of $40,000 for the unspeakable offence of wearing Adidas shoes on the field during a game without covering the three stripes with white tape.

Under the circumstances, it was hard to draw any benefits from such tie-ins, and Adidas decided to try another entry. It proclaimed that it would be making a measured comeback in football by signing five university teams, in which it would invest all its resources. Over at Nike they weren't overly impressed when they heard that the first team would be the University of Nebraska.

As it struggled to catch up with many wasted years in the football business, Adidas admits that it made some "ugly mistakes." The Mace line of cleated shoes, which was meant to herald the brand's return to American football fields, turned into such a disaster that the players ended up wearing soccer boots. But Tom

Osborne, Nebraska's football coach, covered up several other embarrassments to help Adidas get back on track in football.

The competition really began to pay attention, however, when they heard that the Adidas men had received a visit from the football coaches of Notre Dame, which possessed an unparalleled heritage. Again, Adidas didn't have any hope of outbidding its rivals, which were all on the case. It still begged for an audience, though, and got a foot in the door through the university's soccer coach.

It took a strong dose of self-confidence and some theatrical skills for the Adidas managers to put on a decent show for Mike Wadsworth, athletic director of Notre Dame at the time. "Everybody else was inviting them to their campus," said Robert Erb. "We had no campus. We just had this warehouse. When they came out we all threw on lab coats, we took them downstairs to the basement, we set up a treadmill, put some blinking lights on, and told them that this was our laboratory."

Beyond these antics, the Adidas men made sure to impress upon their guests that they wanted to team up with them for the benefit of Notre Dame. They had cleverly brought along pictures reminding Wadsworth that Nike, their current partner, had sometimes produced shirts with the Swoosh at the front and the university's name at the back. With Adidas, Notre Dame would always be in front.

The news that the august Notre Dame University had picked the three stripes didn't go unnoticed among others in the American sports business. The all-sports marketing pact was evaluated at $5 million per year for five years, much more than the going rate. From then on, Adidas America regularly received phone calls from other universities fishing for an offer. But the call that transformed the prospects of the company in American team sports came from New York.

. . . .

The Yankees had just hired Derek Schiller, a young marketing executive, to offset soaring costs by raising marketing revenues.

With David Sussman, the general counsel of the New York Yankees, and Rick White, an independent consultant, Schiller was entertaining the thought of an unprecedented breakout sponsorship deal. They had come up with an endorsement concept that would give Adidas stupendous exposure in Yankee stadium, at an equally stupendous price.

At the same time, it was almost certain that such an agreement would drag Adidas into a conflict with Major League Baseball (MLB), which was in the middle of finalizing its own all-encompassing deal with Reebok and Nike. If the Yankees decided to break out, the league could almost forget about their joint endorsement deal.

Still, Robert Erb didn't hesitate. "His response to our phone call made it all happen," said Derek Schiller. "The others treated this as just another call. But he said he would jump on a plane and meet with us in New York the next day. Adidas reacted so quickly that we just never got the chance to talk with the others in any meaningful way."

Adidas America judged that the prize would justify the troubles. Teaming up with the Yankees on such a scale would have untold repercussions for the brand, not only in New York but in the rest of the country, too: the name would be out there on the team uniforms, on the outfits of all the staff, underneath the score board, on the first base line, the third base line, the rain covers—everywhere.

Just a few days after the opening talks, Robert Louis-Dreyfus himself headed to New York and introduced himself to George Steinbrenner, owner of the Yankees. Again, in a matter of days, the Adidas and Yankees managers got together in Tampa, Florida, where Steinbrenner had his business interests. In March 1997, they were all ready to reveal that Adidas and the Yankees had signed a ten-year deal worth about $93 million, which was the largest sponsorship awarded to an individual American sports franchise at the time.

To mark the occasion, Robert Louis-Dreyfus and Christian Tourres turned up in George Steinbrenner's box at Yankee stadium for the opening game of the season. Nike attempted to steal the Adidas show by handing out Nike caps outside the stadium and announcing that Michael Jordan would turn up to greet Steinbrenner, but the basketball player was politely turned away.

Until then, baseball hadn't been a priority for any of the largest sports companies. Nike even spent more on soccer than baseball. But once Adidas obtained its deal with the Yankees, baseball suddenly turned into a sports marketing battlefield. It was described as "a bomb of Ruthian proportions," and the explosion was ugly.

Adidas and the Yankees had attempted to prevent a legal brawl by excluding some rights from the deal, but that wasn't sufficient to prevent outrage at the league. By the beginning of May, the New York Yankees and Adidas were suing all of the other twenty-nine teams, along with several baseball officials and MLB's marketing team. The antitrust suit filed in Florida alleged undue interference in their deal.

It would take almost precisely one year for the dust to settle. The volley of lawsuits ended with an out-of-court settlement that enabled Adidas and the Yankees to go ahead with their deal nearly as intended. Adidas gave up on the Yankee uniforms, in exchange for other apparel licensing rights for other MLB teams.

All those who knew the fabric of the American sports business realized just how decisive the deal could be. "It legitimized the Adidas brand in American sports and beyond," said Schiller. Loyal to Adidas, the team's managers went out of their way to boost the brand, constantly providing introductions for individual athlete contracts and encouraging all of the players to wear the three stripes on the field.

Yet again, the Yankees pact was heavily questioned by international managers. As they saw it, Adidas had signed an exorbitant check without any rights for the Yankees uniforms or merchandise. Nearly $100 million seemed a big price to pay for a few billboards in New York. But Robert Louis-Drefus stood firm, certain that the glitz of the Yankees would rub off on the three stripes.

By 1998, with the young basketball players on their roster, a raft of universities, and the New York Yankees, Adidas America could celebrate its return to the forefront of the American sports business. By then, sales had begun to take off. At the time of the takeover by the Strasser crew, revenues were estimated at $215 million, but two years later they had nearly quadrupled, to $840 million. Six years into the deal with Sports Inc., Adidas America's turnover reached $1.6 billion.

The Yankees agreement marked the last high-profile contribution of Robert Louis-Dreyfus. His time at Adidas culminated with the victory of the Adidas-clad French soccer team in the 1998 world championships. Jubilant crowds poured onto the Champs-Elysées in Paris, where Adidas had hired a terrace and laser-beamed its optimistic slogan, "La Victoire est en nous," ("Victory is in us"), on the Arc de Triomphe. Shortly afterward the chief executive appeared to lose interest, failing to turn up at meetings and ducking issues that required tough decisions. Only a handful of executives and friends were aware of the fact that Louis-Dreyfus was fighting leukemia.

Uncertain of the outcome, he had begun to prepare for his estate. He could no longer be bothered to deal with petty in-fighting or to haggle for weeks on sponsorship deals. "I just thought, what the heck," Louis-Dreyfus admitted. "We were making lots of money anyway." The sloppiness began to show throughout the organization, and he decided to throw in the towel.

cool cats

On a warm evening in October 1997, scores of intrigued guests assembled at the Fox Studios in Los Angeles. They were welcomed to the middle of a film set with façades that were meant to represent New York buildings. As they sipped their cocktails, a raft of well-known broadcasters, athletes, and assorted celebrities chatted around them.

The event was part of an uncharacteristically glitzy international Puma sales meeting, held in Santa Monica. The company's executives could then widely reveal that Puma had indirectly partnered with the Fox network, which explained the presence of all the familiar faces from the American film and television business.

Towering above them was Jochen Zeitz, a young German manager in a sharp suit who had been parachuted into the hot seat at Puma. After an embarrassing series of failures and continuing losses at Puma, the company's bankers were downright wary when Zeitz was introduced to them in June 1993. Tall, athletic, and preppy, with blond hair, the thirty-year-old looked as if he had walked in straight from his college graduation. Sure enough, there would be yet another restructuring plan, and yet another bill for the bankers.

But those at Puma who had worked with Zeitz over the past two years, when he had been marketing manager, could have testified that he was something special. Focused to the point of coldness, he always knew exactly where he was going—and so far, he always got there.

Jochen Zeitz had all the hallmarks of a wunderkind. He studied medicine before switching to business school and was fluent in six languages. During a stint at Colgate-Palmolive, in Hamburg and New York, he had learned the ropes of marketing. But it was his determination and his steely personality that set him apart.

Predictably, Jochen Zeitz began by wielding a tall ax. "There will be no sacred cows," he insisted. Just like Robert Louis-Dreyfus, on the other side of town, Zeitz laid off hundreds of people, reorganized production, and cut out business units that had no place in a company with ambitions to make profits. After less than two years, Puma had returned to profits. The young chief was prepared to invest again—and he found just the right friends to hold the pursestrings.

The pact unveiled in Santa Monica stemmed from an agreement sealed in November 1996 between Zeitz and New Regency, the film production company behind such blockbusters as *Pretty Woman, A Time to Kill,* and *War of the Roses.* The production firm belonged chiefly to Arnon Milchan, an Israeli citizen of such mysterious charm that he drew comparisons with Jay Gatsby.

Milchan built his wealth on citrus production and alleged weapons deals for Israel—"everything from nuclear triggers to rocket fuel," an American broadcaster put it. He lived the life of a jet-setting mogul, with multiple abodes and "a tall Scandinavian blonde in every port."

But most interestingly, Arnon Milchan had come to believe that film, broadcasting, and sports could form a heady entertainment mix. A former member of the Israeli soccer team, he regularly played tennis and avidly watched the sport. And to make the cocktail yet more intoxicating, he resolved to invest in an inspiring sports brand.

After a rebuff from Adidas in the early nineties, Milchan arranged for a meeting with Jochen Zeitz. While the chief executive was reluctant to share influence at the company, he had to acknowledge that Milchan's contacts could be most interesting for Puma, not to mention his deep pockets. The wealthy producer entered the Puma capital in December 1996, buying 12.5 percent at a cost of about $80 million, with an option to acquire another 12.5 percent.

At the time, Milchan still owned 60 percent of New Regency, while the remaining shares were held by an impressive cast of international tycoons, ranging from Kerry Packer, the Australian media magnate, to the Kirch Group in Germany, to Warner Bros. in Los Angeles. But in September 1997, Milchan's business relocated to the Fox compound after News Corp, Rupert Murdoch's media empire and owner of the studios, teamed up with New Regency and snapped up 20 percent its shares.

That evening in Los Angeles, Jochen Zeitz held a forceful speech to introduce Puma's new partners and to outline the company's investments in the American market. Arnon Milchan spoke at more length about his own interest in sports and his pride in partly owning Puma. As many of the guests saw it, the Santa Monica party was the turning point for the Puma brand.

. . . .

Since the late eighties, Puma had barely ceased to decline. The company's ill-advised forays in the discount market had apparently tarnished the brand's reputation beyond repair in the United States. By 1996 it reached sales of just $25 million, surviving on a few soccer boots and batches of cheap sneakers. It was credited with a humiliating market share of just 1 percent, and even that might have been rounded off generously on account of nostalgia by the market researchers.

Once he had finished cleaning up, Jochen Zeitz decided that

Puma should be relaunched from the United States. He began by buying back the American rights to the brand, which had fallen into the hands of Puma's former Scandinavian owners. Then he hired Jim Gorman, a former Nike executive and Adidas board member, to head up the American subsidiary in Boston.

A former middle-distance runner, Gorman had achieved his fastest ever time at the trials ahead of the 1972 Olympics in a pair of Pumas. He was convinced that, just like him, thousands of American sports people and retailers would have distinct memories of Puma. "Some people felt you couldn't kill the brand, because it was already dead," Gorman said, "but it wasn't." Among the startling statistics, Puma had just 1 percent of the sports market in the United States, but in consumer surveys, about 70 percent of respondents said they knew and recognized the brand.

To emphasize the decisive aspect of the American investments, Jochen Zeitz and his future wife, Birgit, lived in Boston for several months. He agreed to invest in a roadshow to display entirely refreshed lines of apparel and, just as Gorman had predicted, he easily obtained meetings with all the leading American retailers.

This came at a time when Nike was at loggerheads with Foot Locker and some other retailers, who resented the company's perceived arrogance and heavy-handed tactics. If Puma could give them a reason to buy more of their products, they would gladly do so. Over the next years Foot Locker, which had once banned Puma from its shelves, would drive Puma's revival in the United States.

Meanwhile, Milchan and his pals vouched for exposure. Once they were on board, Puma suddenly obtained prime-time advertising space on Fox, including a slot just before the Super Bowl in January 1998. The Fox executives couldn't justify giving it away entirely, but at a cost of about $400,000 it was still almost free. Milchan held the doors wide open for Puma in Hollywood, enabling it to set up shop in the Santa Monica studios and to get the Formstripe into movies like *X Men*.

As the partnership deepened, New Regency gradually increased its share ownership of Puma. Between the film production company and individual investments by some of its partners, the Hollywood men raised their ownership to 40.25 percent of the sports company. Arnon Milchan and David Matalon, New Regency's chief executive, took their seats on the Puma board along with Peter Chernin, chief operating officer of Newscorp.

The American shareholders inundated the Puma managers with suggestions for investing in sports and entertainment. David Matalon once called to let Gorman know that he had been talking to the Dodgers. He didn't seem to realize that, judging from the size of the Adidas pact with the Yankees, any endorsement deal with the Dodgers would probably have cost about four times Puma's entire American turnover!

The contacts of the Regency men proved more useful when Arnon Milchan, who had a personal interest in women's tennis, exchanged thoughts with Richard Williams, father of Venus and Serena. The two men both felt that sports and entertainment went together, and that women's tennis could be built into a much more exciting show. A charismatic young woman with a daring dress sense, Serena Williams was exactly the sort of player who could bring some buzz to the courts.

Serena's managers negotiated shrewdly. They rejected offers from Reebok and Nike, and turned to Arnon Milchan instead. With Puma, they could be assured that Serena would get her own commercials, and that she would be allowed to wear clothes that fitted her personality. And they obtained a deal that was built to a large extent around incentives.

The point was that the WTA's rules prevented Serena Williams from fully taking part in its tournaments, due to her young age. The negotiations with Puma were based on her ranking in 1997, which still wasn't very impressive. But Richard Williams was convinced that, once she fully integrated the WTA Tour, his daughter would wreak havoc on the circuit. She had already caused a major upset at the Ameritech Open in Illinois when, ranked 304th, she had beaten both Monica Seles and Mary Pierce.

So Serena's lawyer, Keven Davis, asked for only a small retainer.

On the other hand, she could quickly earn a lot more money from her Puma deal if she progressed through the WTA ranks or won any Grand Slam tournaments.

Just weeks after the deal was signed, in January 1998, Jochen Zeitz watched his bill from the Williams family grow exponentially. By the end of the year, Serena had surged to the twentieth position in the WTA rankings, adding up to costs of more than $2 million for Puma.

Still, the tie-in was precisely in line with the strategy that Jochen Zeitz envisaged. On the back of Milchan's investments, he invented an entirely new business, which he defined as "sports lifestyle." It consisted of a clever mix between Puma's sports heritage and its high-fashion flair, which was neatly embodied by Serena Williams: a formidable athlete, she eagerly wore tight-fitting outfits, bright yellow dresses, and knee-length socks, which all strikingly revealed Puma's cool factor.

. . . .

William "Tank" Black, an agent in the football business, had heard about Puma's new friends, and in 1998 he figured that they might be willing to make a splash with his new client: Vince Carter, a young guard and spectacular dunker from Daytona Beach, Florida.

There had been such noise around Milchan and Fox that Black didn't hesitate to talk big bucks. Coming just after the deal between Adidas and Tracy McGrady, he reckoned that Carter was worth about $50 million for ten years. Had he known that Puma was still making only about $40 million in the United States, he may have turned to another brand.

Jim Gorman immediately made it clear that the millions wouldn't happen. Due to a player lockout, which prevented the season from starting until early February 1999, he managed to bring the price down to $350,000 per year, potentially compensated by large royalties on sales of Carter-related products. On the other hand, it was agreed that the deal would be further reduced or altogether scrapped if Carter were picked by a Canadian or a minor American team.

Carter was drafted fifth by the Golden State Warriors in San Francisco, but he was traded on the spot to the Toronto Raptors. As far as Puma was concerned, that meant that the deal was off. Tank Black still insisted that they reopen negotiations and accepted another substantial cut, bringing the contract down to $150,000 per year, paired with specific incentives.

But once the lockout ended, Carter ripped through American basketball courts, to be named Rookie of the Year 1999. Sneaker executives were swarming around him, so that the deal with Puma suddenly seemed very meager.

To begin with, Vince Carter claimed that his Puma shoes didn't fit him. He then claimed that Puma had failed in its marketing obligation to make a signature shoe for him—they only made a shoe called "Vinsanity," touted as "the favorite shoe worn on the court by Puma athlete and NBA superstar Vince Carter." The player made it clear that he wanted out of his Puma deal, and he started wearing other brands.

Jim Gorman repeatedly warned Black against any such moves. "Jochen Zeitz is a man of honor, he's not going to accept that," he told the agent. "You're cheating. Don't go down that path, because we'll fight it and even though you think you'll be able to push it really hard and break it, you're going to have a fight."

But Carter ignored the warnings. By the end of November 1999, his agency confirmed that he was walking away from his ten-year deal with Puma. The basketball player "no longer endorses Puma products and Puma is not authorized to use his name," PMI ProSports Marketing stated, insisting that Puma hadn't lived up to its promotional obligations.

Just as Gorman had predicted, Jochen Zeitz hit the roof. Milchan hired a lawyer from the entertainment business, and after long, drawn-out talks, they all headed for arbitration in Boston. Unimpressed by Black's arguments, the arbitrators precisely calculated what the Carter deal might have been worth for Puma.

At that stage Carter was billed as the next Michael Jordan, so the supposedly missed earnings were phenomenal. By April 2000 the arbitrators had reached a verdict: unmoved by Carter's arguments, they ordered him to pay actual damages and punitive damages amounting to $15.9 million. To make matters worse, they issued an injunction that would prevent Carter from endorsing or wearing any brand competing with Puma for three years. By the time the lawyers had reached a settlement to remove the injunction, allowing the player to sign with Nike, Carter's bill reached nearly $19 million. The sabotaged agreement with Vince Carter turned into the most profitable deal Puma America had ever made.

. . . .

The Carter settlement came at a euphoric time for Puma. Earlier that year, the brand had reaped huge benefits from an investment in Logo Athletics, a company specializing in licensed products for the sports leagues. Since Nike and Adidas had muscled into that game, Logo Athletics was in financial trouble. In 1998, Jochen Zeitz agreed to buy 30 percent of the company, in exchange for the right to place Puma on the shirts of some of the teams under Logo Athletics contracts.

The deal was most judicious in American football. Under the agreement with Logo Athletics, Puma suddenly appeared on television screens every weekend, featuring on the shirts of twelve smaller teams. But the mood was altogether jubilant in January 2000 when the Super Bowl pitted the Tennessee Titans against the Saint Louis Rams: the leaping cat was woven into the sleeves of every uniform on the field that day. It was an extraordinary boon for Puma, given the fact that the cost of television spots around the Super Bowl reached up to $3 million for just thirty seconds.

The heightened exposure came just at a time when the athletic shoe business was under pressure. Other sneaker companies and retailers reacted by slashing prices, but Puma distinguished itself by doing exactly the opposite: in the middle of the squeeze, it came up with exclusive lifestyle ranges made by celebrated designers.

By the end of 2000, Puma's American sales reached nearly $80 million, and they would expand exponentially over the next years. The U.S. expansion fueled a stunning growth run for the Puma Group, which saw its sales multiply fivefold in as many years. Zeitz was celebrated as an iconic, new-style German entrepreneur. And the mixture of sports and fashion was more than juicy, yielding higher profit margins for Puma than any of its large competitors had.

The sports lifestyle recipe that Puma applied in the United States worked just as well elsewhere. As time went by, the brand could indulge in somewhat larger investments, but they always came with a twist. Instead of clashing head on with Adidas and Nike, it went into Formula One, profiting from the absence of its rivals to near-monopolize the paddock. When it designed new shirts for the Cameroon soccer team, Puma caused a furor by making them sleeveless. And when it wanted to make a splash in European soccer, it went for the Italians and their flair.

The investors who pumped money into Puma's revival were well rewarded. In the first ten years that Zeitz ran Puma, its share price multiplied more than sixteenfold. When Arnon Milchan exited Puma in 2003, at a mouth-watering profit, he was swiftly replaced by heirs to the Herz family, a German family that had made a fortune in the coffee business.

As Puma began to recover, Adidas was quick to denigrate its smaller neighbor as impish and a has-been. Pointing to the brand's lifestyle products, Adidas haughtily contended that Puma was not a competitor. "It's not a sports company," they said. But in fact, Puma had come back at such speed that the gap had become much smaller.

Just a decade after they teetered on the brink of the abyss and the Dasslers bailed out, both Adidas and Puma were back in shape. After Adidas moved to the former U.S. Army base in Herzogenaurach in 1993, the two companies were even reunited on the same side of the Aurach River. But they would have to re-invent themselves all over again in the next years, in the battle of the new global sports behemoths.

high noon

While athletes prepared to battle it out in the Greek summer heat, dozens of guests waited in line to pick up their passes for the 2004 Olympics. Amid the buzz that preceded the opening of the Games, small-time officials on their way to the stadium mixed with business heads who had invested millions in the Olympics. Among them were two of the most influential chiefs in the business: Herbert Hainer, Adidas chief executive, and Paul Fireman, the man behind Reebok.

Although they spent much of their time fighting each other, the two men stopped for a friendly handshake. In such a tight-knit industry they could not avoid doing business together from time to time, and they got on well. They even agreed to meet for coffee later that day on Paul Fireman's yacht, *Solemates*, anchored in the port of Athens.

Herbert Hainer's arrival at the helm of Adidas, about four years earlier, had stirred little enthusiasm. Filling the boots of Robert Louis-Dreyfus was never going to be easy, but it seemed an insurmountable challenge for a thoroughly unglamorous German with a moustache, a somewhat stiff demeanor, and an accent straight out of a British war comedy.

The son of a Bavarian butcher, Hainer worked harder than others to pursue his studies. They were financed partly by his soccer skills, which earned him a small income as a regular on the second-division team of Landshut. Then he spent his summers slaughtering pigs and cows for his parents. But he distinguished himself from his two brothers by often taking up a position behind the cash till. "I liked playing with money," he said.

Hainer already had several years of rigorous training at Procter and Gamble when Adidas came along. The timing could not have been worse: he joined the company in April 1987, just two weeks before Horst Dassler's death. He then weathered permanent frustrations to rise through the ranks, and after the Louis-Dreyfus years, many agreed that Hainer would bring badly needed discipline back to Adidas.

The German chief immediately made his agenda clear. Adidas had become bloated and complacent: he would cut out scores of redundant executive positions and introduce much more rigorous working methods. No longer would Hainer tolerate the ad libbing that had flourished under Louis-Dreyfus.

While sports remained Adidas's core business, it moved beyond the sports fields with its Originals range and by teaming up with such designers as Stella McCartney and Yohji Yamamoto. The Japanese designer made an entire line of three-striped garments and sneakers, called Y3, which propelled the three stripes from the locker rooms to the catwalks.

When it came to sports marketing, Herbert Hainer didn't hesitate to compete head on with Nike, leading to a massive inflation of soccer partnerships. Among the most interesting calls was the acquisition of a 10 percent stake in Bayern Munich, the German soccer club. For Chelsea, the London club that saw its fortunes pick up miraculously after its takeover by Roman Abramovich, the Russian oil billionaire, Adidas forked over an estimated $188 million for eight years. And its deal with Real Madrid, the Span-

David Beckham, the epitome of the modern sports marketing business.

ish soccer team, was upgraded in 2004 to the record sum of about $37 million per year.

The inflation was equally flabbergasting in basketball. Adidas and Kobe Bryant terminated their disappointing relationship in 2002. On the other hand, that same year, the company signed a deal with Tracy McGrady that would almost certainly stretch until the end of his career. At about the same time, the company lost an unprecedented bidding war for LeBron James, which Nike won with $90 million over seven years—just behind Nike's highest-paid endorsee, golfer Tiger Woods, on a $100 million deal.

Even American soccer, so long snubbed by the sneaker companies, was not immune to such formidable price hikes. In 2004, Adidas obtained an all-encompassing deal with Major League Soccer to outfit all of its teams, for an estimated $150 million for ten years.

Herbert Hainer placed many chips in the Chinese sweepstakes as well. In a striking case of reverse globalization, the country that was once regarded as a sneaker manufacturing ground turned into a buzzword for the global sporting goods behemoths.

Chinese sales multiplied at a dizzying speed, with each of the leading brands opening thousands of stores.

The company rethought its advertising and launched a global campaign with the tagline "Impossible is nothing," featuring the most emblematic Adidas players and teams. The ads earned scores of awards. Among many other visuals, they showed David Beckham's improbable free kick at Selhurst Park, and Zinédine Zidane rising from his deprived neighborhood in Marseilles to stardom at Real Madrid.

None of the improvements Herbert Hainer brought about at Adidas could be encapsulated in such an improbable line. Yet the unassuming German delivered, time and again. The company became more hardhitting; its sales increased at a steady rate, and its shareholders were duly rewarded.

As the results began to speak, Herbert Hainer shaved his moustache and shed his Louis-Dreyfus complex. The defensive attitude of the early days made way for a firm handshake and a confident laugh. As he summed it all up himself, "The best managers aren't the ones who have plenty of ideas. They are the ones who can pick one or two ideas and execute them impeccably."

One of the few problems that still chagrined Hainer at the time of the Athens Olympics was the brand's American situation. In spite of repeated management changes and heightened investments, the three stripes remained merely a small irritant for Nike. Far from lifting its American market share as promised, Adidas had actually lost yet more ground to the American company. The German chief was all the more receptive to Paul Fireman's own complaints.

. . . .

Since its heydays in the late eighties, Reebok had continued to make its presence felt as the third international brand in the business. It rivaled Nike in basketball, invented all-encompassing deals with American sports leagues, and attracted urban youngsters through deals with rappers like Jay Z and 50 Cent. Yet the Reebok brand had lost much of its zest, and it never matched the huge hits it had scored in the previous decade.

To begin with, the company's management became unstable once Reebok went public and shareholders asked Paul Fireman to step aside in 1987. Eleven years and a few chief executives later, Reebok had become so rudderless that Fireman was called back to the rescue. Still, he had to leave several times over the next years due to heart surgery and never truly found his feet at Reebok. "By the time I got the company back, I just didn't know how to put it back together again," he admitted.

Reebok continued to ride high in the United States, where Fireman sealed a raft of unmatched licensing deals. It began with the National Football League (NFL), which launched an in-depth review of its licensing business in 1999. With licensing revenues of about $3 billion that year, the NFL was generating more business from licenses than any other league at the time. But rights to outfit the teams were scattered among Nike, Adidas, Puma, and Champion, and there was a dollop of side deals for other companies to produce NFL leisure apparel and related merchandise. Commissioner Paul Tagliabue acknowledged that many of the NFL-stamped products were of dubious quality, and therefore backed the suggestion to place more of the business into fewer reliable hands.

Paul Fireman's pitch hit the nail on the head. "You ought to be ashamed of yourselves," he railed. "You made people pay to do things that they shouldn't do to keep a little piece of the pie. Nobody is making any money. You're a brand that's great on the field but horrible off the field. When you give a product to a guest that comes to your suite to watch the game, I have to believe you cringe."

The NFL managers must have indeed felt a tinge of embarrassment because in December that year they awarded Paul Fireman a massive, ten-year merchandising deal that would put all the NFL teams in Reebok uniforms from 2002 and gave the company extensive rights to make NFL leisure products. The company apparently paid more than $250 million to grab a share of the NFL licensing business.

Fireman resorted to the same hardball tactics with David Stern at the National Basketball Association (NBA). When Stern told the

Reebok chief that he was about to sign an all-encompassing pact with Nike, Paul Fireman shot back: "Do you want to be a hostage? You know they want it all their way. Their brand is more important than your brand. If you want that, do it. If you don't, change your mind and talk to me." By August 2001, Reebok had obtained a ten-year marketing deal for all NBA teams, worth $200 million.

Reebok battled just as hard with Nike for the most prominent basketball players. Paul Fireman lured Sonny Vaccaro away from Adidas, benefiting from his relationships through the ABCD camp. The contract with Allen Iverson was renewed in 2001 at an estimated $60 million, to last until the end of his career, and Reebok ran away with Yao Ming.

A bidding frenzy had erupted around the Chinese player after the country's authorities allowed him to leave the country and he went on to be drafted by the Houston Rockets in 2002. Yao Ming's endorsement was regarded as an extraordinary opportunity for the sports brands to raise their profile in China, the new el dorado of the sports business.

Yao himself had learned a thing or two about the American sports business. "When the Nike guys come in, I put on Reebok. When the Reebok guys come by, I put on Nike," he laughed. By the time Yao Ming had tired of changing shoes, he had signed a whopping deal with Reebok: his ten-year contract could be worth up to $100 million, depending partly on the growth of Reebok sales in China and the player's own achievements.

But over the years, Fireman became disturbed by the intensity of the fight with Nike and the attitude of the managers on the other side, as he perceived it. "Nike always think of whoever is their number one opponent as a warlike enemy," he said. "They're insane, sick, disgusting, I think." What was most hurtful for Reebok was the strength of Nike's American market position. Fireman alleged that Nike bullied its retailers, which made it increasingly tough for Reebok and others to obtain shelf space.

The balance of power between Nike and the retailers shifted dramatically when Foot Locker, by far the largest sports retailer in the United States, caved in to Nike's demands. In response to tightened trading conditions, Foot Locker briefly stopped selling Nike products. Adidas and Reebok could have seized the opportunity to lastingly conquer shelf space, but they didn't.

Instead Foot Locker had to admit that it could not do without Nike, further tightening the brand's grip on the market. "Then I knew that neither Adidas nor us would ever rise to enough market share to take them on with any real impetus," said Fireman. "So I decided that the only way to do it is by taking the two brands that represent the two sides of the equation."

On Paul Fireman's boat in Athens, after a bit of small talk with Herbert Hainer, the Reebok chairman began to moan about Nike again. "Could we maybe do some things together?" he ventured. At a follow-up meeting in October 2004, at Reebok's sleek head offices in Canton, Massachusetts, the German chief executive was stunned to hear that Fireman was prepared to fold his business into Adidas. "Paul acknowledged that, in this case, he would have to surrender control to us," said Herbert Hainer. "He agreed to step down. After all, he was sixty and he had already undergone five heart bypasses."

By August 2005, the two were ready to reveal that Adidas had issued a bid to take over Reebok, at a price of about $3.8 billion. Paul Fireman and his wife, Phyllis, who still owned about 17 percent of Reebok, stood to earn roughly $800 million.

The principle behind the blockbuster deal was to continue running Adidas and Reebok almost independently, but the complementary aspects of the two brands would be thoroughly exploited. Adidas would cultivate its heritage as a team-oriented brand, while Reebok would deal with more aggressive stars.

The tie-in would beef up Adidas's business in the United States, which had never recovered fully from its double knockout by Nike and Reebok in the eighties. Arguably Reebok's most enticing asset, its long-term and all-encompassing deal with the NBA, was swiftly transferred to Adidas. Conversely, Reebok could benefit from the Adidas firepower in Europe and Asia, where the American brand had barely registered until then.

But perhaps most fundamentally, the megadeal reshaped the

Herbert Hainer, Adidas chief executive, and Paul Fireman, the man who made Reebok, team up to tackle Nike.

sports business, pitting Adidas and Reebok squarely against Nike. It was the most spectacular move in a wave of consolidation that had been going on for several years, leaving only a handful of middle-size sports brands under family ownership. Many others had been integrated in billion-dollar conglomerates with several brands—just as Horst Dassler had envisaged three decades earlier.

Taking just the leading brands, the acquisition of Reebok brought Adidas much closer to the Oregon behemoth. It pitted the seemingly untouchable Nike brand, with sales of about $13 billion, against a combination of about $10 billion for Adidas and Reebok together—close to $7 billion for the Adidas brand and $3.2 billion for Reebok. The deal redrew the battle lines as the sporting goods titans prepared for their next clashes. They were bracing themselves for a massive showdown, to take place on German soccer pitches.

. . . .

All the protagonists had prepared several years in advance. Over the previous decades, the stakes had risen consistently, but nothing could compare with the rush of the 2006 World Cup, to be held on German soil. It would unleash a marketing extravaganza of unmatched proportions, at an estimated cost of about €250 million for Adidas. It was the company's ultimate chance to prove that, for all of Nike's advances, soccer still belonged to Adidas.

The campaign orchestrated by Adidas bore all the hallmarks of a military operation. The bombardment began many months before the Adidas Teamgeist ball started rolling on German pitches: huge billboards featuring the brand's most admired players started sprouting up around the world, while launches of national jerseys and boot designs were whipped up into large-scale media events.

Held in Nuremberg, the company's international marketing meeting in March 2005 featured enough soccer players to form an all-time favorite team, from Zinédine Zidane to Michael Ballack. There was Sepp Blatter, the FIFA chairman, who had given Adidas yet another deal as official partner of the international federation. Nearby sat Franz Beckenbauer, head of the World Cup's organizing committee.

As the opening ceremony came closer, the battle reached television screens. Viewers were pelted with slick commercials featuring the most prestigious soccer stars. David Beckham, Kaka, and Lionel Messi all proclaimed that "Impossible is Nothing." The campaign even had its own monument, the *Adidas World of Football*, a smaller but otherwise exact replica of the Berlin Olympic stadium, erected on the lawn of the Reichstag, the country's parliament building.

Nike had come a long way since it started to get into soccer in earnest in 1994. It upped the pressure at the next edition, heavily banking on its $160 million deal with the Brazilian squad. Even in the United States it could savour the rewards in terms of publicity, when Brandy Chastain celebrated her winning goal at the women's World Championship in 1999 by lifting her shirt and displaying a black Nike bra. Then it dramatically raised the stakes in European football by signing mammoth deals with Manchester United and Barcelona F.C., reaching $200 million for five years.

This time, Nike egged on Adidas by declaring that it had become the international market leader in the soccer business. It claimed to have caught up with several decades of Adidas inventions and investments. In a somewhat puerile showdown, the two fired at each other with astronomical figures of shirts and boot sales.

Ironically, it was Puma that would feature most abundantly on the shoulders of soccer players during the World Cup. Pelé was wheeled out for commercials, and Puma secured its presence on the pitch by obtaining endorsements from the largest number of teams: twelve squads for Puma, against six for Adidas and eight for Nike. Even if many of the Puma endorsees were startup African teams, they still filled television screens for two weeks—and the brand had taken a head-start for the next tournament, which would take place in South Africa.

After all the buildup, the end game in Germany was a repeat of the fiercest derby in the sports business, featuring the three-striped French team against the Puma-clad Azzuri. With a much tighter budget than its competitors and a mixture of luck and flair, it was the smallest of the large contenders that ended up lifting the trophy with the Italian players.

· · · ·

There was no way that anyone catching a glimpse of the event could escape the hoardings lining the pitch or the pervasive presence of the sponsors. Since Horst Dassler had opened the floodgates, international companies had continued to pour their money into sport—and on an ever larger scale.

The zealots who roamed around Olympic villages in the seventies to track down and remove any corporate logos would have had a fit at the latest edition of the Games, and there was worse to come: Adidas spent an estimated $80 million to outfit officials and the Chinese team at the opening and medal ceremonies of the 2008 Olympics in Beijing—a combination that Horst Dassler himself could only have contemplated in his wildest dreams, and the ultimate example of collusion between the interests of sports, business, and politics.

The sports business has changed beyond recognition since the Dasslers invented it. Long gone were the days when a sneaky employee could simply leave a pair of boots in the locker room with a couple of banknotes. Hushed conversations had been replaced by the shuffling of lawyers' loafers in the corridors of huge sports agencies. And some of the unassuming athletes who were grateful just to go along for the ride had turned into millionaire superstars who, under pressure, might just about agree to tie their own laces.

Adi and Rudolf Dassler could never have begun to picture it all.

epilogue

The Americans

BILL CLOSS, GARY DIETRICH, and RALPH LIBONATI, the men who spread Adidas in the United States in the early days, earned more from the buyout than they could ever spend. Ralph Libonati was the least fortunate of the three: he agreed to take over the helm at Pony, the American brand that was partly owned by Horst Dassler. He was unable to redress the ailing Pony, and he died prematurely. Gary Dietrich retired to a plantation in North Carolina and a breathtaking mansion in forested Montana. Bill Closs continued to dabble in the tennis business with Nike, otherwise enjoying his stupendous view on Lake Flathead, Montana.

JIM WOOLNER, KARL WALLACH, and LEE STOCK, the managers behind Puma in the United States, struggled to come to terms with the dismissal of their company, Beconta, as the brand's American distributors. Unlike their Adidas counterparts, they were poorly rewarded for their remarkable contribution to the Puma story. Lee Stock remained for several years as president of

Puma USA but passed away in 2006. Woolner retired to his mansion in White Plains, New York, occasionally enjoying visits from the likes of Reggie Jackson. Wallach opted for a rugged retreat in Colorado.

The Family

INGE DASSLER and KARIN ESSING, the two eldest daughters of Adi and Käthe, both retired from business after the sale of their stake in Adidas. Karin and her husband remained in Franconia, where she died of cancer in 2006; while Inge moved to the Bahamas. Her former husband, ALFRED BENTE, who aptly steered much of the company's expansion in Germany, started a new life in Portugal.

BRIGITTE BAENKLER, the third Dassler daughter, continued to run the former Sporthotel opened by her parents in Herzogenaurach, which she bought back from Bernard Tapie and renamed the Herzogspark Hotel. She turned it into a highly rated establishment, with a wide range of sports facilities and photographs of her illustrious parents adorning the walls.

SIGRID DASSLER, the youngest of the four daughters, moved to the Bahamas with her children. Her former husband, CHRISTOPH MALMS, was placed at the head of ISL, the sports marketing company founded by Horst Dassler, which was declared bankrupt in May 2001. A Swiss prosecutor spent several years investigating the circumstances of the failure, but by then the Malms relationship had disintegrated.

SUZANNE DASSLER, daughter of Horst and Monika Dassler, lost her last financial interest in the family's business with the bankruptcy of ISL. When Sepp Blatter, FIFA chairman, alleged that the Dasslers had been behind illicit payments in the sports business, Suzanne forced a gag order on him. She moved to Switzerland and decided to reconcile with the rest of the family. Her brother, ADI DASSLER, JR., briefly owned a restaurant in Los Angeles and set up a small sneaker company called AdiOne. Like his father, he died prematurely, in October 2006, defeated by cancer at the age of just forty-three.

GERD DASSLER, second son of Rudolf Dassler, retired and remained in Herzogenaurach. He resides on Christoph Dassler Strasse with his second wife, Lydia. They live in the house with the large garden that Gerd inherited from his father as part of the acrimonious settlement with his late brother, Armin. He admits that the family disputes still give him nightmares.

FRANK DASSLER, eldest son of Armin Dassler and grandson of Rudolf Dassler, caused a furor in Herzogenaurach in June 2004 when it was announced that he had been appointed head of legal affairs at Adidas. He courageously broke the absurd taboo that made it unthinkable for a Puma heir to cross the river. Longtime Puma employees fumed that Frank's father, Armin Dassler, must be turning over in his grave. IRENE DASSLER, Armin's widow, expressed the same views in a local tabloid. She privately retracted her statements and congratulated Frank on his prestigious appointment. He lives in Herzogenaurach with his wife and child.

The Investors

ANDRÉ GUELFI, Horst Dassler's former sidekick, continued to cultivate his skills as a wheeler-dealer. This briefly landed him in jail, when he was arrested in connection with the Elf bribery scandal. He was accused of acting as an intermediary for the French oil company in its efforts to secure exploration deals. He was sentenced to a three-year suspended sentence, but the prosecution appealed, requesting a firm prison sentence instead. During a stay at La Santé Prison in Paris, Guelfi resided in a cell adjacent to Bernard Tapie. The two became friends when Tapie noticed that Guelfi could not walk comfortably around the courtyard and offered the older man the loan of his Adidas sneakers. The two later concocted deals together in Russia.

BERNARD TAPIE was incarcerated for his part in another bribery scandal at Olympique de Marseille. Due to his personal bankruptcy, he could not return to business. He switched to acting, obtaining a lead role as Inspector Valence in a French TV cop series and starring in a play titled *Un Beau Salaud* (*A Neat Bastard*). At the same time, Tapie led a crusade against Crédit Lyonnais, claiming that he was fleeced in the sale of Adidas. French judges provoked an outcry in September 2005 when they deemed Crédit Lyonnais guilty and awarded unprecedented damages of $165 million to Bernard Tapie (to be forked over by French taxpayers). However, in October 2006, the Court of Cassation dashed Tapie's hopes of a spectacular financial recovery by rejecting this verdict and referring the case back to the appellate court.

ROBERT LOUIS-DREYFUS briefly backed up Bernard Tapie's case and hired him as a manager at Olympique de Marseille. However, this startling tie-in was short-lived. Louis-Dreyfus remained the owner of Olympique de Marseille, which brought him nothing but losses and harassment. At the same time he built up a thriving telecommunications arm in the Louis-Dreyfus family empire. He often works from a palazzo on Lake Lugano, where he welcomes guests in a pair of Adidas flip-flops.

FRANÇOIS-HENRI PINAULT, chairman and chief executive of Pinault Printemps Redoute (PPR), a French retail and luxury conglomerate, caused a stir in April 2007 when he confirmed that the company had bought a blocking minority in Puma and had offered to take over the rest. The owner of Gucci and many other luxury labels, PPR thus officially sealed a new alliance between sports and high fashion. While Puma was declared almost worthless in the early nineties, the PPR bid placed its value at nearly $7.1 billion.

sources

This book is based on five years of research, entailing many days in dusty archives and countless interviews around Europe, the United States, and Japan. The interviews ranged from telephone conversations to repeated daylong encounters. Some of the sources have kindly provided internal documents and personal correspondence.

The contents are further documented through clippings from *Die Süddeutsche Zeitung, Die Frankfurter Allgemeine, Handelsblatt, Bildzeitung, Die Zeit,* several regional German newspapers, *Stern, Spiegel, WirtschaftsWoche, Le Monde, Libération, Le Figaro, Les Echos, Le Quotidien de Paris, Le Nouvel Observateur, De Telegraaf, Vrij Nederland,* the *Financial Times,* the *Wall Street Journal, Il Sole 24 Ore, Sports Illustrated, L'Equipe, Sportstyle,* and *Sporting Goods Intelligence.*

The cinema has played its own part in documenting the history of sport. Among its output most relevant to this book are *Das Wunder von Bern* (Sönke Wortmann, 2004), *The Tokyo Olympics* (Kon Ichikawa, 1964), and *Chariots of Fire* (Hugh Hudson, 1981).

Adidas and Puma both provided stacks of annual reports, press releases, and other company documents. I have drawn some early anecdotes from a manuscript written by Hermann Utermann, a German historian, about the story of Adi Dassler. This was never published, and the rights were acquired by Adidas. The company itself published a substantial history of its beginnings—although it incidentally obliterated the forties.

Quotes that do not appear in the references below are issued from unrecorded conversations with sources who wished to remain anonymous.

Prologue

"mostly hype and hair": *The Times*, 12/01/07.

"Let's be honest": Grant Wahl, in *Sports Illustrated*, 12/01/07.

"radically transform": David Bond, in *The Daily Telegraph*, 12/01/97.

"David was the most unaffected guy": Steve Martin, telephone conversation, August 2003.

"Would you like to make a friend?" and rest of the Beckham anecdote recounted by Paul McCaughey, interview, 23/07/03, London.

"I could not have guessed": interview, Thierry Weil, 24/09/03, Herzogenaurach.

Chapter One: The Dassler Boys

Details in this chapter are drawn to a large extent from the reference books cited on page 364 and 366, as well as from articles by local historians. Further details were gathered in informal conversations with elder people related to the Dasslers, their neighbors, and friends. Manfred Welker, a local historian who lives just across from the former Dassler house on Hirtengraben, has thoroughly studied Dassler family history.

Registration for NSDAP membership : Bundesarchiv Berlin, NSDAP-Zentralkartei.

Background on sports under Nazism mostly from the reference books cited on page 366, predominantly *Stürmer für Hitler*, and Richard Mandell on the Berlin Olympics.

"animal qualities," as quoted in *In Black & White*.

"Rudolf was a bit of a peacock": Betti Bilwatsch, interview, 08/07/04, Lauf an der Pegnitz.

"She was a serious person": from *Der Mann der Adidas war*.

"The relation to my brother": letter from Rudolf Dassler to the managers of Beconta, Puma's longtime American distribution company, dated March 19, 1969. The letter was sent to Beconta after the revelations in *Sports Illustrated* regarding payments at the 1968 Mexico Olympics, which referred to the Dassler feud. "You have a right to learn the truth," Rudolf wrote in the opening paragraph.

"Heil Hitler": correspondence as part of an investigation by the finance authorities into suspected illegal profits, in May 1944, which led to a fine of 4,000 reichsmark (State Archive of Nuremberg, Regierung von Mittelfranken, 78/ 3930–1).

"It was Adi Dassler": telephone conversation with Hans Zenger, March 2005.

Chapter Two: Two Brothers at War

Assignments of shoe companies under the NS-regime: files of the Wirtschaftsgruppe Lederindustrie (Bundesarchiv Berlin R13, XIII).

Details regarding Adi Dassler's assignment in the Wehrmacht: from Utermann.

"Kampf" and "Blitz": price list included in the wartime investigation of Gebrüder Dassler by the finance inspection, State Archive of Nuremberg.

Request of Russian workers: correspondence, Fachgruppe Schuhindustrie der Wirtschaftsgruppe Lederindustrie, Landersarbeitsamtsbezirk Bayern (Bundesarchiv Berlin, R13 XIII, 250).

"Rudolf bluntly rejected": Betti Bilwatsch, interview, 08/07/04, Lauf an der Pegnitz.

Anecdote on Maria Ploner: from conversation with Frau Ploner in Herzogenaurach.

"Here are the bloody bastards": anecdote and quote from Betti Bilwatsch, interview, 08/07/04, Lauf an der Pegnitz.

"In 1941 my brother": from Rudolf Dassler's letter to the Beconta managers.

"I will not hesitate": extract from a letter written by Rudolf Dassler, as quoted by Käthe Dassler in her statement to the denazification committee on 11/11/1946 (Adolf Dassler denazification file, Archiv Amtsgericht Erlangen, Akte 625/ VI/ 14B46).

"My brother-in-law" and the details on the parachuting boots patent: from Käthe Dassler's statement to the denazification committee, 11/11/1946.

Rudolf Dassler's war tale: compiled from his written description of his wartime activities; his more formal statements to the U.S. authorities; the denazification file of Adolf Dassler; and the investigations of the U.S. authorities into the wartime activities of Rudolf Dassler, archived by the intelligence service of the U.S. Army and declassified for the purpose of this book, under the Freedom of Information Act.

Tale of Rudolf's last war months: unofficial statement by Rudolf Dassler, titled "Politische Zuverlässigkeit," dated 06/06/1945, written on Dassler letterhead.

"My disapproval " and "I expected that": statement by Rudolf Dassler to the American authorities, dated 01/07/46, Hammelburg (Rudolf Dassler file, United States Army Intelligence and Security Command, Fort George G. Meade).

"When I came back": from Rudolf Dassler's letter to the Beconta managers.

Liberation of Herzogenaurach: *Kriegsende und Neubeginn, Herzogenaurach 1945*, published by Heimatverein Herzogenaurach, Klaus-Peter Gäbelein.

Chapter Three: The Split

Background on American internment camps: Allierte Internierungslager in Deutschland nach 1945, Lutz Niethammer, in Von der Aufgabe der Freiheit, Akademie Verlag.

Testimony by Friedrich Block: in a statement to the American authorities in Hammelburg, 30/06/46, included in the U.S. intelligence file.

Findings of U.S. investigating officer: in U.S. Intelligence Service file.

All arguments and witness accounts put forward by Adolf Dassler were extracted from a letter to the Spruchkammer (the jurisdiction in charge of the denazification file), Höchstadt/ a.d. Aisch, dated 22/07/1946, and appendices (Adolf Dassler's denazification file).

"Rudolf Dassler further accuses my husband": Käthe Dassler's statement to the denazification committee, 11/11/1946.

"The speeches held inside and outside": ibid.

Mitläufer verdict: issued by Spruchkammer Höchstadt a.d. Aisch, Sitz Herzogenaurach, on 22/11/1946, Adolf Dassler's denazification file.

Registration of the three stripes: confirmed in a letter by Dr. Wetzel, patent lawyer, dated March 31, 1949.

Rudolf Dassler's remark to Sepp Herberger: Deutschlands grösster Familienkrach, *Neue Illustrierte Revue*, 02/02/1968.

Details on Sepp Herberger in Switzerland: from Leinemann's book and the feature film *Das Wunder von Bern*, by Sönke Wortmann.

Puma's claim: contained in an ad placed before the World Cup, in which they boasted that the winners of the 1954 German league championships, Hannover 96, had won the title in Puma boots with screw-in studs.

"If Adi felt": interview, Horst Widmann, 13/01/05, Herzogenaurach.

"He was particularly prolific": interview, Heinrich Schwegler, 05/02/04, Herzogenaurach.

"Sometimes we made mistakes": interview, Peter Janssen, 03/07/03, Herzogenaurach.

Details on Schiele agreement: from interview, with Ray Schiele, Jr.; and on Simeon Dietrich: from his nephew Gary Dietrich, 12/08/04, Condon, Mont.

Chapter Four: Olympic Handouts

"My father wasn't exactly bubbly": quote from *Revolution im Weltsport*, which provides most of the details on Horst Dassler's childhood.

Details on the Sports Depot: provided by Ron Clarke in correspondence, June 2005, and from his book *The Measure of Success*.

"None of the American companies": telephone conversation with Al Oerter, November 2004.

"It was a blessing" and most of the background on the early days of Adidas in California: from Chris Severn, telephone interview, June 2005; same for other Severn quotes in this chapter.

"They were just": telephone conversation with Bobby Morrow, March 2005.

"It was a huge embarrassment": interview, Dick Bank, 03/11/06, Los Angeles.

"Rudolf wanted a child": interview, Betti Bilwatsch, 08/07/04, Lauf an der Pegnitz.

"The relationship was not easy": interview, Peter Janssen, 03/07/03, Herzogenaurach.

The Hary precedent: particularly well documented in *Making a Difference*.

"I gave him shoes" and "it was truly hurtful": interview, Werner von Moltke, 29/07/03, Nieder Olm.

"an outrageous sum" and next Onitsuka quotes: from Kihachiro Onitsuka, in his biographical booklet, "My life history," which was initially published by *Nikkei* in 1990.

"I remember": quote from Henry Carr originally published in the *Detroit News* in 1998.

"like a dash for a train": as quoted by Wallechinsky.

The Mills anecdote: as told by Dick Bank, interview, 03/11/06, Los Angeles.

Chapter Five: The Alsatian Plot

Georges-Philippe Gerst, son of the owners of the Vogel plant bought by the Dasslers, provided much of the background on shoe production in the Alsace and the early days of Adidas France, in a telephone interview, in January 2005.

"He just didn't care": interview, Alain Ronc, 20/06/03, Boulogne.

Revolving dinner anecdote: correspondence with Pat Doran.

"Horst, you are interfering": interview, with André Gorgemans, 06/02/05, Munich.

"You weren't sleeping?": interview, with Thomas Bach, former Adidas sports marketing manager and later IOC member, 28/07/03, Tauberbischofsheim.

"He asked if my prospective wife": interview, Alain Ronc, 20/06/03, Boulogne.

"It was exhilarating": interview, Johan van den Bossche, 30/01/04, Clichy.

Anecdote of Horst Dassler's discovery of Fabara: by Manuel Conte, operations manager of Adidas Spain, 26/01/07, Zaragoza.

"Otherwise he asked": interview, Jean-Claude Schupp, 30/04/04, Monaco.

Background on Beconta and Walter Blaskower: chiefly provided by Karl Wallach, telephone interview, 20/03/07. Further documentation was provided by Sam Lessin, grandson of the late Lee Stock, the third leading executive at Beconta and later president of Puma USA.

"The old man" and "we offered to have him chauffeured": interview, Irene Dassler, 13/01/05, Nuremberg.

Chapter Six: Dirty Tricks in Mexico

"It's time for black people": Harry Edwards, as quoted in *In Black & White*.

"They got the money": "No Goody Two Shoes," by John Underwood, *Sports Illustrated*, 10/03/69.

"He will either become part": as remembered by Jim Woolner, interview, 31/10/06, White Plains, N.Y.

"The whole container" and "they came to fetch us": interview, Peter Janssen, 03/07/03, Herzogenaurach.

"I placed it in my handbag" and "they walked over": interview, Irene Dassler, 13/01/05, Nürnberg.

"She cried her eyes out": Art Simburg as quoted in a translation of a story in the *New York Post*, 03/05/72, by Paul Zimmermann.

"The detention was dreadful": ibid.

"Just two hours later" and "they firmly advised us": telephone interview, Karl Wallach, 20/03/07.

Dick Fosbury anecdote and quote: from encounter at the world athletics championships in Paris, August 2003.

Chapter Seven: The Puma Swinger

"It was most unusual" and "Sure, he was a swinger": telephone interview, Karl Wallach, 20/03/07.

"the situation was just too ridiculous" and "quite astonished": correspondence with Hans Henningsen, from June 2004 to March 2005.

Details of the Pelé pact: further provided by Helmut Fischer, former advertising manager at Puma, and Hans Nowak, formerly in sports promotion at Puma.

Most of the Clyde anecdote and all quotes from Karl Wallach in this context: issued from telephone interview with Karl Wallach, 20/03/07.

"faster than a lizard's tongue": an unnamed opponent quoted in Walt Frazier's biography in the NBA online encyclopedia.

"Frazier's smooth, sultry style": issued from the same biography; the sportswriter was unnamed.

"He was the epitome of cool": interview, Jim Woolner, 31/10/06, White Plains, N.Y.

Chapter Eight: Stars and Stripes

"I hit the jackpot": from *"Doc": The 50-year Sporting Goods Sales Odyssey of H. B. Hughes*, as told to Carlton Stowers, private edition.

"The growth was exponential" and "we were ordering": interview, Gary Dietrich, 12/08/04, Condon, Mont.

"I once requested an entire container": interview, Bill Closs, Sr., 13/08/04, Big Fork, Mont.

"Based on a commitment": interview, Bill Closs, Jr., 08/08/04, Palo Alto, Calif.

"Once we had finished": interview, Peter Rduch, 06/02/03, Herzogenaurach.

"Horst thoroughly prepared": interview, Gerhard Prochaska, 10/08/02, La Baume de Transit.

Most details on the launch of the Superstar and all quotes from Chris Severn: derived from a telephone interview with Severn, June 2005.

"I got really annoyed": telephone conversation with Stan Smith, 05/04/05.

Anecdote on the Jacksons: from correspondence with Margaret Larrabee.

"Horst asked us": interview, Günter Sachsenmaier, 23/11/04, Ottersthal.

Chapter Nine: From Rags to Riches

"I'm not interested": as quoted by Uwe Seeler, German soccer star in the sixties and close friend of Adi Dassler, interview, 04/02/05, Hamburg.

"Every athlete in Munich": telephone interview with John Bragg, March 2005.

Details on the early days at Nike: drawn to a large extent from *Swoosh*, notably the anecdote on Bill Bowerman in Munich.

Guzzling contest anecdote: as recounted by John Bragg, telephone interview, March 2005.

"Horst, you won't spare me anything!": Adi Dassler, as quoted in *Horst Dassler: Revolution im Weltsport*.

"You must be out of your mind": as recounted by Günter Sachsenmaier, 23/11/2004, Ottersthal.

"He had it all in his head": interview, Alain Ronc, 20/06/03, Boulogne.

"This gave the impression": correspondence with Georges Kiehl, who further provided the details on Cali.

"They were putting the squeeze": interview, Bill Closs, 13/08/04, Big Fork, Mont.

"In our frenetic drive": interview, Alain Ronc, 20/06/03, Boulogne.

"The situation was crazy enough": interview, Peter Rduch, 06/02/03, Herzogenaurach.

"When German managers": interview, Jean Wendling, 23/09/03, Bitschoffen.

Chapter Ten: Soccer Punch

The anecdotes surrounding Cruijff's contracts with Cor du Buy: from the former distributor's files, including stacks of press clippings, original contracts, correspondence and internal memos.

"complete codswallop": from correspondence between Du Buy and his lawyer in the Cruijff case.

"the truth of the matter": the judge as quoted in nearly all national Dutch newspapers the next day.

"We would be grateful": letter to Johan Cruijff in Du Buy files.

"Dear Horst": letter from Horst Dassler contained in the Du Buy files, just like the reply.

Further details on the Cruijff dispute with the KNVB: derived from interviews with Jan van de Graaf (18/04/05, Etten-Leur), head of the unit that distributed Adidas in the Netherlands at the time, and Jan Huijbregts (19/04/05, Leusden), secretary-general of the KNVB.

"elegance," "inventiveness" and "genius": foreign newspapers as quoted in *Tor!*

"He didn't want to know" and "some extra money": interview, Horst Widmann, 10/02/05, Herzogenaurach.

"It was phenomenal": interview, Gerd Dassler, 02/07/03, Herzogenaurach.

"It was a thorny matter": interview, Irene Dassler, 13/01/05, Nuremberg, same for following quotes from Irene Dassler in this chapter.

Anecdote of secret meetings between Adi and Rudolf Dassler: based on a single source, Horst Widmann, who remembered arranging the encounters.

Chapter Eleven: Under the Influence

"I'm fine, John": as recounted by John Boulter in interview, 25/09/02, Saverne.

"There were these general secretaries" and "the gold service": interview, Gerhard Prochaska, 10/08/02, La Baume de Transit.

"Those who had never": interview, André Guelfi, 30/07/03, Paris.

Anecdotes on the Terrasse Hotel relayed by Jacky Guellerin, interview, 03/05/04, Courbevoie.

"He had the amazing ability" and "at the end of an evening": interview, Patrick Nally, 22/07/03, London.

Details on Christian Jannette's involvement: mostly provided by him, interview, 23/09/03, Illkirch.

"My opinion is that": Stasi reports into the activities of Horst Dassler and Adidas, by informant "Möwe." Quote extracted from a report titled "Adidas und Einfluss auf verschiedene Organisationen und Wahlen in den internationalen Sportgremien," undated. (Zentralarchiv, der Bundesbeauftragte für die Unterlagen des Staatssicherheitsdienstes der ehemaligen Deutschen Demokratischen Republik, archive number 15825/89). Same for following quotes from this informant.

"There was nothing we could do": interview, Gerd Dassler, 02/07/03, Herozgenaurach.

"When a sports official": interview, Gerhard Prochaska, 10/08/02, La Baume de Transit.

Morocco anecdote: as recounted by Blagoje Vidinic, interview, 22/11/04 in Strasbourg.

Description of Champion d'Afrique: issued from the full collection of the magazine since its inception at the Bibliothèque Nationale in Paris.

Ali anecdote: by John Bragg, telephone conversation, March 2005.

Other details about the American arm of the sports political team: described by John Bragg and Margaret Larrabee, Mike's widow, in correspondence.

"Horst had an incredible intellect": John Bragg, telephone conversation, March 2005.

Chapter Twelve: The Bountiful Game

"The struggle was between": Keith Botsford, *Sunday Times*, 16/07/74.

"I left the celebrations early": interview, Blagoje Vidinic, 22/11/04, Strasbourg, same for entire anecdote.

"They were talking as friends": interview, Eric Drossart, 19/01/04, London.

Anecdote on Dell's start in the sports business: by Donald Dell, interview, 07/11/06, Washington, D.C.

Details on the early days at West Nally: provided mostly by Patrick Nally, interview, 22/07/03, London.

"He fired instructions": ibid.

Background on Coca-Cola's involvement in sports marketing: partly from *For God, Country and Coca-Cola*, by Mark Pendergrast, Collier Books, 1993.

Patrick Nally provided most of the background on the early dealings of SMPI, and investigations by German news magazines, particularly *Stern* and *der Spiegel*, added some details.

"From the beginning": extracted from Sepp Blatter's written replies to author's questions.

"They had discussions": interview, Christian Jannette, 23/09/03, Illkirch.

"Horst openly talked": interview, André Guelfi, 30/07/03, Paris.

Chapter Thirteen: The Clandestine Empire

Le Coq Sportif history: drawn to a large extent from Emile Camuset's book.

Anecdotes on the court tussles between Le Coq and Adidas: backed up by court rulings.

"I went over": interview with André Guelfi, 30/07/03, Paris.

André Guelfi's life story: compiled from Guelfi's autobiography as well as articles in *Le Monde*; the book *Forages en eaux profondes*, by Airy Routier and Valérie Lecasble, regarding the Elf bribing scandal, Bernard Grasset, 1998. Fatima Oufkir has formally denied that André Guelfi, one of her husband's closest associates, took advantage of his "suicide" to plunder his Swiss bank account, during her and her children's atrocious captivity. She described her ordeal in a book called *Les Jardins du Roi*, Michel Lafon, 2000.

"Between the two of us": interview, André Guelfi, 30/07/03, Paris.

"When someone came": interview, Johan van den Bossche, 30/01/04, Clichy; also the source for the Heller anecdote.

"Horst sometimes pretended": interview, André Guelfi, 30/07/03, Paris.

"In such a jumble": Jean-Marie Weber as quoted in *Revolution im Weltsport*.

Le Coq Sportif's story in the United Kingdom: as recounted by Robbie Brightwell, interview, 26/10/04, Congleton.

Background on Roberto Muller: by Muller himself, interview, 16/08/04, New York.

"flashes of genius": interview, Larry Hampton, 23/07/03, Wimbledon.

Anecdote on the bowl of cocaine: by André Gorgemans, among others.

"Sometimes I wondered": interview, Robbie Brightwell, 26/10/04, Congleton.

"She completely flew off": interview, Dieter Passchen, 05/02/04, Herzogenaurach.

"Adi Dassler was livid": interview, Horst Widmann, 13/01/05, Herzogenaurach.

"One day he was walking": interview, Karl-Heinz Lang, 11/01/05, Scheinfeld.

Chapter Fourteen: Olympic Friends

"Pavlov was like a kid": interview, Christian Jannette, 23/09/03, Illkirch.

Details on Samaranch's intimate relationship with the Franco regime: from Andrew Jennings books.

"He distinguished himself": interview, Christian Jannette, 23/09/03, Illkirch, who further recounted the details of the encounter between Samaranch and Dassler in Barcelona.

"for every task": interview, Gerhard Prochaska, 10/08/02, La Baume de Transit.

"You have just spoken" and next anecdote: interview, Frank Craighill, 08/11/06, Maclean, Va.

Anecdote of Sportshotel bugging: provided by Gary Dietrich, 12/08/04, Condon, Mont.

"And all of a sudden": interview, Jörg Dassler, 24/09/03, Herzogenaurach.

"He was permanently hiding": interview, Klaus Hempel, 07/04/04, Luzern.

"He quizzed me" : interview, Christian Jannette, 23/09/03, Illkirch.

"He fired off letters": interview, Didier Forterre, 30/01/04, Paris.

Details about the genesis of the Olympic programme: provided mostly by Jürgen Lenz and complemented by the book by Michael Payne, then at ISL, who went on to became marketing manager for the IOC.

"the right question": interview, René Jäggi, 06/04/04, Kaiserslautern.

Chapter Fifteen: The Return

"Herr Lenz": anecdote from Jürgen Lenz, 07/04/04, Lucerne.

"fell head over heels": interview Roberto Muller, 16/08/04, New York.

Discovery of the odd dealings: by Marcel Schmid in several telephone conversations, April 2005.

"international crook": as recounted by Marcel Schmid.

"One hour cost": interview, André Guelfi, 30/07/03, Paris.

Tales of disappearing documents and customs police raid: by Patrick Nally, Didier Forterre, Klaus Hempel, and several others whose offices were searched.

"There were entire periods": interview Günter Sachsenmaier, 23/11/04, Ottersthal.

Anecdote of the management ultimatum: by Klaus-Werner Becker, interview, 06/04/04, Basel.

"I'm at a crossroads": Horst Dassler quote as relayed by Jean Wendling, interview, 23/09/03, Bitschoffen.

"countless reasonable proposals": Walter Meier as quoted in Horst Dassler, *Revolution im Weltsport*.

Chapter Sixteen: Collapse

"You have to kill them": as reconstructed by Bill Closs, Jr., interview, 08/08/04, Palo Alto, and Bill Closs, Sr., interview, 13/08/04, Big Fork, Mont.

"I told them": interview, Bill Closs, Sr.

"They inspected the sample": interview, Günter Sachsenmaier, 23/11/04, Otters-thal.

"Adidas refused": interview, Horst Widmann, 13/01/05, Herzogenaurach.

Anecdote of the meeting between Horst Dassler and Phil Knight: as relayed by Larry Hampton, interview, 23/07/03, Wimbledon, and in *Swoosh*.

A witness of Horst Dassler's meetings in Havana was Joe Kirchner, former textile apparel manager at Adidas in Germany and later special envoy in the Adidas USA office, who is behind the anecdote of the Los Angeles bank vault as well. Rich Madden, then head of Adidas USA, contended that he had been dismissed at least partly because he refused to carry one of the suitcases stuffed with cash.

Details of Nike's preparations for the Olympics: from *Swoosh*.

"costly and ephemeral show": Horst Dassler, quoted in *Swoosh*.

"Los Angeles was a massive": interview, Günter Pfau, 06/02/04, Herzogenaurach.

All quotes and anecdotes on entertainment promotion: from Angelo Anastasio, telephone interview, September 2005.

"As a junior in high school": Donald Dell, interview, 07/11/06, Washington, D.C., while further details on the Michael Jordan endorsement were revealed in *Swoosh*.

Details on the relationship with Patrick Ewing: from Dave Morgan, interview, 02/11/06, New York.

Details on the early days of Adidas USA: from Rich Madden, interview, 15/08/04, Summit, N.J.; Don Corn, interview, 07/08/04, Carlsbad, Calif.; and Bart Stolp, interview, 07/11/06, Wilmington, Del.

"Adidas would not have": interview, Rich Madden, 15/08/04, Summit, N.J.

"We had devoted our lives" and "the next day": interview, Gary Dietrich, 12/08/04, Condon, Mont.

Chapter Seventeen: The Emperor Strikes Back

"It basically defeated" and much of the advertising anecdote: Tom Harrington, interview, 07/08/02, Bruchkobel.

"It was the most hostile": interview, Ingo Kraus, 29/07/03, Frankfurt.

"I want to be a leisure brand": Horst Dassler, quoted by Tom Harrington.

"Our catalogues and flyers": interview, Peter Rduch, 06/02/03, Herzogenaurach.

McMahon anecdote: recounted by Dave Morgan, interview, 02/11/06, New York.

"It was such a shocking sight": interview, Blago Vidinic, 22/11/04, Strasbourg.

"This felt like a conspiracy": interview, Michel Perraudin, 03/07/03, Herzogenaurach.

"While he was waiting": correspondence with Pat Doran.

"My friend Horst" and details of deal between Adidas and Ilie Nastase: from interview with Ilie Nastase, 09/12/04, Paris.

"Unfortunately my illness": memo to board members, dated 31/03/87.

"It was a gripping sight": interview, Johan van den Bossche, 30/01/04, Clichy.

"What in the hell": interview, Donald Dell, 07/11/06, Washington, D.C.

"an unostentatious, modest man": *Abendpost*, obituary by Dieter Gräbner, date unknown.

"the most powerful man in sports": *Düsseldorf Express*, date unknown.

"tireless, but not selfless genius": *Abendpost*, obituary by Dieter Gräbner, date unknown.

Chapter Eighteen: Puma's Demise

"Tiriac has the air of a man": John McPhee, in his book *Wimbledon: A Celebration*, as quoted in *Sports Illustrated*, 6/22/1987 (Kirkpatrick, Curry).

"Horst was very upset" and the rest of the WFSGI anecdote: relayed by Kihachiro Onitsuka during an encounter at the ISPO fair in July 2005.

"They needed money right away" and "little piece of yellow paper": interview, Jim Woolner, 31/10/06, White Plains, N.Y.

"There was no need": interview, Gerd Dassler, 02/07/03, Herzogenaurach.

"He told me he needed": interview, Richard Kazmaier, who provided most of the details on the American fiasco as part of an interview in Boston, 18/08/04.

"kind of crazy": interview, Frank Dassler, 10/03/03, Herzogenaurach.

"the retailers told us": interview, Uli Heyd, 09/02/05, Herzogenaurach.

"Puma is looking for a buyer": Horst Dassler, as quoted in *WirtschaftsWoche*, 13/03/87.

"You have lost your business": from the memory of Jörg Dassler, interview, 24/09/03, Herzogenaurach.

"As the bankers put it": interview, Frank Dassler, 10/03/03, Herzogenaurach.

"the books were filled": interview, Hans Woitschätzke, 14/03/05, Barcelona, same for following quotes and anecdotes.

"Put it this way": interview, Irene Dassler, 13/01/05, Nuremberg.

Chapter Nineteen: Shark Attack!

"Think of a shark": interview by Axel Thorer, in *Playboy*, no. 10, 1990.

"The inventories were clogged": interview, Roddy Campbell, 23/07/03, London.

"When Hannibal trekked": *Esquire*, no. 2, 1991.

"For several days": interview, Johan van den Bossche, 30/01/04, Clichy.

"As soon as the boss": interview, Jean Wendling, 23/09/03, Bitschoffen.

"We shipped it into Kazakhstan": interview, Roddy Campbell, 23/07/03, London.

Peter Ueberroth fêted in *Time* magazine: 1/7/1985 (Lance Morrow).

"They didn't spare us" and "this man imposed himself": Suzanne Dassler as quoted in *France-Soir*, 14/07/90.

"The speed of the collapse": interview, Carl-Hainer Thomas, 12/01/05, Erlangen.

"very arrogant impression": interview, Gerhard Ziener, 22/09/03, Darmstadt.

"it was a done deal": interview, Michel Perraudin, 03/07/03, Herzogenaurach. This meeting with Klaus Jacobs was remembered in the same terms by Hermann Homann and Axel Markus.

Chapter Twenty: The Sellout

Details on Bernard Tapie: from *Le Flambeur* and countless other books written on his roller-coaster life.

"All the people who fight": interview, Bernard Tapie, 03/03/04, Paris.

"the impression that Tapie" and "it appeared that his slate": interview, Ulrich Nehm, 02/07/03, Munich.

"the shareholders have one last request": Gerhard Ziener, as quoted by Laurent Adamowicz, telephone conversations between April and May 2005.

"we don't know him": *Le Figaro*, 13/07/90.

"where will the money come from?": *Le Quotidien de Paris*, 09/07/90.

"Bernard just told them": Laurent Adamowicz, telephone conversations between April and May 2005.

"how would you like": Bernard Tapie, quoted by Laurent Adamowicz, idem.

"He called us very excitedly": interview, Michel Perraudin, 03/07/03, Herzogenaurach.

"A day when I'm not": Tapie, as quoted by Klaus Müller, interview 15/01/04, Berlin.

"René Jäggi was sitting there": interview, Tom Harrington, 07/08/02, Bruchkobel.

"I feel like I've bought": Bernard Tapie, quoted by Axel Markus, interview 23/09/03, Nuremberg.

"For nearly two years": interview, Gilberte Beaux, 23/11/02, Paris.

Chapter Twenty-one: Stir It Up

"It is the end of an era": Cindy Hale's letter as quoted in *Sportstyle*, 20/12/1993.

"You can't run on the deck": conversation with John Horan, 15/08/04, Long Beach Island, N.J.

"This industry is like Snow White": Phil Knight at the opening of the 1978 Nike sales meeting, as quoted in *Swoosh*.

"They seemed to be" and "I was truly blown away": interview, Peter Moore, 09/08/04, Portland, Ore.

"We all had goose bumps": interview Bernd Wahler, 22/09/03, Bensheim.

"They got everything": interview, Peter Rduch, 12/01/05, Nuremberg.

"Nobody wants": Karl-Otto Lang, as quoted by Peter Moore, interview, 09/08/04, Portland, Ore., idem for rest of this conversation.

"We should have done this": reactions as relayed by Cindy Hale-Yoshimura, interview, 11/08/04, Portland, Ore.

"In the summer heat": interview, Tom Harrington, 07/08/02, Bruchkobel.

"He could give someone": interview, Cindy Hale-Yoshimura, 11/08/04, Portland, Ore.

"It was like running through a swamp": interview, Tom Harrington, 07/08/02, Bruchkobel.

"He was like Elvis": interview, Cindy Hale-Yoshimura, 11/08/04, Portland, Ore.

Mass resignation of business unit managers: described by Jan Valdmaa, then head of the business unit for running and later international marketing manager, interview, 05/08/02, Munich; and Bernd Wahler, interview, 22/09/03, Bensheim.

Chapter Twenty-two: Triple Bluff

"made a few bob": interview, Stephen Rubin, 29/04/03, London.

"B.T.F. SA and Pentland": press release by Pentland Group plc, dated 07/07/92.

"In all the deals we did": interview, Stephen Rubin, 29/04/03, London.

Further details on the management bid and the due diligence by Stephen Rubin were extracted from interviews with other leading executives at the time, including Bob McCulloch, interview, 30/04/03, Stockport, and Tom Harrington, interview, 07/08/02, Bruchkobel.

"an awful amount of trouble": interview, Stephen Rubin, 29/04/03, London.

"purposely destabilized": interview, Gilberte Beaux, 23/11/02, Paris.

"the investigations have revealed": press release by Pentland Group plc, dated 15/10/92.

"it was bluff": interview, Stephen Rubin, 29/04/03, London.

"no liquidity at all": interview, Axel Markus, 23/09/03, Nuremberg.

"How do you think?": Axel Markus quoted by Herbert Hainer, interview, 10/02/05, Herzogenaurach.

"Robert Louis-Dreyfus" note: interview, Jean-Paul Tchang, 11/10/04, Paris.

"By then I had quit" and other Tchang quotes in this chapter: interview, Jean-Paul Tchang, 11/10/04, Paris.

"I was the nit-picker": interview, Christian Tourres, 22/11/02, Paris.

"the rot, the cancer, the gangrene": François Bayrou, then secretary-general of the center-right UDF party, quoted in *Le Monde*, 18/02/93.

"Not a bad deal": interview, Robert Louis-Dreyfus, 23/05/02, Caslano.

"In the eyes of many investors": Laurent Adamowicz, telephone conversations between April and May 2005.

Chapter Twenty-three: The Comeback

"I can't tell you when": Robert Louis-Dreyfus, as quoted by him as part of an interview on 23/05/02 in Caslano, same for next quotes.

"the only way": Rob Strasser, as quoted in *The Oregonian*, 23/03/93.

"Listen David": anecdote recounted by Eric Liedtke, interview, 19/10/06, Herzogenaurach, same for Starks anecdote.

"it was the first time": John Horan, quoted in *The Oregonian*, 16/10/94.

"Europeans wouldn't know": interview, Peter Moore, 09/08/04, Portland, Ore.

"Some European managers": interview, Bernd Wahler, 22/09/03, Bensheim.

"we figured": interview, Peter Moore, 09/08/04, Portland, Ore.

"Strasser was a phenomenal character": interview, Christian Tourres, 22/11/02.

"It was announced briefly": *Intern*, October 1993.

"center-stage personified": Jay Edwards, as quoted by *The Oregonian*, 09/11/93 (Mike Francis).

"tried to make a coup" and "couldn't manage his pocketbook": interview, Robert Louis-Dreyfus, 23/05/02, Caslano.

Chapter Twenty-four: Soccer Punch II

"It was next to no money!" and "Phil Knight rejected out of hand": interview, Alan Rothenberg, 03/11/06, Los Angeles.

"When you visit the Nike headquarters": telephone interview, Sunil Gulati, April 2007.

"In our view there was an implied goodwill": interview, Robert Erb, 02/11/06, New York.

"just couldn't get their act together": interview, Alan Rothenberg, 03/11/06, Los Angeles.

"there was a lot of anger": interview, Robert Erb, 02/11/06, New York.

"Sporting event?": "The Zillion-Dollar Games," in *The Economist*, 20/07/96.

"Take this thing": interview, Steve Wynne, 08/02/05, Munich.

Chapter Twenty-five: Sneaker Wars II

"Sonny was absolutely sure": interview, Robert Erb, 02/11/06, New York.

The story of the deal between Adidas and Tracy McGrady: outlined by Robert Erb and described in more detail in *Sole Influence*.

"The NFL guys would stand": interview, Steve Wynne, 08/02/05, Munich.

"Everybody else was inviting them": interview, Robert Erb, 02/11/06, New York.

"His response to our phone call" and "It legitimized the Adidas brand": telephone interview, Derek Schiller, May 2007.

"I just thought, what the heck": interview, Robert Louis-Dreyfus, 23/05/02, Caslano.

Chapter Twenty-six: Cool Cats

"There will be no sacred cows": interview, Jochen Zeitz for an article in *Management* magazine, 25/04/02.

"everything from nuclear triggers to rocket fuel": *NBC News* as quoted in *Los Angeles Magazine*, Arnon Milchan profile by Ann Louise Bardach, April 2000.

"Some people felt": interview, Jim Gorman, 30/10/06, Boston.

Anecdotes around Serena Williams and Vince Carter: lean strongly on this interview, with Jim Gorman, and newspapers listed above.

Further details were provided by some of the lawyers involved. The exact amount of the settlement reached between Puma and Vince Carter could not be officially confirmed. However, the sums emerged in 2004 in a federal court in Columbia, where Vince Carter and Tank Black faced each other. Black, who was then in federal prison for money laundering and other charges, wanted Carter to pay him $9 million for commissions on endorsement deals and $5 million in damages. Carter countersued, demanding that Black reimburse him $18.9 million in relation to the Puma case, as reported by *USA Today*. The Carters said they had "no comment concerning Puma."

Chapter Twenty-seven: High Noon

"I liked playing with money": interview, Herbert Hainer, 10/02/05, Herzogenaurach.

"The best managers aren't": ibid.

"By the time I got": interview, Paul Fireman, 01/11/06, Lancaster, Penn., same for next Fireman quotes in this chapter.

"When the Nike guys come in": Yao Ming, as quoted by Brook Larmer.

"Paul acknowledged that": interview, Herbert Hainer, 10/02/05, Herzogenaurach.

Other facts and figures in this chapter are derived from the author's daily coverage of the sports business since 1999, and from thousands of miles of press reports around the soccer World Cup in Europe.

bibliography

The Dasslers, Adidas, and Puma

Adi Dassler, Wilfried Geldner, Berlin: Ullstein, 1999.

"Adi Dassler: from the beginnings to the present," a history manual of the Adidas-Salomon Group, by Karl-Heinz Lang and Renate Urban.

Comment Adidas devient l'un des plus beaux redressements de l'histoire du business, by Eric Wattez, Paris: Editions Assouline, 1998.

Der Mann der Adidas war, unpublished biography of Adolf Dassler, by Hermann Utermann, 1983.

"'Doc,' the 50-year Sporting Goods Sales Odyssey of H. B. Hughes," as told to Carlton Stowers, private edition.

Horst Dassler: Revolution im Weltsport, by Paulheinz Grupe, Munich: Hase & Koehler, 1992.

Making a Difference, Adidas-Salomon, 1998.

Rudolf Dassler 70, *Privatdruck*, 1968.

Sneaker-Story: der Zweikampf von Adidas und Nike, by Christoph Bieber, Frankfurt-am-Main: Fischer, 2000.

Stadtbuch Herzogenaurach, Aus der 1000-jährigen Geschichte Herzogenaurachs, 2003.

Sports History

Ajax, the Dutch, the War: Football in Europe during the Second World War, by Simon Kuper, London: Orion, 2003.

Cien años de leyenda, 1902–2002, Real Madrid, La Coruña: Everest, 2002.

The Complete Book of the Olympics, by David Wallechinsky, London: Aurum Press, 2000.

In Black & White: The untold story of Joe Louis and Jesse Owens, by Donald McRae, London: Scribner (Simon and Schuster), 2002.

King of the World: Muhammad Ali and the Rise of an American Hero, by David Remnick, New York: Random House, 1998.

"Les Jeux Olympiques, d'Athènes à Athènes," Paris: L'Equipe, 2003.

The Nazi Olympics, Richard Mandell, Champaign: University of Illinois Press, 1987.

The Rise and Fall of the Third Reich, by William L. Shirer, Simon and Schuster, 1960.

Sepp Herberger, Ein Leben, eine Legende, by Jürgen Leinemann, Reinbek bei Hamburg: Rororo, 1998.

Stürmen für Deutschland, die Geschichte des Deutschen Fussballs von 1933 bis 1954, by Dirk Bitzer and Bernd Wilting, Frankfurt am Main: Campus Verlag, 2003.

Stürmer für Hitler, Vom Zusammenspiel zwischen Fussball und Nationalsozialismus, by Gerhard Fischer and Ulrich Lindner, Göttingen: Verlag Die Werkstatt, 1999.

3:2, Die Spiele zur Weltmeisterschaft, by Fritz Walter, Munich: Stiebner Verlag, 2000.

Soccer Culture

Tor! The Story of German Football, by Ulrich Hesse-Lichtenberger, London: WSC Books, 2002.

Elegance Borne of Brutality: An Eclectic History of the Football Boot, by Ian McArthur and Dave Kemp, Haywards Heath: Two Heads Publishing, 1995.

Morbo: The Story of Spanish Football, Phil Ball, London: WSC Books, 2003.

Brilliant Orange: The Neurotic Genius of Dutch Football, by David Winner, London: Bloomsbury, 2000.

Those Feet: A Sensual History of English Football, by David Winner, London: Bloomsbury, 2005.

1974: Wij waren de besten, by Auke Kok, Amsterdam: Thomas Rap, 2004.

Once in a Lifetime: The Extraordinary Story of the New York Cosmos, by Gavin Newsham, London: Atlantic Books, 2006.

Soccer in a Football World: The Story of America's Forgotten Game, by David Wangerin, London: WSC Books, 2006.

Sports Biographies

Blessed, by George Best, London: Ebury Press (Random House), 2001.

Fanny Blankers-Koen: een koningin met mannenbenen, by Kees Kooman, Amsterdam: L. J. Veen, 2003.

Günter Netzer: Aus der Tiefe des Raumes, by Günter Netzer and Helmut Schümann, Reinbek bei Hamburg: Rowohlt, 2004.

Kinderen van Pheidippides, de marathon, van Abebe Bikila tot Emil Zatopek, Kees Kooman, Baarn: Tirion Sport, 2005.

Max Schmeling: An Autobiography, edited by George von der Lippe, Chicago: Bonus Books Inc, 1998.

Mr. Nastase: The Autobiography, by Ilie Nastase and Debbie Beckerman, London: Collins Willow, 2004.

My Side, by David Beckham and Tom Watt, London: Collins Willow, 2003.

Operation Yao Ming: The Chinese Sports Empire, American Big Business and the Making of an NBA Superstar, by Brook Larmer, New York: Gotham Books, 2005.

Playing Extra Time, Allan Ball, London: Sidgwick and Jackson, 2004.

There's Only One David Beckham, by Stafford Hildred and Tim Ewbank, London: John Blake Publishing, 2002.

The Way It Was, Stanley Matthews, London: Headline Books, 2000.

Sports Business

De betaalde liefde, by Marcel Maassen, Nijmegen: Uitgeverij SUN, 1999.

Broken Dreams: Vanity, Greed, and the Souring of British Football, by Tom Bower, London: Simon and Schuster, 2003.

The Football Business, by David Conn, Edinburgh: Mainstream Sport, 1997.

Foul! by Andrew Jennings, London: HarperSport, 2006.

Great Balls of Fire: How Big Money Is Hijacking World Football, by John Sugden and Alan Tomlinson, Edinburgh: Mainstream Publishing, 1999.

The Great Olympic Swindle, When the World Wanted Its Games Back, by Andrew Jennings, London: Simon and Schuster, 2000.

The Lord of the Rings, by Vyv Simson and Andrew Jennings, London: Simon and Schuster, 1992.

Das Milliardenspiel, Fussball, Geld und Medien, by Thomas Kistner and Jens Weinreich, Frankfurt am Main: Fischer, 1998.

Minding Other People's Business: Winning Big for Your Clients and Yourself, by Donald Dell, New York: Villard Books, 1989.

The New Lord of the Rings, by Andrew Jennings, London: Simon and Schuster, 1996.

Olympic Turnaround, by Michael Payne, Twyford: London Business Press, 2005.

Der Olympische Sumpf, by Thomas Kistner and Jens Weinreich, Munich: Piper, 2000.

Die Spielmacher, by Thomas Kistner and Ludger Schulze, Stuttgart: Deutsche Verlags-Anstalt, 2001.

Sole Influence: Basketball, Corporate Greed, and the Corruption of America's Youth, by Dan Wetzel and Don Yaeger, New York: Grand Central Publishing, 2000.

Business Biographies

Comment ils ont tué Tapie, André Bercoff, Paris: Michel Lafon, 1998.

Conflicting Accounts: The Creation and Crash of the Saatchi & Saatchi Advertising Empire, by Kevin Goldman, New York: Touchstone, 1998.

Le Flambeur, la vraie vie de Bernard Tapie, by Valérie Lecasble and Airy Routier, Paris: Grasset, 1994.

L'Original, by André Guelfi, Paris: Robert Laffont, 1999.

Tapie, l'homme d'affaires, by Christophe Bouchet, Paris: Editions du Seuil, 1994.

Sports Brands

Le Coq Sportif, by Emile Camuset, private edition, date unknown.

Just Do It: The Nike Spirit in the Corporate World, by Donald Katz, Holbrook, Mass.: Adams Media Corporation, 1994.

No Logo, Naomi Klein, Toronto: Albert A. Knopf, 2000.

Swoosh: The Unauthorized Story of Nike and the Men Who Played There, J. B. Strasser and Laurie Becklund, San Diego: Harcourt Brace Jovanovich, 1991.

acknowledgments

A few years ago, Adidas employees were sent out to clean an old storage room in Herzogenaurach. They were stunned to find, at the back of the hangar, boxes full of old shoes. Karl-Heinz Lang, a longtime Adidas technician, took upon himself the task of sorting through the rotting cartons and cleaning up the most valuable remains. The result is a row of cupboards in Scheinfeld containing the spikes worn by Jesse Owens as well as Muhammad Ali's boots and many other treasures. Thanks to Karl-Heinz Lang for leading me through this superb display, which speaks more than a shelf-full of books. To share this with a wider audience, he is working on setting up an Adidas museum in Herzogenaurach. The project is steered by Frank Dassler.

Renate Urban, Lang's assistant in Scheinfeld, patiently helped me to visualize modern shoe production by leading me through the adjoining plant. This turns out small runs of standard soccer boots as well as handmade series for David Beckham and other high-maintenance players.

While this book remains entirely independent, I am most grateful to the leading executives of Adidas and Puma for their welcome and assistance. Due to the contentious family history behind the two companies, neither of them has comprehensive archives. However, both have kindly provided me with extensive access to all their public documents and arranged many interviews with current employees.

Much to their credit, the people in charge of press relations at Adidas and Puma accepted that I would portray their companies' history as I uncovered it, with their controversial past and dubious dealings. Although they never attempted to influence the contents of the book, they apparently trusted me to make it clear that their current management could not be held responsible for such actions. I can only hope that I have not undermined their belief in such an unusually open attitude.

I am most indebted to Jan Runau and Anne Putz, in charge of media relations at Adidas, for their enthusiasm and cooperation. They repeatedly welcomed me in Herzogenaurach, went out of their way to dig up useful facts, and opened doors that would otherwise have remained closed.

The night I spent at the Puma head offices, holed up in a meeting room with scores of fascinating documents and an empty pizza box, oddly ranks as one of the fondest memories in these five years of research. I still wonder how I resisted the temptation to roam through the empty corridors. Thanks to Ulf Santjer, head of media relations at Puma.

I owe the most thrilling moments of this project to all the people who agreed to share their memories for this book. For many of them, their time at Adidas or Puma was the most intense period in their professional life. Their testimony was often fraught with the passion of these times—the excitement of the games, the ferocity of the battles with the other side. I discovered some astonishingly forceful personalities, fascinating storytellers, and amazingly kind individuals.

Many of the people I interviewed do not appear in this book. This is such a complex story, and there are so many angles to it, that I had to eliminate some of them. If you are frustrated about this, I sincerely apologize, but you can be assured that the exercise was worse for me.

As I researched the company's war history, I was stunned by the diligence of German and American archivists. They spent hours answering my queries and came forward with invaluable advice.

More thanks are due to colleagues, friends, or both. Among those who provided guidance, encouragement, or just a patient ear as I crashed in their living rooms on my travels, blabbering on about stripes and wildcats, are: Jeroen Akkermans and Annemieke Wapperom, Erin Barnett, Thierry Cruvellier, Alain Franco, Machteld van Gelder, Albert Knechtel, Simon Kuper, David Winner.

I was particularly impressed with the generosity of Andrew Jennings, the British journalist who uncovered large-scale corruption in Olympic circles. Andrew is so genuinely passionate in his disgust of such wrongdoings that he enthusiastically assisted the newcomer on his patch. My research on Horst Dassler's infiltration of sports organizations leaned heavily on Andrew's revelations.

The concept for this book may never have turned into a manuscript at all without Eugenio Di Maria, editor and publisher of *Sporting Goods Intelligence Europe*. I met him in Munich about seven years ago, when I attended my first edition of ISPO, the industry's international trade fair. As I reported for him over the next years, he patiently shared his unparalleled knowledge of the European sports industry. He provided me with unique insights and introduced me to more people than I could have hoped to meet by myself. It has been an immense privilege to work with such a passionate and demanding editor. Eugenio may not be held responsible for the contents of this book, but I owe much of it to him.

David Luxton, my English agent and partner at Luxton Harris, took a risky gamble. After all, a Dutch woman residing in France, investigating two German sports companies, and delivering an

English-language manuscript did not seem an obvious proposal. I am most grateful for David's steadfast support, his quiet reassurances, and his unwavering confidence in the project.

I could not have wished for a more dedicated editor than Emily Takoudes at Ecco for this American version of my book. Olympic Games keep her glued to her television screen and she has spent several years in Germany, which was a most promising start, but her patient guidance and sharp editing proved equally valuable to finalize this American manuscript.

My deepest gratitude goes to a person very close to me who abhors soppy personal notes at the end of acknowledgments and shall therefore remain anonymous.

Nîmes, July 2007

index